NEVEAH
and the
ANGEL of DEATH

One City's Quest to Bring a
Child Killer to Justice

HARLAN ABRAHAMS

For information contact
Harlan Abrahams
Denver, Colorado
harlanabrahams@aol.com
www.harlanabrahams.com

Abrahams, Harlan
NEVEAH and the ANGEL of DEATH:
One City's Quest to Bring a Child Killer to Justice

ISBN: 978-1-938859-49-6

1. Child abuse
2. Criminal justice
3. Domestic violence
4. Law and public policy
5. Law – murder – true crime
6. Gallegos, Neveah Janey
7. Montoya, Angel Ray

Cover photograph courtesy of the family of Neveah Gallegos

Cover design by NZ Graphics

Printed in the United States of America
At the
Tattered Cover Press

This book is dedicated to the memory of
NEVEAH GALLEGOS

To the cause of eradicating child abuse

And, as always, to my wife Carolyn

TABLE OF CONTENTS

FOREWORD by MITCH MORRISSEY

As the Denver District Attorney, I am honored to have the responsibility of carrying forward and building on a legacy of commitment to eliminate violence against women and children. It is a professional and moral pledge that I have made to my community and to myself. We devote countless resources in the effort to work together with other government and community-based agencies to collaboratively raise the bar on how we prevent and react to these violent acts. We must be the collective voice of our community as these acts tear at the fabric of all of our lives.

Each and every day, my staff at the District Attorney's Office works to be the best that we can be at bringing justice to our community. Included in our mission is holding ourselves and our partners accountable for individual and institutional performance. Every injury and every death is a sign that we are not at our destination and every sign motivates us to work harder and smarter to improve.

Harlan Abrahams has written an insightful and in-depth account of the murder of little Neveah Gallegos, the man who murdered her, and the mother who stood by and let it happen. The story is heart-breaking. Harlan does not shy away from graphic details, so the reader can understand the heinous crime that was presented to the jury. Harlan is clear and direct in reporting the facts of the case and the trial. At the same time, he conveys the profound emotions that permeated the years of seeking justice.

Every violent death is treated with a determination to find justice, but the death of a child carries a particular burden. Harlan helps us feel the despair experienced by Neveah's family at not being able to prevent the terrible death of such a small girl as well as the spirit and resolve of the outstanding prosecution team, police officers, and investigators.

There were many others who also became invested in the outcome of the trial. You see, this case differed from other baby murders in that Angel Montoya tried, and succeeded for a while, to conceal the small body. In an unprecedented community effort, law enforcement and civilians searched area neighborhoods for Neveah. Teams of volunteers, off-duty officers and concerned citizens looked under bushes, in alleys and in dumpsters as the city waited with sad resignation for the inevitable discovery.

Harlan brings that time and other pivotal events to life by illuminating individual personalities and meticulously recounting the broader picture. One of the distinguishing aspects of this book is its intimate narrative focus on the case from the perspectives of a dozen of the participants – family, witnesses, jury and police. His description of the jury members is particularly interesting as this is an aspect of true crime reporting that is often overlooked.

In the first half of his book, Harlan weaves into the narrative a deep legal and policy analysis of the problem. In this way, he demystifies the process without distracting from the absorbing true story. The trial is reported during the second half of the book and Harlan accurately brings to life the drama and pathos that brought the jury to its verdict.

In my opinion, it is inconceivable that Angel Montoya did not abuse Neveah's mother. There are irredeemable people in this world, and Angel Montoya is one of them. There is strong evidence that he physically abused and terrified other children – one testified against him during Neveah's trial. Anyone not convinced of the long-term damage caused by experiencing or witnessing abuse should have seen that little boy's terror when in the proximity of Angel Montoya.

In Denver, public servants in the criminal justice system realize that many people are reluctant to come forward to ask for help, as they are concerned about possible consequences for themselves. Tragedies could be averted if people had greater trust in law enforcement; however, for a variety of understandable reasons many at-risk people will not call us in times of crisis. One innovative solution being implemented in Denver is the creation of one place where a victim of domestic violence can find help from counselors, advocates, medical providers and, optionally, the police. This is one place where victims can access counseling for themselves and their children, and have questions answered about legal issues, housing, employment options, or public benefits.

The Rose Andom Center will reduce barriers to services and promote easier access to both law enforcement and community-based agencies. The Rose Andom Center will create a "wraparound" service delivery model that will marshal many domestic violence-related resources in the community into a coordinated system. This reduces the number of places victims must go for help, and increases the likelihood of successfully utilizing resources to end the abuse in their lives and their children's lives. If we can change the system by making the process simpler, we can stop the cycle of abuse earlier — saving lives, taxpayer money, and children's futures.

We cannot bring Neveah back, but we can honor her memory by doing all that we can to prevent another tragedy. I appreciate what Harlan Abrahams has done to help us remember so that we continue to move forward.

Mitch Morrissey
October 2013

Photo courtesy of the family of Neveah Gallegos

ONE: THE LAWYER in the PARKING LOT

Three-year old Neveah Gallegos—strangled, stuffed in a duffle bag, and buried under a log and a tire—did not capture the attention of the national media. She did, however, capture the conscience of a community: her family and friends, the police and prosecutors, even a jail house snitch whose cell was next to the cell of a guy named Angel Ray Montoya. After hearing Angel Ray talk about dumping the child's body, the snitch wrote some letters to the police and prosecutors.

Those letters became one of four breakthroughs in a case that began officially on Friday, September 21, 2007, in a small parking lot in the Golden Triangle of Denver. At 3:01 p.m. on that sunny afternoon, a young woman crossed that parking lot and accosted a lawyer leaving her office early for Yom Kippur. The lawyer was wearing tennis clothes and holding a cell phone to her ear, finishing a call.

The young woman was short and heavyset. She had long dark hair pulled back in a ponytail. Her face was round and full. She wore a light-colored T-shirt and dark pants, and she was clutching something in her hands: a little girl's jacket, which looked pink in the late-day light. She appeared dazed and approached slowly from the back side of the parking lot, asking for help, asking to use the lawyer's cell phone.

The lawyer stepped back. Her antennae were twitching. Something wasn't right. A veteran of 25 years of civil litigation and real estate experience, the lawyer prided herself on carefully observing her surroundings, especially in a transitional mixed-use neighborhood like the Golden Triangle, adjacent to downtown. She wasn't about to put her cell phone in the hands of this strange woman.

Instead she asked, "What's wrong?" She had to ask it twice.

"In the alley," said the young woman in a low voice, "they … took my baby in the alley."

Instantly the lawyer dialed 911.

It couldn't have taken more than two rings for the operator to answer. But on some level, during that moment, the lawyer thought it was odd the young woman wasn't acting more hysterical. After all, if her baby had just been kidnapped!

The 911 operator came on the line and the lawyer simply reported: "I'm at 1080 Cherokee and there's a woman here who says her baby was just taken from her in the alley."

The operator asked the lawyer to put the young woman on the line. The lawyer surrendered her cell phone. The young woman took it and started talking. She said she was walking in the alley between 10th and 11th behind Cherokee with her daughter, and a white car pulled up, and a tall white man with a full red beard got out and grabbed her daughter and pulled her into the car.

As she spoke, the young woman's voice grew louder and her manner became more animated. She said the man with the red beard warned her that if she told anybody, he would hurt her little girl. By now the young woman was sobbing.

And though she was still on the cell phone, sirens already were approaching. This didn't surprise the lawyer since the parking lot was only a couple of blocks from police headquarters. She motioned the young woman toward the front sidewalk and waved at the patrol cars, which were slowing down as they reached the corner.

When the patrol cars stopped and the first uniformed officers got out, the lawyer gestured at the young woman and said, "That's her"—then stepped aside.

The next 128 minutes turned surreal. A dozen police cars— marked and unmarked—converged on the scene, sealing off the parking lot from both the street side and the alley side. Located between a gray concrete residential loft building and the one-story brick building where the lawyer worked, the parking lot is relatively small, long and narrow. It holds about thirty cars.

Earlier there had been only three cars and a small restaurant truck parked in the lot.

Now it was crawling with police—male and female, in uniforms and in plainclothes—and flashing lights were splashing the sides of the buildings in lurid reds and blues. The parking lot started to look like the sound stage from some CSI crime drama, though no yellow tape defined its limits, and it was not the flattened, fictional, two-dimensional version seen on TV. It was three-dimensional and real. It engaged all the senses.

These were waters into which the lawyer never waded. She had decades of experience and plenty of street smarts, but hers was a world of contracts and surveys and title commitments and egomaniacal businessmen who got sued in civil courts. And while she knew lots of lawyers who made their living in the criminal justice system—prosecutors and defense counsel alike—she had always avoided their untidy world.

Yet now she found herself inside a genuine crime scene, ordering itself into structure, on her very doorstep. She saw the police cruisers that had created a perimeter around the block flashing their reds and blues like echoes of the lights spinning around the parking lot. She saw officers come and go, talking to each other, talking into cell phones and radios. She answered the occasional question, remembering an additional detail or two.

But mostly for 90 minutes, though no one had asked her to stay, the lawyer just stood around the parking lot, near the entry to her building, overhearing much of what the young woman was telling the police, the same basic story with an added phrase or some different wording here or there. She was coming from—or going to—Denver Health with her daughter, who was three—or was it four? Some things weren't too clear. But this much was:

In the alley over there, a white car pulled up and a white man with a full red beard got out and grabbed the young woman's daughter and pulled her into the car and warned her not to tell anyone and sped away.

At some point during the re-telling, the lawyer called her secretary inside the one-story building and told her what was happening. At some point her secretary brought a bottle of water for the young woman and left soon after with the only other person who was still inside. At some point a neighbor from the gray concrete lofts on the other side of the parking lot leaned out his window and asked what was going on, and the lawyer said: "She says someone took her kid or something like that."

And at some point a uniformed police officer asked the lawyer if he could go inside to use the rest room and she said, "Sure." She buzzed open the security door and went with him into the building, realizing she had just consented to a warrantless entry by the police.

At this time, the one-story building where the lawyer worked was vacant on the first floor, awaiting new tenants. The basement was, however, fully occupied by the unstructured offices and storage spaces of the real estate developer and restaurateur with whom the lawyer worked. A metal and concrete stairway led from the entry area to the basement.

The lawyer took the police officer down the stairway, walked him through the office and storage space, showed him the rest room in the back, and left. After more than a few minutes, she glanced at her watch. It was taking a long time for the police officer to use the facilities and return. She figured he must be using the opportunity to snoop about the big open space, orderly here and cluttered there, confirming the bona fides of the lawyer's background story.

No matter. One route from the rest room to the stairway would have taken the officer past the desks and spaces occupied by the lawyer, her secretary, and the developer. A different, lesser-used route would have taken him past the office space of the person who had left earlier with the lawyer's secretary, the work areas of the people who ran the developer's restaurants, and a load of unused tables and chairs and dusty fixtures.

Nothing remotely connected to the crimes the officer was investigating. Eventually he was back in the parking lot and the next thing the lawyer knew—a minute or two before 4:30—she was being asked to go to the station with another police officer and give a statement to a "homicide detective," or maybe it was the "homicide department." Either way, the lawyer put two and two together.

Whatever had happened to the little girl, it had gone from a kidnapping to a killing. The lawyer knew this because she knew the legal definition of a homicide: the killing of a human being by another human being. It was basic bar exam material.

But hearing the word spoken by a real live police officer in a real live situation, about that poor little girl, the lawyer's heart skipped a beat. It felt like it was swelling inside her chest.

Now people who knew the lawyer wouldn't have been surprised. They would say her heart was one of her most notable characteristics. Adjectives used to describe her often included "big-hearted." Others were smart, ethical, practical, wise, and self-assured. She had a famous sense of humor and an uncanny way with people.

And she was kind beyond belief.

She had grown up on Long Island, gone to college in Binghamton, and moved to Colorado in the late 1970s. Since earning her law degree in 1983 from Denver University, she had served as a partner at several area law firms and as in-house counsel to the real estate developer who had recently purchased the one-story brick building at 1080 Cherokee. She had married for the first time at forty-five, only five years before, and she showed a mighty maternal instinct when it came to her two stepdaughters and her two younger nieces.

It mattered little that her stepdaughters carried none of her blood or that her nieces were both Chinese orphans who had been adopted by her brother and sister-in-law. The lawyer had bonded with them—and they had bonded to her—anyway.

So, too, it mattered little that the lawyer had never set eyes upon the little girl whose name she didn't even know, but whose jacket looked pink in the late-day sun. The lawyer's heart—her giant, empathetic heart—went out to that little girl.

The solemnity of what was happening around her also pressed upon the lawyer. In only 90 minutes, starting when she hit 9-1-1 on her cell phone, an Amber Alert had been issued and soon cancelled. Now she was going to police headquarters to be interviewed by a homicide investigator. She felt uncomfortable in the grungy tennis clothes she was wearing, having played with a friend from noon to 2:00 and having returned to her office only briefly for a wrap-up of necessities before the weekend. Seemed like a lot of the people she was dealing with were leaving early for Yom Kippur.

While the lawyer and her husband were both Jewish, they were not observant. Seldom did they venture to synagogue or temple. They didn't light candles and they certainly didn't fast. For them Yom Kippur was just an excuse to hurry home to spend some extra time together.

So when the lawyer had left her office early in her grungy tennis clothes on that sunny Friday afternoon, she had thought nothing of their unseemly condition. She'd go home and shower. She'd grab some dinner with her husband and they'd watch Bill Maher together.

But all that changed when that chubby young woman approached her in the parking lot.

Now the lawyer re-entered the empty one-story building and went downstairs to her office space and quickly pulled on jeans and a top—nothing fancy, but better than her tennis clothes—and took a minute to call her husband and tell him she would be late. Then she went back upstairs to the parking lot, got into an unmarked car, and rode with a female plainclothes officer to the station a couple of blocks down the street.

It was after 4:30 and before 4:40 p.m.

On the way to the station the lawyer asked her escort if it was true the police were now investigating a homicide. She needed to hear it, not deduce it. She didn't want the news coming from herself. The female officer answered, sadly, yes they were.

By now the lawyer's emotions were boiling. She had been keeping herself pretty well composed under the circumstances. True, she had suffered a bad moment when she was alone in the basement changing clothes, but she had pulled herself back together quickly. Now, however, tears she had successfully held at bay were threatening to invade her eyes. She took a long deep breath and composed herself one more time. Then she was led down a nondescript hallway and seated in a nondescript interview room across a plain table from a plainclothes detective.

The videotaped interview of the lawyer began at 4:43 p.m. The detective had dark hair that was well-trimmed and he appeared without a jacket, in his shirt sleeves and a tie. He started by asking the lawyer, "How you doin' today?"

She said, "I was doing fine," and her tone was anything but upbeat.

He didn't ask for elaboration. Instead he introduced himself without giving his first name: "I'm Detective Estrada, okay?"

Then he went over the Video Interview Advisement Form, reciting his badge number —"ninety six zero five zero"—and identifying the room as "interview room A." He also included a temporary case number—"zero seven six four five four seven seven"—that later morphed into a different number. In fact, every 911 call that is made is given a temporary case number, sometimes many case numbers if there are many calls about the same event. If that event results in a criminal case in district court, then it is assigned a court case number. The transcript of the lawyer's interview says "Court Case No. 09-CR-10170 & 09-CR-10201" at the top of each page, indicating it would not be until 2009 that the case was assigned a court case number.

Next Detective Estrada went over the lawyer's basic personal information: name, address, date of birth, and phone numbers. The lawyer confirmed for the record that she was not under the influence of any drug, narcotic or alcohol, that she was making her statement voluntarily, and that she understood her interview was being recorded.

He asked if she knew why she was being interviewed. She said yes, and began a description of the events of the past two hours, starting when the young woman approached her in the parking lot. When she got to the part about handing her phone to the young woman, Estrada asked if the lawyer could hear what the young woman was saying to the dispatcher.

The lawyer said yes, and described what she could hear of the conversation.

He asked, "When she approached you, and you were on the phone … she appear upset?"

The lawyer said, "She seemed … I would use the word a little more dazed or odd."

The whole situation, from the lawyer's perspective, seemed very off-putting.

Estrada asked, "How was her demeanor when she was on the phone with the dispatcher?"

"She was crying at that point," said the lawyer, "talking louder at that point. When she first started talking to me, she wasn't talking all that loud. [Now she was] much more upset in the obvious sense of the way, you know? Oh my God, I just want my baby, kind of breaking down sobbing … more emotional or animated than when it was just me."

He stayed with the theme of the young woman's demeanor—her emotional state—for another moment before he asked about the little girl's jacket: "You couldn't see if the jacket was soiled or anything? It just appeared to be a pink jacket?"

"It didn't appear to be soiled when I just saw it in her hand," answered the lawyer.

Next they went over the story the young woman told the police when they arrived at the parking lot. The lawyer had nothing new to add, no license plate numbers or other leads.

Estrada asked her to draw a picture of the parking lot and the surrounding buildings and the approximate locations of the vehicles that were in the lot and where she was when she left the building and where the young woman was when the lawyer first noticed her. The lawyer drew the picture that later became People's Exhibit #3 in Court Case No. 09-CR-10170.

Estrada asked, "And where does she say that her daughter was taken from?"

"I heard her tell one of the officers that she was taken from the alley, she said by the PBS building … I'm guessing she's referring to the building that would be immediately behind …"

Estrada interrupted: "The loft." He meant the old brick loft building that was on the north side of the one-story building at 1080 Cherokee, not the gray concrete loft building that was on the south side of the parking lot where the drama unfolded.

She said, "Up there [but] I can't swear to you that that's the PBS building."

He asked her nonetheless to put a mark where she thought the young woman meant her daughter had been taken. She marked the map and then labeled the streets and again indicated where the few vehicles were parked in the lot.

At 5:04 p.m. they took a break and Estrada left the interview room. When he returned he asked the lawyer to describe the young woman.

The lawyer said, "She was, I believe, Hispanic … long brown hair pulled back in a ponytail or a clip at the back of her head. I believe she was wearing a light-colored T-shirt."

"Do you know what color?"

"I wanna say tan … and dark pants, perhaps black … um, she was shorter than me, I would say five four … medium to heavy build."

Estrada concluded the interview at 5:08 p.m.

At the time, the lawyer didn't know the name of the young woman or the little girl. In fact, she couldn't pinpoint when, during her 90 minutes in the parking lot, the young woman had been taken away by the police, though she knew it was sometime before she had gone with the female officer to the station.

So many questions came to mind. Was the young woman—the mother—suspected of killing her own child? Or was it someone else? And how did they know it was a homicide and not a kidnapping?

The lawyer offered to walk the short distance back to the parking lot but Detective Estrada wouldn't hear of it. Instead he drove her back, going straight up Cherokee, against the one-way traffic sign. They pulled in front of the parking lot and now it truly did resemble the stereotypic TV crime scene, complete with garish yellow tape stretched this way and that to seal it off.

Estrada told the uniformed officer who was guarding the crime scene to let the lawyer out. The officer undid enough yellow tape to let the lawyer's car pass through. She drove home and told her husband everything. Then she cried in his arms.

* * *

Scenes like these are all too common. According to data from the U.S. Department of Health and Human Services:

For FFY 2011, more than 3.7 million (duplicate count) children were the subjects of at least one report. One fifth of these children were found to be victims [and] the remaining four fifths of the children were found to be nonvictims of maltreatment. The duplicate count of child victims tallies a child each time he or she was found to be a victim. The unique count of child victims counts a child only once regardless of the number of times he or she was found to be victim during the reporting year.

For FFY 2011, 51 States reported (unique count) 676,569 victims of child abuse and neglect. The unique victim rate was 9.1 victims per 1,000 children in the population … the national estimate of unique victims for FFY 2011 was 681,000 …

■ Victims in the age group of birth to 1 year had the highest rate of victimization at 21.2 per 1,000 children of the same age group in the national population.

■ Victimization was split between the sexes with boys accounting for 48.6 percent and girls accounting for 51.1 percent. Fewer than 1 percent … were of unknown sex.

■ Eighty-seven percent of (unique count) victims were … African-American (21.5%), Hispanic (22.1%), and White (43.9%).

Moreover, 80% of all child abuse is perpetrated by parents.

The Kempe Foundation for the Prevention and Treatment of Child Abuse and Neglect—located in Denver—is among the many organizations devoted to ending child abuse. Its web site gives these definitions of the principal types of maltreatment:

Neglect = Failure to provide for a child's basic needs

Physical Abuse = Physical injury as a result of hitting, kicking, shaking, burning, or otherwise harming a child

Sexual Abuse = Anytime a child is used for sexual gratification

Emotional Abuse = Any pattern of behavior that impairs a child's emotional development or sense of self-worth

And the following graph from the web site of ChildHelp.org— derived from earlier U.S. government statistics—shows the problem is actually getting worse, not better:

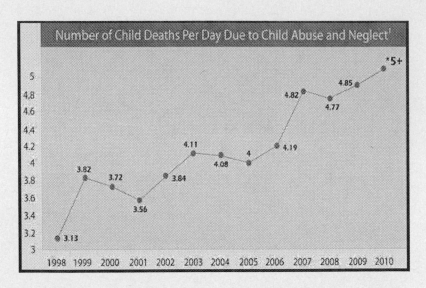

Number of Child Deaths Per Day Due to Child Abuse and Neglect[1]

The ChildHelp.org web site also emphasizes the pervasiveness of the problem—"child abuse occurs at every socioeconomic level, across ethnic and cultural lines, within all religions, and at all levels of education"—and addresses the terrible costs of child abuse in America:

> About 30% of abused and neglected children will later abuse their own children ... About 80% of 21 year olds that were abused as children met criteria for at least one psychological disorder. The estimated annual cost of child abuse and neglect in the United States for 2008 is $124 billion. Children who experience child abuse and neglect are 59% more likely to be arrested as a juvenile, 28% more likely to be arrested as an adult, and 30% more likely to commit violent crime.

There are real children's lives at stake, right here in America, not somewhere half way around the world. The story of Neveah Gallegos is notable because it validates many of the statistics set forth above and, more importantly, because it illustrates two of the most important failures that haunt the child abuse landscape:

The failure of the mother to protect her child from a known abuser *and* the failure of the child-and-family service agencies to intervene effectively to prevent child abuse when the facts and circumstances warrant intervention. In this case, the mother— Miriam Gallegos—the young woman who accosted the lawyer in the parking lot—was the girlfriend of Angel Ray Montoya. Though she knew all about his ugly history, she left her daughter alone with him.

In May of 2012 a jury convicted Angel Ray of first degree murder for the death of Neveah. The side of the story that focuses on her tragedy touches our hearts, to be sure. But the soul is stirred by the side that focuses on the community's quest to bring her killer to justice.

For many long months—nearly five years—that quest consumed the lives of family and friends, police and prosecutors, and eventually judges and juries. This is their story.

* * *

Many photos were taken of the scene in the small parking lot at 1080 Cherokee that late September afternoon. One of them sticks in the minds of many who have seen it. In particular it sticks in the mind of Detective Mark Crider, the red-headed father of two young daughters who became the lead homicide investigator on the case.

In the photo the lawyer, several police officers, and the young woman—Neveah's mother—are standing around in a cluster, not far from the entrance to the one-story building where the lawyer worked. They are talking and gesturing among themselves.

It must have been an unguarded moment. For the camera clearly caught a snicker on the face of Miriam Gallegos.

TWO: THE FAMILY and ANGEL RAY

Neveah Janey Gallegos was born under "a full moon, a blue moon"—according to her grandmother Janet—on August 1, 2004, at St. Joseph's Hospital in Denver. At the time Miriam was seventeen, still in high school, and unwed. In fact, Miriam claimed she didn't know who the father was, so none was listed on Neveah's birth certificate. Janet and her older sister Vera attended Miriam during her brief labor and the uneventful birth.

Janet and Vera were always there.

Janet was born in Durango 48 summers before Neveah, the third of three sisters, eleven years younger than Vera, the oldest. A baby brother arrived a few years later. The family moved to Montrose when Janet was still young. They were a close-knit family, though Janet was especially tight with Vera.

Janet says: "She more or less raised me ... I think of her as my second mother."

Vera is the nickname everyone uses for Genevieve Alvira, who evolved into the matriarch of the family after marrying Joe Vigil in 1964. She and her siblings had children and their children gave them grandchildren. On holidays they would congregate at Joe and Vera's modest home on South Yukon in Lakewood, just west of Denver proper. Photos from family events show Neveah laughing at Vera's house. Janet was almost always present. And usually Miriam wasn't.

These photos give faces and shapes to the family. In them Vera looks short and stout with a round cheerful face and strait dark hair cut chin-length. She complements Joe, who is thin and tight and silver-haired. They are a warm and stable couple. They've lived in that same house in Lakewood since they bought it in 1974. Their son grew up in that house. And despite her battle with multiple sclerosis, Vera worked successfully for twenty-six years as a tax examiner for the Colorado Department of Revenue. She had just retired when Neveah was born.

By then Janet was a small rounded woman, taller than Vera but on the short side nonetheless, with a quiet voice and long braided hair that had turned mostly gray over time. Since 1984 she had worked as a certified nursing assistant's aide, most recently at the Alzheimer's unit at the Villas at Sunny Acres, an assisted-living facility. She did basic patient care: "I feed, I bathe. I do activities, daily living, assist the nurses."

In the midle-1980s Janet started seeing a man named Leon Maestes. He fathered both of her daughters: Miriam, born April 25, 1987, and Cathy, born February 7, 1990. While the four never lived together as a family, Leon did play a role in his daughters' lives until Miriam was ten.

Miriam and Cathy were close in their early years. Janet has compared their personalities: "Cathy is very ... into technology ... culinary arts, the food. And she is very smart. She is ... very responsible." Miriam, by contrast, "communicates very well. She was into music. She was in symphony chorus. She was a smart girl." And until she was in middle school, Miriam was a good student who got good grades.

Still all was not well in the Gallegos household. Incidents of domestic violence scarred Janet's relationship with Leon. Once, with Miriam and Cathy watching, Leon pulled a gun on the family. By the time Janet ended their toxic relationship, the abuse had taken its toll.

On November 16, 1996—when Miriam was nine and the stresses were building inside the family—Janet threw a book at Miriam and hit her in the face. The next day Miriam arrived at Goldrick Elementary School with a light purple bruise on her cheek. This triggered an inquiry by the Denver Department of Social Services. Miriam was interviewed and stated her mother had hit her on the face with her hand because she had been goofing off and not listening when her mother was telling her to do her homework. She said it was the first time Janet had ever hit her and she was not fearful of returning home.

When Janet was contacted, she confirmed she had been having difficulty with Miriam that night and that she had hit her. Janet said she had lost her temper when Miriam started talking back to her, but expressed remorse after hitting Miriam, and said she had never hit either of her daughters before. The Social Services report said Janet was very forthcoming in her statement and appeared to understand the need for intervention. The caseworker found both Janet and Miriam were cooperative. The case was closed at intake and the report concluded the incident was an isolated one. Later Janet said: "We were discussing something. I can't remember what. But what happened, I tossed a book and it hit her. Okay. All right. Yes."

It wasn't a memory Janet was proud of. So she got rid of Leon and bought herself a nice little house on Lipan Street and worked hard to make a decent life for herself and her two young daughters.

Still it seemed like nothing she could do could stop Miriam from following a disturbing path. Middle school was not a time of positive development. It started small, with Miriam breaking household rules like curfews. Then she began leaving the house and staying away for hours, then days, then overnights. Sometimes she would not come home for weeks. One time she stayed away for months.

Janet was frantic. She had no idea where Miriam—now thirteen or fourteen—went when she left the home like that. Thinking there was "nothing really I could do," Janet would still file a runaway report whenever Miriam disappeared for more than a day.

"I filed more than ten runaways for her," Janet recalled. "It was just redundant. Every time. It never changed."

Eventually, every time, Miriam would come back home. And every time, even if she had been gone for months, Janet would let her back in: "Because she's my daughter. That's her home."

When Miriam was sixteen and supposedly going to high school, she told Janet she was pregnant. She lived at home during the rest of her pregnancy; she was covered by Janet's health insurance; and Janet went with her for almost all of her prenatal checkups. Janet also helped Miriam improve her diet during this time. The pregnancy advanced normally.

On the night of July 31, 2004, Miriam suffered a number of contractions. She went to the hospital with Janet and Vera but, according to Janet, "she wasn't ready. She was in false labor. She wasn't dilating yet so they sent her home."

The next night she went into labor for real so back to the hospital they all went. "We took her in around three and Neveah was born … at 4:00 in the morning … she had just gotten there and it wasn't too long [before] she delivered."

Returning to the little house on Lipan, things seemed to get off to a decent start. Sure, it was noisy, busy, and hectic, with a hard-working mother—one with no car—two teen-aged daughters, and one newborn baby. But Neveah was a beautiful child, an easy child, never colicky or ill, a child who slept peacefully through the night. And Miriam was breastfeeding Neveah some of the time while she was "going through W.I.C."

W.I.C. stands for Women, Infants, and Children. It is a program funded primarily by the U.S. Department of Agriculture and operated in Colorado by its Department of Public Health and Environment. The program provides nutrition education and supplemental nutritious foods to women who are pregnant or breastfeeding and to children under five.

According to Janet: "Through W.I.C. they would help her … with the milk and weighing the baby and checking the baby's weight. And then she went through the doctor at La Mariposa for her immunizations, for her well baby check-ups."

Of course Janet went to almost all of Neveah's regular check-ups at La Mariposa clinic, which was just around the corner from her home. And she was always happy to hear the doctors confirm what she knew already: Neveah was developing normally.

Photos of Neveah from that year show a dark-haired little girl with smooth caramel-colored skin and big dark eyes. She loved music and got along well with other people. By the time she could stand on her feet, she was dancing and smiling and laughing. By the time she could eat solid foods, she was hooked on pizza, spaghetti, and Taco Bell.

And by that time, Miriam was again steering off course. Throughout Neveah's first year, Miriam had increasingly taken less and less responsibility for her. She routinely passed Neveah off to her mother or younger sister Cathy. Though Miriam might sleep with Neveah and take her for walks, she left the diapers and the baths and the heavy lifting to others.

Janet talked about the bond she forged with Neveah during those months: "She lived in my household. We were – I more or less raised Neveah. She was like my child."

Still no one could contest that Janet was spread pretty thin. Enter Vera, the matriarch. Together with Janet and Cathy, she began taking rounds with Neveah. The three formed a triumvirate that assured Miriam's inattention would not become neglect.

The danger of that was very real. For by the end of Neveah's first year, Miriam was back in high school, enrolled in a charter school program at the "Life Skills Center" at nearby 10th and Cherokee Street. And while that sounded great to all concerned, it was little more than a cover for Miriam's slide back into her old ways.

For while Neveah—they called her Veah—bonded more and more with Grandma Janet, Auntie Cathy, and Great Aunt Vera, her mother Miriam started staying away from home like she did before Neveah was born. At first it was just a night or two. Then weeks or a month or two at a time.

Janet never knew where Miriam was.

Meanwhile, as Neveah plunged deeper into her second year, she was putting on weight and getting taller and starting to walk and talk.

She would ask Janet: "Are you tired, Grandma?"

Or she would say to Cathy: "You are going to school."

Or to Vera: "You take care of me, Auntie."

She loved watching *Dancing with the Stars* on the television and Leonardo DiCaprio in *Titanic*. She also loved Elmo and Dora the Explorer, and she looked at lots of picture books, favoring those with pop-ups. Janet would get her used children's books with words in them, and Neveah would open them up and look at them intently, even though she couldn't read the words.

Miriam became less of a presence in Neveah's life. She dropped out of her charter school program, got a job, and rented an apartment. She refused to tell Janet where she was working or where she was living. She rarely visited the little house on Lipan Street and usually made Cathy or Vera deliver Neveah to her at some grocery store or other place.

Miriam wasn't there to see how much Neveah came to love the tortillas grandma Janet made. Or to witness the expansion of her diet into bacon and eggs every morning. Or to watch her splash and frolic in Vera's little inflatable swimming pool. Or to deal with her transition to the potty, which would lag behind her other skills.

Miriam was too busy falling in love with Angel Ray Montoya.

* * *

During the second half of Neveah's second year, she began living a double life. There was the happy, healthy, loving Neveah who basked in the protective love of Janet, Cathy, and Vera. Then there was the Neveah that came to fear the man who insisted on being called "Daddy Ray."

Neveah didn't have the luxury of asking abstract questions. Why wouldn't an alienated, overweight, unwed mother with low self-esteem and a conniving way about her fall in love with Angel Ray?

Two years older than Miriam, he was reasonably handsome with a whiff of gang about him. He had a sturdy physique and a fine tattoo on his forearm. His hair was thick and black, cut close on the sides, longer on top. His moustache and chin growth seemed wispy but his eyes—dark, hooded, and steely hard—warned against taking him too lightly.

Janet didn't know much about Angel Ray. All she knew was that, sometime early in 2006, Miriam had acquired a boyfriend. She brought him to the little house on Lipan Street two or three times that spring. Once, if Janet recalled correctly, he came with his niece and nephew.

But Janet never liked the guy. He was leading her daughter down a path that would include a bust for possession of pot and a guilty plea to possession of drug paraphernalia. Two incidents in particular caused Janet escalating concern. They cemented her distaste for Angel Ray Montoya.

The first incident occurred in the spring of 2006, during one of the visits by Miriam, Neveah, and Angel Ray to Janet's house on Lipan Street. Later Janet recalled:

"I was upstairs in Cathy's room and they came upstairs, Neveah and Ray and Miriam to her room … He sat down Miriam and they put Neveah in a playpen. And Miriam was crying and she wouldn't stop crying. And he was … kneeling down next to her, and he told her to stop crying. And he was whispering in her ear and … he was getting more controlling with her to stop. She needed to stop crying."

And what was Neveah doing in her playpen? She was staying put because Daddy Ray had told her, "You need to stay there in the playpen."

But what else was Neveah doing?

"She is watching her mother. She was upset. Neveah was upset because her mother was upset … she was very tense. She was just watching what was going on … I told Miriam … I didn't appreciate that in my house. I told her if it didn't stop, I would call the police."

By then Neveah was reaching her arms out to Janet: "She was, come on grandma … [But] he just looked at Miriam, you know? And I went to get Neveah and Miriam said just to leave her alone. Just leave her."

Still Janet wasn't taking orders from her wayward daughter. She reached out for Neveah.

Angel Ray spoke up: "Just leave her there. Don't take her. Don't get her out."

And that was all it took for Janet to know she did not want this man anywhere near Neveah. She said to Miriam, "This is Neveah's house, Miriam … he's gonna push the wrong buttons here … you better tell him because I'll call nine, one, one. He does not tell me, my granddaughter, you, anything."

After that Janet could never feel comfortable with Angel Ray in the house. That look of anger in his eyes when he was insisting on leaving Neveah in her playpen simply wasn't natural. But it wasn't until the second incident—in July of 2006—that Janet became truly alarmed.

According to Janet, Miriam was working at the McDonald's "right by his mother's house on Alameda and Broadway … and we had went that morning to pick up Neveah and she had left her with Ray … and she says, 'Well Ray's gonna bring her at ten o'clock.' [But] it's already eleven, twelve o'clock and we said, 'We're just gonna go get her' … so we went to his mother's house and … he came to the door and he was just looking at us, you know? And he wouldn't bring the baby out. So Cathy says, 'I'll go get her.' And so Cathy went and she says, 'I'll stay here until Miriam gets here with the baby.' [Meaning she'd stay with the baby until Miriam got there.]"

Vera, who was driving the triumvirate that morning, later recalled "while we were at McDonald's, uh, Miriam came to our table and she said, 'Auntie,' she said, 'the baby is bleeding and I don't want you to make a deal out of it' … And I said, 'Where is she bleeding from?' And she said, 'Oh, it's like a diaper rash.' And so, uh, after that I didn't really think much about it."

She wasn't thinking about it, in particular, as she and Janet drove away while Cathy stayed behind with Ray and Neveah at his mother's house. Later, however, Janet said: "So [Cathy] was worried about her. Ray was acting real funny, you know?"

At the time Janet told Cathy: "Go get Neveah, we'll leave, so we can go," but Cathy insisted on staying put until Miriam got there. Then they'd bring Neveah home together.

That evening Cathy and Miriam arrived at Lipan Street with Neveah. Miriam started to change Neveah's diaper, then she paused and said, "There's a little bit of bleeding, don't worry about it." Janet noted that Miriam "changed her real quick and she says she'll be okay. It was already late so Neveah was tired. She was only two …"

Janet thought maybe Neveah had scraped herself. She asked Miriam how that odd bit of bleeding—vaginal bleeding—had happened. "And she says, 'Oh, it's okay, it's okay.' You know, so Neveah went to sleep and in the morning I changed her, and there was a big vaginal area … and I called my sister, I says, 'There's—she did something to her.' You know, somebody did something to her. And so we took her to Denver General."

In the interview Janet gave on July 17, her 50th birthday, to Detective Roger Weir and Barbara Pierce of the Department of Human Services, she described the bleeding in more detail: "She had gotten up and, uh, I changed her diaper and there was blood in the, on the tissue that I was wiping her with … So, uh, I kept wiping and it was more blood so I, you know, was concerned … I saw blood on her labias and, you know, that's when I called Miriam."

Miriam, of course, said it was nothing, just a diaper rash, which indeed Neveah did have at the time—but not on her genitals. And now Neveah was clotting! Janet turned to Vera.

Vera remembers the call. Janet said, "The baby's really bleeding."

Vera asked, "Where is she bleeding from?"

Janet said, "Like blood clots, just like a menstrual period."

Vera said, "Hey, she's only, not only but two years old yet … That's not normal … Don't change her again … Wait till I get there … Janet, don't change her diaper again … I'll come down and take you to the hospital with her."

While Vera was on her way to pick up Janet and Neveah, Janet called Miriam and Miriam said she wanted to go with them, so they picked her up outside Angel Ray's house before going to Denver General—a/k/a Denver Health—a few blocks away. Vera sat in the waiting room.

Janet hovered over Neveah in the ER. In the corner Miriam called Angel Ray. And while Janet didn't catch all of what was said, that's when she learned something about Angel Ray that his jury wouldn't hear. It provoked such an argument that Janet came out and said to Vera, "Will you come in with us? Because Miriam is just verbally attacking me and I'm just kind of worried that we're gonna get into it in there."

So Vera joined them in the emergency examining room.

That's when, according to Janet, "Miriam started telling us he was not supposed to be around the kids and he was, uh, he had done something to a little boy, his other girlfriend's little boy … [She said] we were gonna get him in trouble because he was gonna go to jail 'cause he was a sex offender. He wasn't supposed to be around kids. And, 'Why did we do that?' And she was really upset with us."

Vera, according to her account, confronted Miriam directly: "We just want to know what happened to her and have her taken care of. We want the truth."

Miriam answered, "Because Ray is not supposed to be around children and this is gonna get him in trouble."

Vera was incredulous: "You're more worried about Ray than the baby?" She pressed: "Why is Ray gonna be in trouble?"

Miriam said, "Well, he's not supposed to be around children because he's gotten in trouble before ... They made up a big story about him, uh, something about another kid."

A police officer—a rookie who admitted he really didn't know what to do—came in with a couple of social workers. Vera recalls, "One was sitting on the floor watching and observing the baby and they kept asking, 'Why is the baby going to your aunt and to your mother for nurturing, why is she not coming to you? Why are you not nurturing your baby?' ... and, uh, Miriam was just sitting there in the corner all distraught and crying the whole time."

To all of them, Miriam insisted she didn't know what had happened—"somebody had to have done it"—but she "claimed Ray wouldn't do something like that to the baby."

Janet didn't buy it. They told her at the hospital there seemed to have been a trauma to Neveah's hymen. Janet believed Angel Ray "did something to her. Because he ... he's sexually molested her, did something and then he knew that if he brought her home [and] we found any, we'd take her to the hospital. Maybe he thought it would be easier to not let her ... come back." Janet's level of concern was raised to alarm.

The next few months were touch and go. A report by the Colorado Department of Human Services described the incident and its aftermath in great detail and bureaucratic style:

[T]he maternal grandmother and mother of two-year old Neveah had brought the child to the hospital due to vaginal bleeding. The physician examined the child and diagnosed a small hymeneal tear. The emergency response caseworker immediately responded to the hospital. The mother reported that she had left Neveah Gallegos alone with her boyfriend, "Ray," on July 14, 2006. He reportedly had given Neveah a bath … The initial medical report indicated that Neveah had suffered a penetration injury but it was inconclusive as to what had penetrated the child. A Denver Police Detective also responded to the hospital.

The officer placed a police hold on Neveah Gallegos for placement with the DDHS and agreed to placement of the child with the maternal grandmother. The officer, in conjunction with the caseworker, ordered that the mother have no unsupervised visits and not reside in the same house with the grandmother and have no contact with Angel Ray Montoya …

The officer and the caseworker checked the DPD's data system and determined that Angel Ray Montoya was a registered sex offender. The officer made contact with Mr. Montoya but he refused to participate in an interview. DPD reported that due to the lack of evidence, there was insufficient probable cause to arrest the alleged perpetrator. The case was transferred to an intake caseworker on 7/16/06. The caseworker completed the safety and risk assessments on 7/17/06. The safety assessment noted no safety concerns.

7/18/06:
The grandmother brought Neveah to the FCC for a culpa scope examination. Dr. Kathryn Wells, Medical Director at the FCC, was consulted regarding the medical findings and after reviewing the results, determined that the injury was to the urethra opening and not the hymen. Dr. Wells stated that although the findings did not rule out sexual abuse, it was much less indicative of sexual abuse than a hymeneal tear, as the injury could have occurred during diapering.

Miriam Gallegos attended the Team Decision Making (TDM) meeting that was held on 7/27/06. A case was opened for services. The TDM resulted in a documented agreement that custody of Neveah was returned to Miriam

Gallegos and Miriam could return to her mother's home. A safety plan was developed that required Miriam to report to DDHS any contact with Angel Ray Montoya. DDHS agreed to provide in-home services for three months, and Family-to-Family resources would be made available to assist Miriam with parenting skills and a GED program. The agreement indicated that Miriam Gallegos would take full responsibility for parenting Neveah with day care assistance from the grandmother and the aunt.

8/02/2006:
The intake caseworker conducted a home visit with Miriam, her mother, her aunt and Miriam's daughter Neveah. The intake caseworker completed a social history interview and observed the home. The intake caseworker informed Ms. Gallegos that the case was being transferred to an ongoing worker. The caseworker noted no safety concerns in her documentation …

8/03/2006:
The caseworker and supervisor concluded that the allegation of sexual abuse was unfounded based upon the inconclusive medical findings, lack of verbal history by Neveah, and the inability to interview Angel Montoya. The department reported that Angel Montoya's whereabouts were unknown.

[Note the report's conclusion that the allegation of sexual abuse was "unfounded"—suggesting it had no basis—rather than "unproven," which would have been a more accurate characterization.]

10/03/2006:
The therapist assigned to work with the family from a contract service provider conducted safety, risk and NCFAS assessments on the family using the Colorado Assessment Continuum. The safety assessment documented safety concerns, and a safety plan indicated that "suspected perpetrator must not have access to the child."

<u>11/13/06:</u>
The therapist called the caseworker and stated she did not have any safety concerns and would like to talk about closing the case. A home visit was conducted on 11/17/06 and the caseworker noted no safety concerns ... The caseworker concluded with the statement "Miriam still has not stated that Neveah was sexually abused by her boyfriend. But she does understand the safety concerns." The closing NCFAS was completed on 11/21/06.

<u>11/17/2006:</u>
A treatment-staffing meeting was held with the caseworker, the therapist, the therapist's supervisor, and Miriam Gallegos. Ms. Gallegos reported that things were going well and the team agreed to close the therapeutic service and to close the DDHS case in one month. Ms. Gallegos again denied having any contact with Angel Montoya.

<u>11/21/2006:</u>
The therapist completed The Colorado Safety Assessment-Plan. The therapist noted that Miriam Gallegos continued to minimize the extent of the injury and deny Angel Montoya caused injury. Miriam Gallegos stated that the suspected perpetrator no longer has contact with the child; therefore current conditions or family actions addressed all identified safety concerns. The Colorado Risk Reassessment was completed with risk level rated at low.

<u>1/02/2007:</u>
Case closed as Miriam Gallegos had complied with her treatment plan, completed the in-home treatment with the community based service provider, continued to do well in the home with her mother, had a job and was connected to community resources. Closing statement indicated ... no child protection concerns at that time.

Happy New Year, Neveah Gallegos. The State of Colorado has concluded you are safe.

* * *

Does a parent in the U.S. have a legal obligation—a recognized duty—to protect his or her child from harm caused by third parties? The answer is not as clear as most people would assume.

Law professor Vincent Johnson and lawyer Claire Hargrove explained in a 2006 article in the *Villanova Law Review* that common law scholars recognized the "special relationship" between a parent and child that would trigger an exception to the general rule that the law would not force a person to become a Good Samaritan: someone who takes *affirmative action* to help someone else who is in harm's way.

So there was plenty of rhetoric about the legal duty of a parent to protect a child from harm. But there was precious little precedent from the courts.

The problem was this duty ran headlong into conflicting common law principles, such as those granting parents immunity from causing harm to their children for purposes of discipline, especially in agrarian settings.

How to set the line between abuse and discipline? The courts couldn't even address the issue until those competing common law principles were abrogated or limited by statute. And so there remain, even in the 21st century, relatively few cases in America that impose a privately enforceable *civil duty* on a parent to prevent harm to his or her child.

Under *child welfare and criminal laws*, there is much more to work with. Colorado, like most states, has detailed statutes that address child abuse in these two contexts. Its Children's Code and Human Services Code set forth the specific terms and conditions under which the state can intervene on behalf of an abused child. However, these statutes still do not expressly declare the parent's affirmative legal duty to protect.

Furthermore, investigators must "take into account accepted child-rearing practices of the culture in which the child participates including, but not limited to, accepted work-related practices of agricultural communities. [And nothing defining the terms used in the statute] shall refer to acts that could be construed to be a reasonable exercise of parental discipline." This means the two common law barriers to intervention remain on the books in the context of Colorado's child welfare laws.

Its Criminal Code and Criminal Proceedings Code likewise provide definitions of child abuse and procedures for prosecuting its perpetrators. Under these statutes, however, the definition of child abuse is worded so it clearly does cover both actions and failures to act: "A person commits child abuse if such person causes an injury to a child's life or health, or permits a child to be unreasonably placed in a situation that poses a threat of injury to the child's life or health, or engages in a continued pattern of conduct that results in malnourishment, lack of proper medical care, cruel punishment, mistreatment, or an accumulation of injuries that ultimately results in the death of a child or serious bodily injury to a child." This statute takes a major step forward.

Fortunately the case law is also catching up. For example, the California Court of Appeals in 2008 faced a case where a father who was prohibited by court order from visiting or staying at the apartment of the mother of his children had been staying with her for a week nonetheless. One night he immersed his one-year old son in a tub of water and other chemicals and threw him against the wall in the mother's presence. The child had been crying but stopped after he hit the wall. Later that night the child started crying again. The father punched the child in the chest and a neighbor heard a series of thuds against the wall that lasted three minutes, after which the child stopped screaming.

During these horrific hours the mother stood by and did nothing to protect her child. The next morning the father woke the mother and told her the child wasn't breathing.

The father then purchased gasoline and took the child's body into the bathroom where he burned it in a bucket in an effort to erase its identifying features. When the police arrested the father, they found the child's body in his van. He was charged with murder and the mother was charged with aiding and abetting.

The trial court instructed the jury that the mother did indeed have a duty to take all steps reasonably necessary under the circumstances to protect her child from harm. On appeal the mother argued the trial judge "incorrectly instructed the jury that a parent may be liable for aiding and abetting ... by intentionally failing to act to protect her child from harm."

After reviewing the single California case and the few cases from other states that had addressed the issue, the appeals court sided with the majority of those cases. It held that "a parent has a duty to protect his or her young child and may be criminally culpable on an aider and abettor theory for an assault causing death and on an implied malice theory for murder where the parent fails to take reasonably necessary steps for the child's protection, so long as the parent, with ability to do so, fails to take those steps with the intent of facilitating the perpetrator's assaultive offense."

The appeals court made clear at the end of its opinion what it thought about the mother's failure to act: "She made no effort to aid her son: she did not scream, call 911, ask a neighbor to help or call for help, or do anything else. Instead, she went to sleep and left her son alone with Lopez [the father] though she knew Lopez had recently punched him and thrown him against a wall ... a reasonable jury could infer that appellant was capable of taking some action to protect her child and that she chose not to do so, but to go to sleep and leave her son alone with Lopez."

* * *

Still Janet didn't know about the cases and statutes that might have helped her save Neveah. When she asked Miriam for custody, so Neveah could be covered by Janet's medical insurance and be given a "stable home," Miriam refused, and Janet didn't have the resources to consult a lawyer about taking custody from Miriam.

Janet didn't know the alternatives that are available to loved ones who won't take "no" for an answer—who wish to push beyond the child welfare agencies. What Janet knew was the Department of Human Services was wrong.

None of its counseling and home visits had done any good. Their reports were a fantasy. The reality wasn't nearly so rosy. By the fall of 2006, Janet was exhausted, working the graveyard shift, caring for Neveah, and worrying about Miriam. Vera began taking Neveah for five nights almost every week, becoming her primary care-giver during the last year of her life.

Again Miriam moved out, rented her own apartment, got a new job, and at some point started seeing Angel Ray again—if she had ever really stopped seeing him. That meant Neveah was again coming into contact with a known sex offender, even if it was only on those increasingly rare occasions when Miriam took Neveah to stay with her for a night or two.

After those visits, Neveah began acting oddly. It was as if the barrier between her two lives was dissolving. She would put her fingers to her lips and say "shhhhhhh" whenever she was asked about "Daddy Ray." And during bath time, Vera noticed that Neveah had started saying, "Don't touch, don't touch," whenever she tried to wash her vaginal area.

Janet and Vera didn't need to read any academic studies to realize Neveah was in danger. But the studies, reports and articles by experts fully supported their fears. A paper published in 2008 by researchers from the University of Virginia painted this sad picture:

Children living in cohabiting households with unrelated males, as well as children being cared for by their mother's boyfriend, are especially vulnerable to maltreatment. Studies consistently find that unrelated males who are placed in a caretaking role with children are disproportionately involved in the physical and sexual abuse of children ...

Children born into a cohabiting relationship are much more likely to see their parents break up than are children born into married families. Consequently, compared to children born into married families, they are much more likely to live in a single-parent household before they reach age 18 and to experience family instability, both of which increase their odds of suffering from neglect ... Men who are not related by biology or by adoption (soon after birth) to the children in their care are more likely to have difficulty controlling their anger when children misbehave or reining in any sexual attraction that they might have toward the children. Accordingly, stepfathers and boyfriends are more likely to engage in abusive behavior toward their step-children or toward the children of their girlfriend.

In other words, an unrelated male who is a registered sex offender should never be left alone with a child. Miriam was shirking her duty to protect Neveah and the bureaucrats were doing nothing about it.

Janet felt powerless. All she could do was remain on edge during those few days—usually two days, twice a month, sometimes less—when Miriam came for Neveah.

Later Janet said, "My sister would go take Neveah to her and she would meet at the store. She wouldn't allow us to go to her apartment."

Predictably under these circumstances Neveah began showing less interest in being with her mother. She was happiest "at home" with her triumvirate: Janet, Vera, and Cathy.

She was comfortable there.

She was safe there.

Neveah turned three in August of 2007. No longer a baby, she was a walking, talking little girl-child, potty trained at last, still in love with Dora and Elmo, showing more interest in her clothes and appearance, and recently taken with those ubiquitous pink princess tennis shoes.

Miriam used the occasion to stay away from Neveah for the next several weeks, leaving her to the triumvirate. Janet was naturally upset: "And you know after awhile Neveah just doesn't think of her mother anymore … but then Miriam starts missing her so she came and got her. Told me she had four days off. And I says, 'How can you work full time and have four days off in a row? You know, how are you going to make ends meet?' She said, 'Well, I'll call you if I have to go to work … [on] Thursday. If not, I'll bring her Friday.' [But] Miriam, her cell phone was disconnected because she didn't pay for it."

So the wheels were set in motion for Neveah's final days on Earth. Miriam would pick her up on Tuesday, September 18, after her mother went to work and return her on Friday, the 21st, unless she had to go to work on Thursday, in which case she would bring Neveah back a day early.

Janet was concerned. Tuesday night to Friday night meant three days with a mother whose sound judgment Janet seriously questioned, and likely also with Angel Ray, that sex offender she was practically living with again.

Neveah stayed overnight with Vera on Sunday, September 16. The next evening, about 9:00, Joe drove Vera and Neveah to Janet's house. Vera sat in the back seat with Neveah. All the way down Wadsworth and Sixth Avenue, Neveah was crying and distraught. She kept saying things like "No mama, no mama" and "Don't take me to my grandma's [Janet's]. Take me to my other grandma's [her great-grandmother's] … I don't want to see mama … I want to see my grandma with the doggy."

Finally Vera asked her, "Why don't you want to see your mother? Is Daddy Ray there?"

Neveah put her fingers to Vera's lips to tell her to be quiet.

When they got to Janet's house, Vera tried to undo Neveah's seat belt but, Vera said later, "She wouldn't let me. She was fighting me off and crying. So I got out of the car. I went to my sister's door and knocked. She answered and I said, 'Neveah is very upset.' And my sister just ran out to the car and got her … she quit crying and she got happy to see her grandma."

The problem was not Janet, of course. The problem was Vera had told Neveah that her mother would be coming to pick her up. That was what upset her.

After taking her inside and calming her down, Janet and Cathy examined Neveah thoroughly during her bath: "We check her good if she's gone." There were no bruises, scratches or cuts on the little girl. She was in perfect health.

The next day—Tuesday—Janet later recalled, "I slept two or three hours in the afternoon, she napped with me, and we went in the afternoon to Little Caesar's to get pizza on the light rail, and on the way back Cathy was to take Neveah because I had to go to work."

They ended up taking the pizza home, however, and instead going to Country Harvest to eat. Then, Janet had to leave in time to catch her bus to work.

Before she left, she put some things together for Neveah in her little pull-along suitcase-backpack. "It had a decal on the front, um, like Dora, but I don't remember exactly … I put [in] some money … for Neveah. In case she needed anything. And I put a note to Miriam."

The note read: "Miriam, please bring back all Neveah's clothes. I bought her some footy pajamas and here's 50 dollars. Please, if possible, after you get settled, pay me back for Neveah, 30 dollars. We can discuss this, and please try to get medical as soon as possible for her, or I will try. We have to meet heads on this, and let me know when you are going to bring her back. Be careful, Mom, Cathy and Neveah."

The extra money was meant to help Miriam with the deposit on her new apartment. Janet, ever the maternal figure, wouldn't write her daughter off. Still inevitably she had to go to work, so she left her precious Neveah with Cathy, and Miriam came to pick her up later that night, and a scene like the one the night before unfolded yet again.

Neveah didn't want to go.

She held onto Cathy and cried, "No mama, no mama!"

Janet, when she was interviewed a month later by Denver Homicide Detective Mark Crider, was able to say exactly why Neveah didn't want to go with her mother:

"Because she knew Ray. She was afraid of him."

THREE: THE DAY of the MURDER

Miriam took Neveah from the protection of the triumvirate and none of them felt there was anything they could do about it. Janet's worries were hardly dampened by the phone call she received from Miriam later in the week, supposedly from the Sports Authority outlet where she was working, supposedly on her day off, supposedly visiting her co-workers, supposedly with Neveah right there, dozing on her knees.

Janet thought Miriam was working at the Sports Authority in Aurora, east of Denver, a fairly long bus trip away. In reality, Miriam was working at the "Sportscastle," the flagship of the Sports Authority chain of 45 stores, located in the heart of Denver at 10th and Broadway, an iconic building whose façade is covered with faux-castle flourishes. Built in 1925 as a Chrysler dealership, the Sportscastle houses six rambling floors of sporting goods and gear.

Little did Janet realize Neveah was so close. Her house was only a mile due west of the Sportscastle. It was located in the heart of the La Alma-Lincoln Park neighborhood, one of Denver's oldest neighborhoods, near downtown. La Alma contains the Santa Fe Arts District, the Museo de las Américas, the Denver Health hospital complex, Denver West High School, an emergency food bank, the Asian and Hispanic Chambers of Commerce, La Mariposa clinic, and about 7,000 residents.

Two-thirds of these residents are Hispanic, Native American, African-American, or mixed. They live in old, small-scale Victorians, narrow row houses, stucco duplexes, and little brick bungalows.

While the crime rate and poverty rate are high in the neighborhood, the pool and recreation facilities at Lincoln Park take the edge off. It's a vibrant environment.

Neveah had plenty of room to run and grow when she was in La Alma.

On the other side of Speer Boulevard, directly to the east, lies Denver's Golden Triangle, formed by 13th Avenue on the north, Broadway on the east, and Speer running diagonally to connect the two and form the third side. In 2007 it was a transitional neighborhood stuck in a gentrification that refused to move forward. A handful of fashionable lofts were scattered among desolate parking lots, low-rise worn-down businesses, and a few decent restaurants.

Just inside the Golden Triangle, a block east of Speer, the little parking lot to the south of the one-story office building at 1080 Cherokee awaited the drama about to unfold.

On the morning of Friday, September 21, none of the triumvirate knew that Neveah awoke within walking distance. Only a half mile beyond the Sportscastle on Broadway, just four blocks further east and three blocks further north, there sat a small apartment house where she was staying with Miriam and Angel Ray.

The address of the apartment house was 1257 Logan Street and it fell on the tacky side of Capitol Hill, Denver's most densely populated neighborhood, stretching from Broadway east to Downing Street, and from 7th Avenue on the south to Colfax on the north. Capitol Hill includes Colorado's gold-domed capitol building and a wide array of mansions, including the Governor's Mansion, upscale condominiums, retail stores and office buildings, good restaurants and cheap cafes, loud night clubs and coffee shops, an old vinyl record shop, a large number of downscale apartments, and an edgy feel, especially the closer you get to Colfax Avenue, Denver's major east-west artery, often said to be the longest Main Street in the Nation.

While many key details of that Friday would not be discovered until further investigation, by that night it was clear: Neveah started her day alive in Unit # 308, a small studio apartment, at 1257 Logan Street and left that unit dead later that afternoon.

Logan is a busy one-way street running north that intersects with 13th Avenue, an even busier one-way street running west, parallel to Colfax and two blocks south. The apartment house at 1257 Logan is one small parking lot and another small apartment house from that busy intersection. The run between the sidewalk and the curb is hard-packed dirt with patchy weeds. What yard there is between the sidewalk and building is covered in white stones except for the cement walk to the three stairs that lead to the entry. Though shaded by an old tree on the north side of the property, the yard is hardly a place where Neveah could have run or played with other kids.

The roof of the building appears flat. The middle 30% of the façade is covered with thin blond stones laid horizontally around the entry way and above it. A curved overhang stretches above a small space in front of the door. To the right and the left of the blond stones are the two apartment wings, built with thin dark bricks, two stories high with a basement whose windows are covered with bars. There can't be more than twenty units in the whole building.

From the outside it is neither horrible nor inviting.

That morning Miriam left her unit in that apartment building and walked the seven blocks to go to work at the Sportscastle. Breaking her promise to her mother Janet, her aunt Vera, and the Colorado Department of Human Services, she left Neveah in the care of Angel Ray Montoya, "Daddy Ray," a registered sex offender who had once choked a girlfriend's son and who had most likely molested Neveah herself the year before.

Already the day was heating up. It had been hotter and drier than usual in Denver all month. People were dressing in cool summer clothes.

Was Miriam sweating by the time she got to work? Was she concerned, in her heart or mind, about leaving Neveah with Angel Ray? Did she even bother to think about it while hustling to the Sportscastle on that warm September morning?

Because if she wasn't thinking about the danger, she should have been. The day before Miriam had noticed Neveah had a bruise on her left cheek, a bump on her forehead, and a scratch on her back. She certainly knew these injuries had to have been suffered—or inflicted—sometime after Neveah came to stay with her and Angel Ray on Tuesday night. After all, Janet and Cathy saw no such marks on Neveah on Monday when they examined her.

But whether or not Miriam was worried, the triumvirate certainly was. Usually Miriam took Neveah for only a day or two. This time the extra day, stretching the visit through Friday, meant extra exposure to Angel Ray. As the day wore on, Janet's anxiety level began to rise.

Even Janet's neighbor, Elizabeth Murray, later expressed concern: "… the truth is, the man who we all think around here is the father, should have never been allowed to see her … because … he was crazy."

By early afternoon that craziness had claimed its victim.

Sometime between 1:30 and 2:00, Angel Ray knocked on the door of a neighbor named Stephen Matthews and asked to use his telephone. Angel Ray seemed upset. His legs were shaking, according to Matthews, "and he seemed to be sniffling, almost to not cry."

Matthews asked Angel Ray if Neveah was okay because he had heard her crying the day before.

Now the fact was Neveah's crying had become a trigger—a hot button—for Angel Ray. Later Miriam testified that she never actually saw him hit Neveah, but he did get increasingly frustrated whenever she cried or got too clingy. And Miriam admitted Angel Ray was less affectionate with Neveah than with his own niece and nephew—suggesting confirmation for the idea that unrelated boyfriends respond differently than real fathers to their girlfriend's children—and he wanted Neveah to act more mature than she was.

Angel Ray brushed aside Matthews' question. "Everything is fine," he said. So Matthews allowed Angel Ray to use his telephone. First Angel Ray dialed directory assistance to get the number for the Sportscastle. Then he called Miriam there.

Her boss answered the phone and handed it to her. Matthews overheard Angel Ray's side of the "frantic call." Later Miriam described it like this: "He was hysterical … He kept telling me, 'I need you to come home. I need you to come home.'" But he refused to tell her why.

Miriam ran the seven blocks home. By this time the day had gotten hot. By this time she must have been worried. By this time she must have been sweating. She arrived at her apartment and at first Angel Ray blocked her from entering. He pleaded with her: "Babe, I didn't do anything. I promise. You have to believe me. I just gave her a sip of water and she collapsed."

Miriam went inside. It was odd: Angel Ray was playing their song, the old R&B favorite, "Always and Forever." And it was hot. The place was all closed up.

Miriam rushed to see Neveah. She found her lying on the bed, covered with an orange and red blanket. She tore off the blanket and saw her daughter was dressed in red sweat pants, a red sweat shirt with a cartoon elephant on it, and her pink princess tennis shoes.

If she had been thinking straight, Miriam might have realized Neveah had been clothed this way to hide the bruises on her body. Why else put her in sweat clothes on such a hot day? It's a common ploy, in fact, that child abusers use every day: cover the evidence, ignore its very existence.

Neveah was not breathing. Miriam could tell she was dead. "She was pale. There was no color to her skin. She was gone." There was "dried crusty blood around her lips and tongue." Still Miriam claimed she tried to "put air into Neveah" by putting her on the floor and attempting CPR on her, but she wasn't able to revive her.

Angel Ray insisted he had done nothing to harm the child. He said he had given her a bath because she had urinated on herself. Afterwards, she'd gotten dressed and had something to eat and drink. And when she took that drink, "she could not breathe, started panting, and collapsed."

He told Miriam he put Neveah in the bed and covered her with the blanket. He told Miriam that he loved her. She and Angel Ray were terrified. He begged her to protect them both: "They're going to blame both of us," he said, according to Michelle Amico, who later became his lead prosecutor. "You know how this is going to look. If you love me, babe, you will think of me too."

Miriam did not want to lose Angel Ray. With Neveah gone, he was all she had left. So instead of calling an ambulance or the police, she agreed to help him cover up the death of her daughter. They conspired together.

First they stuffed Neveah's body into a "white trash bag with yellow handles" and then they stuffed the white trash bag inside a "black trash bag" and then they stuffed the black trash bag inside a royal blue duffel bag with white lettering on it. Miriam later described how she had to force Neveah's body into the white trash bag, head first and folded into a sort of fetal position because she was too tall to fit inside the bag. She described Neveah's body as being stiff and said they placed blankets around it inside the duffle bag to make it appear more bulky.

Then they talked about what to do. It was Miriam's idea to take the body somewhere and dispose of it. They decided she would fabricate the fake kidnapping story and try to sell it to the police in order to buy time for Angel Ray to get away and dispose of the body.

They left the apartment together. They walked to the alley behind the building and went their separate ways. The last Miriam saw of Angel Ray, he was walking north up the alley, carrying the royal blue duffel bag with Neveah's body inside.

Miriam wandered the nine blocks from her Capitol Hill apartment house to the alley behind the parking lot at 1080 Cherokee in the Golden Triangle. There she saw a woman in tennis clothes emerging from the one-story office building. The woman was walking toward a white Audi A6 parked in the lot. She was holding a cell phone to her ear.

Miriam walked toward the woman. Whether she was acting dazed and confused or was truly dazed and confused, only Miriam could say. She asked the woman to use her cell phone.

The woman looked skeptical, took a step back, and asked, "What's wrong?"

She had to ask it twice.

Miriam answered in a soft voice: "In the alley ... they ... took my baby in the alley."

The woman in the tennis clothes still would not hand over her cell phone. Instead she dialed 911 and that became the official beginning of the inquiry into Neveah's death. The cops arrived almost immediately. Lights were flashing blue and red, and the parking lot was swarming with police officers. It was turning into a genuine crime scene.

Miriam repeated the story she had told during the 911 call: her daughter had been kidnapped.

* * *

While American law remained ambivalent toward the privately enforceable civil duty of a parent to protect a child, and Colorado's child welfare laws failed to do anything about the danger Angel Ray posed to Neveah, the criminal law was ready to spring into action. In fact, four different sets of laws were triggered by the 911 call made by the lawyer in the parking lot.

First there was the *substantive criminal law*. Ever since the earliest days of the Republic, it has been clear that "common law crimes" are not recognized in the U.S. Accordingly judges, whether state or Federal, cannot create or define the elements of a crime. In other words, at the Federal level, if the government wants to create or define the elements of a crime that falls within its jurisdiction, then Congress must enact legislation, a statute, to do so. So too at the state level, if the government wants to create or define the elements of a crime that falls within its jurisdiction, then its state legislature must enact a statute to do so.

In Neveah's case, several substantive crimes seemed to have been committed. Initially the system thought it was dealing with a kidnapping. An Amber Alert was issued. Kidnapping protocols were initiated. Soon, however, "probable cause" existed to suspect very different crimes. These ranged from relatively minor infractions, like the false reporting of the child's kidnapping, to the most serious felonies society recognizes, including homicide. The exact legal elements of these crimes, created and defined by the Colorado General Assembly, would come into play—and become subjects of fierce argumentation— over the next five years of investigation and judicial proceedings.

But the most serious of these crimes would need a body to make them stick. And at the time, while Miriam was standing in the parking lot, telling her lies to the police, she was hoping Neveah's body would not be found, at least not right away. She was hoping her kidnapping story would give Angel Ray time to dispose of it. At one point she even felt a snicker cross her face as she thought about it. Unfortunately for her, that instant was caught on camera—the first of two times she would be caught on camera looking that way. It became a piece of evidence.

Second there were the *evidentiary and procedural laws and rules* that govern how criminal investigations and proceedings are conducted. These, too, would become bones of contention in the legal battles waged over the fates of Miriam and Angel Ray. And while she was as oblivious to these laws and rules as she was to the legal elements of the crimes she might have committed with her boyfriend, the police were not. From the moment they got the 911 call from the lawyer, they acted with upmost professionalism, mindful of the procedural and evidentiary rules that would apply in any subsequent proceedings. Eventually, their efforts would be rewarded.

Third there were a variety of Federal constitutional protections enshrined in the *Bill of Rights* that came into play. They included the Fourth Amendment:

> **The right of the people to be secure in their persons, houses, papers, and effects, against unreasonable searches and seizures, shall not be violated, and no Warrants shall issue, but upon probable cause, supported by Oath or affirmation, and particularly describing the place to be searched and persons or things to be seized.**

The Fifth Amendment:

> **No person shall be ... subject for the same offense to be twice put in jeopardy of life or limb; nor shall be compelled in any criminal case to be a witness against himself, nor be deprived of life, liberty, or property, without due process of law...**

The Sixth Amendment:

> **In all criminal prosecutions, the accused shall enjoy the right to a speedy and public trial, by an impartial jury of the State and district wherein the crime shall have been committed, which district shall have been previously ascertained by law, and to be informed of the nature and cause of the accusation; to be confronted with the witnesses against him; to have compulsory process for obtaining witnesses in his favor, and to have the Assistance of Counsel for his defense.**

And the Eighth Amendment:

> **... nor [shall] cruel and unusual punishments [be] inflicted.**

These are among the "fundamental rights" that lie at the core of our constitutional system. Justice Benjamin Cardozo, writing in 1937, called them "the very essence of our scheme of ordered liberty." Each of these rights would play an important role in the unfolding tragedy of Neveah Gallegos.

Fourth and finally there were those *provisions of the state's constitution that applied* even though the comparable provisions of the U.S. Constitution did not apply. That's because the "fundamental rights" located in the Fifth, Sixth, and Eighth Amendments apply equally to the states and to the Federal government. In the arcane vernacular of the Supreme Court, they have been "incorporated" through the due process clause of the Fourteenth Amendment.

However, some rights—in particular the right to grand jury indictment and arguably the right to bail—have never been "incorporated" and therefore do not apply to the states unless their own state constitutions or statutes create those rights.

Still, virtually all states, including Colorado, do provide for bail and roughly half still have grand juries. Colorado's rules governing the rights to bail and grand jury indictment would likewise come into play in the cases against Miriam Gallegos and Angel Ray Montoya.

How, then, did the authorities conduct themselves in light of the rules that governed them?

And, from their perspective, what took the case from a kidnapping to a homicide?

* * *

Since the Fourth Amendment was fully applicable, the police could not just barge into Miriam's apartment. And they hardly had time to get a proper search warrant from a judge, since they were operating under the assumption there had been a kidnapping and precious seconds were ticking away. So they did the next best thing. They asked Miriam for permission to enter her apartment to get a photo of Neveah to broadcast in connection with the Amber Alert.

When Miriam gave them permission, she sealed her fate and that of her boyfriend.

Short versions of the transformation of the case from kidnapping to killing filled the media. Longer versions appeared in two documents with similar wording, both signed that evening by Detective Joseph Delmonico: the Statement of Probable Cause signed in support of the initial arrest of Miriam Gallegos and the Affidavit and Application for Arrest Warrant (the "Affidavit") signed in support of the initial arrest warrant issued for Angel Ray Montoya. That Affidavit ended with the conclusion that there was "probable cause to believe Angel Montoya; DOB: 01/19/85; committed the crime of Murder in the First Degree."

An even more complete public version of the transformation of the case came after 18 months of hard work, in the April 2009 Arrest Warrant that accompanied the Indictment of Angel Ray. The following account of the hours between 3:00 p.m. and 7:40 p.m. that Friday blends the accounts found in the Affidavit and the Arrest Warrant. Discrepancies are noted.

The officers who arrived "on scene" at the parking lot immediately engaged Miriam. She repeated her kidnapping story—the white car, the red-bearded man. Information on the kidnapping suspect was "quickly aired over Police Radio."

Meanwhile, the responding officers noticed that Miriam was clutching a small child's jacket, pink or purple, but was not carrying a purse or diaper bag. This seemed odd to them.

Next, according to the Arrest Warrant: "Gallegos provided the officers with the key to her apartment so they could obtain a photograph to aid in the search for Neveah."

Specifically, according to the Affidavit, Miriam told Sergeant Troy Zimmerman where she lived and gave Sergeant Zimmerman "verbal permission to enter this apartment to obtain a current photograph" of Neveah. Sergeant Zimmerman immediately went to Unit # 308 at 1257 Logan Street to obtain this photo and "upon entry noticed what appeared to be a paper towel on the floor of the living room that had blood or some other type of bodily fluid on it."

Detectives from the Child Abuse Unit quickly joined the responding officers at the parking lot at 1080 Cherokee. They began talking to Miriam in an effort to gather further information. When Detective Matthew Cisneros began speaking with her, she "spontaneously stated to Detective Cisneros she and her boyfriend who she named as Angel Montoya were scared and put the baby into a bag."

That's all it took.

"Detective Cisneros verbally advised Ms. Gallegos of her Miranda Rights and Ms. Gallegos was then transported to Denver Police Headquarters and not questioned any further ... Then at Denver Police Headquarters, Ms. Gallegos was formally advised of her Miranda rights again and she waived them and agreed to speak with detectives." She told her story over and over to Detective Mark Crider, among others.

Meanwhile the later Arrest Warrant tells a slightly different version. Crank the time line back to the little parking lot. Miriam gave her key to Sergeant Troy Zimmerman.

He and other officers "responded to 1257 Logan Street, Apartment #308 in an effort to obtain a photograph of Neveah and to secure the apartment to make sure no one entered. While the officers were at that location they performed a neighborhood survey."

During their survey, they questioned Stephen Matthews. He told them he had listened while Angel Ray had called another person on his phone, and that he had "heard Montoya telling the other person that it was an emergency and that he/she needed to come home."

The officers at 1257 Logan relayed this information to Detective Cisneros, who was talking to Miriam at 1080 Cherokee. "Gallegos was confronted with this information and she admitted that Neveah was actually dead. She admitted that Montoya had removed Neveah's body from the apartment earlier that day. She confessed the kidnapping story was false."

Note in the Affidavit there is a "spontaneous" admission by Miriam, whereas in the later Arrest Warrant her admission comes in response to being confronted with Stephen Matthews' account of Angel Ray's phone call to Sports Authority. Another version, one from the media, blurs the lines and says Miriam started confessing when she was confronted with the paper towel that showed signs of bodily fluids. Whichever version is correct—and they are not necessarily inconsistent in any material way—Miriam started spilling her guts in the parking lot and that is when the case went from being a kidnapping to being a killing.

Initially, according to the Arrest Warrant, Miriam told Detective Cisneros that Angel Ray called her to come home and when she got there "Neveah was thirsty and needed some water." Miriam claimed "that Neveah's body temperature was hot and that she had urinated a little bit. Gallegos stated she gave Neveah a drink and she collapsed on the floor … During the interview Gallegos said that she attempted CPR on Neveah but that her eyes rolled back into her head and she stopped breathing. Gallegos told the detective she saw blood around [Neveah's] tongue and mouth" but insisted Angel Ray "would not do anything to harm Neveah."

So Miriam went from a false kidnapping story to a false story where Neveah was still alive when Miriam arrived home.

However, later during the same interview with Detective Cisneros, Miriam "changed her story" and began telling the version where Neveah was already dead and lying in bed under the orange and red blanket when she arrived home. That story became the one she stuck with throughout the long months and years ahead.

* * *

According to the Arrest Warrant, Angel Ray was located at about 7:35 p.m. at 13th and Lincoln in the Capitol Hill neighborhood, only a couple of blocks from the apartment house at 1257 Logan Street. He was wearing a hooded sweatshirt with the hood drawn over his baseball cap. And he was carrying a "small blue duffle bag."

Detective Mike Ryan stopped Angel Ray and confirmed his identity. Angel Ray, according to some accounts, tried to escape, to no avail. Detective Ryan asked Angel Ray what he was doing in the area. Angel Ray said he was looking for a job.

"Detective Ryan asked Montoya if there was anything in the bag and Montoya said no … Detective Ryan told Montoya the police were looking for him and that he thought Montoya knew why. Montoya responded by asking if he could talk to his girlfriend."

Detective Ryan looked inside the blue duffle bag but Neveah's body wasn't there. "He did find a small blanket and towel in the bag. The bag was measured and determined to be 24 inches in length."

Though the Arrest Warrant does not say so—it jumps ahead in time—Angel Ray was arrested on the spot and taken to Denver Police Headquarters where he was booked and bedded for the night. It appeared in the space of less than five hours the homicide had been solved.

The only problem was, of course, there was no body.

Homicide Detective Mark Crider was at police headquarters at 13th and Cherokee when the 911 call came in. It was, he said, a "big deal." There was a kidnapping only three blocks away! The police moved quickly. They were on it "fast and hard," according to Detective Crider.

"Tons of cops and tons of detectives" descended on the small parking lot at 1080 Cherokee. And in fact, the case transformed from a kidnapping to a homicide, Detective Crider's bailiwick, in less than an hour, while Miriam was still being interviewed in that parking lot.

Since it was still during the day shift, the duty sergeant was in charge of assigning cases to his detectives based on their current workloads, their schedules, and like considerations. As soon as the word came in that the case had become a homicide, Detective Crider said to his sergeant, "Hey, I'd like to have this."

His sergeant said, "It's yours."

That's how Detective Crider became the lead investigator of the death of Neveah Gallegos. It would haunt him for the rest of his life.

FOUR: THE POLICE and the SEARCH

On his desk at police headquarters, Detective Crider has taped a single word: PRIVILEGE. It's enough to remind him of a phrase he came across a long time ago:

"No greater honor will ever be bestowed on an officer, or a more profound duty imposed on him, than when he is entrusted with the investigation of the death of another human being."

Detective Crider figures "every now and then we forget the honor and privilege we have in speaking for a victim who can no longer tell their story."

He is a modest, earnest, thoughtful man. He is not like Hollywood's version of a swaggering homicide cop. He is a detective's detective, deeply committed to the public service he performs and constantly aware that his public is composed of real human beings. He is the guy who finds their bodies and carries them out; he attends their autopsies and investigates their deaths; and he works tirelessly to bring their killers to justice. It's his privilege.

Detective Crider was born in Virginia but moved with his family to the Tampa area when he was roughly six. After graduating from high school in Brandon, Florida, he enlisted in the Air Force. During his six years in the Air Force, serving as a security officer—a cop—he was stationed for a time in the Philippines. There he met his wife, a Filipina.

After leaving the Air Force, Detective Crider and his wife returned to Florida, where he served at the St. Petersburg police department for 3-1/2 years. He started on patrol, as young recruits do, cutting his teeth, and worked his way up. He had always wanted to be a cop.

"You know," he would later say, when asked why, "this is going to sound corny as all, but it was just the opportunity to make a difference and help people. I enjoyed that. I still enjoy it to this day. Again, it may sound corny, but that's the truth."

Late in his stint in St. Petersburg, Detective Crider and his wife took a vacation to visit a friend in Colorado. They fell in love with the state. When they got back home from their visit, he applied for jobs with several different Denver area law enforcement agencies. In 1995 he was hired by the Denver Police Department and after completing its academy, he was assigned to patrol District Six: the downtown area, Capitol Hill, Five Points, and Lincoln Park—some of the same neighborhoods that later would play such key roles in the life and death of Neveah Gallegos.

For seven years Mark Crider patrolled Denver's inner city before he became a detective. His first year as a detective was spent in Domestic Violence and his second year was spent in Child Abuse. Then he went into Homicide. At the time of the Angel Ray Montoya trial in the spring of 2012, he had been a homicide detective for eight years, investigating all sorts of killings, suicides, and suspicious deaths.

Yet however grim his day job might be, Detective Crider's personal life is filled with joy. After living for a few years in Denver, he and his wife adopted two daughters, both from China. People tell them how lucky those two girls are to have been taken out of their circumstances and brought to America and given such wonderful lives, but the Criders see it as a blessing on them, for their daughters have given them so much. Together the family lives a life of service that stretches beyond the confines of dad's employment.

On Christmas Day in 2008, for example, the now-defunct *Rocky Mountain News* ran a story about people helping people. It included this passage:

> Nine-year-old Yusha Crider knocked on the stranger's door. A man's voice called from the other side: "Come on in!"

Yusha and her family pushed open the door and walked into the apartment in the Thomas Bean Tower, a subsidized senior housing complex in downtown Denver.

"Merry Christmas!" said Mark Crider, of Littleton. "We're with Meals on Wheels."

They handed Charles H. Williams a hot meal in a tin-foil dish, a small carton of milk, a paper bag with rolls and a wrapped present, all prepared by Volunteers of America.

Williams smiled and thanked the Criders. He then asked them to pray with him. They all stood in a circle, hands clasped, and bowed their heads.

The Criders wished Williams well, picked up their boxes and bags and went on to the next apartment. This was their second Christmas volunteering.

Mark Crider, a detective with the Denver Police Department, said he heard about the VOA program from a district attorney.

On Thursday, they were among more than 80 families who delivered about 1,100 meals and gifts across Denver.

Mark Crider said the holiday program is a great way to teach his daughters the value of giving. "We get more out of it than we put into it."

Williams said he appreciated the Criders' visit. "That was really nice of them," he said, looking at the present wrapped in white tissue paper and a green ribbon. "This is the only thing I'll get."

So F. Scott Fitzgerald was right: "Action is character."

Detective Crider's actions reveal his character and nothing more need be said. Physically, he's an unassuming man of average build, with close-cropped reddish hair, well-proportioned, almost boyish features, and clear blue eyes that go well with his usual business attire: light blue spread collar shirt, striped tie, dark suit, small pistol in holster on his hip, and gold badge on his belt. He listens to classic rock.

Imagine him on September 21, 2007, at police headquarters, as Neveah's drama unfolded. Initially it came in as a kidnapping, so the Child Abuse Unit was the first to respond. But as soon as Miriam admitted Neveah was not kidnapped—she was dead—it became a homicide and Detective Crider's department took over, though it would continue to tap into the expertise of its colleagues in child abuse. This all took place quickly, while Miriam was still in the parking lot.

What prompted Detective Crider to volunteer for the case? Was he interested in child homicides because of his background in child abuse? Later he confirmed: "Yeah, I think that it's just from my child abuse background … They're horrible cases to work, but they're good, good cases in the same sense … In child abuse, they're just good victims to work for. Homicide or not homicide, any kid case you get a good victim … to help motivate you at times when you need some motivation."

Little was needed, however, on that sunny Friday afternoon when the Denver police jumped "fast and hard" on Neveah's case. As soon as he heard Miriam's admission in the parking lot, Detective Cisneros took her into custody, verbally advised her of her Miranda rights, and transported her without further questioning to police headquarters three blocks away.

At headquarters, Miriam was more formally advised of her Miranda rights—that bundle of warnings grounded in the Fifth and Sixth Amendments, as dictated by the Supreme Court's 1966 decision in *Miranda v. Arizona*, and commonly delivered by police in real life, on TV, and in the movies for decades now:

"You have the right to remain silent. Anything you say can and will be used against you in a court of law. You have the right to consult with an attorney and to have your attorney present during questioning. If you cannot afford an attorney, an attorney will be provided to represent you at no cost."

Miriam formally waived her rights and started talking to Detectives Cisneros and Crider. They were still talking to her when Angel Ray was arrested by Detective Ryan at 7:35 p.m. From that moment on, the focus of the case shifted to finding Neveah's body.

* * *

In a homicide investigation, finding the victim's body is almost always critical. Usually, the term *corpus delicti* means the actual physical body, but the law gives the words a more precise meaning that does not necessarily require the actual production of the body. Legally, the term means the state in a homicide case must establish that the person alleged to have been murdered is in fact dead, and that the death was caused by the criminal act of another.

In other words, there must be a death of one person at the hands of a second person.

Technically these two requirements may be met by *circumstantial evidence*. But the problem of the corpus delicti is especially difficult whenever the prosecution cannot produce the victim's body or once it is produced, a cause of death cannot be determined.

This should surprise no one. A case built entirely upon circumstantial evidence—where no witnesses to the crime can testify, no body of the victim is found, and no forensic evidence ties the defendant to the crime—should be hard to prove. A jury should be exceedingly reluctant to convict a defendant under these circumstances.

After all, in the U.S. a person cannot be convicted of the heinous crime of murder without *proof beyond a reasonable doubt and the presumption of innocence.* These concepts date to Biblical times. They are the stuff of popular novels and movies and TV shows, and they are the key to understanding the verdicts in cases like O.J. Simpson and Casey Anthony.

The "presumption of innocence" is recognized in the constitutions of many nations and in the Universal Declaration of Human Rights. In the U.S. the "presumption of innocence"— like separation of powers, checks and balances, Federalism, and the right to privacy—is not stated explicitly, in those exact words, in the nation's Constitution. However, the Supreme Court has held the "presumption of innocence" is implicitly included among the "fundamental rights" that are built into the protections of the Bill of Rights, which have been "incorporated"—or made applicable to the States—through the Due Process Clause of the 14th Amendment.

And along with the "presumption of innocence" comes the high evidentiary requirement of "proof beyond a reasonable doubt." Nearly five years after Neveah's death, the jury in the case against Angel Ray would hear the judge's instructions on the legal meanings of these words. They would become the subject of argumentation by the lawyers.

But on Friday, September 21, two less abstract factors drove the police and prosecutors to launch a massive search for Neveah's body: the simple human need to find that little girl and the simple physical reality that every minute spent looking for her was another minute of decomposition.

After three days or so, the forensic evidence begins to deteriorate rapidly and the cause of death becomes much harder to prove.

* * *

On Saturday morning, Angel Ray appeared in court and asked for a public defender. As soon as he was appointed to represent Angel Ray, attorney David Turner filed motions to restrict the police and prosecutors from questioning Angel Ray and from taking samples of his DNA. The prime suspect wasn't talking and his accomplice—Miriam—didn't know where he had stashed the body of her daughter.

The search intensified, focusing on the greater Capitol Hill neighborhood. The police looked everywhere for the body. They checked Dumpsters and alleyways with bloodhounds and hands sheathed in plastic gloves. The media reported:

> On Saturday, top law enforcement officials issued a disturbing plea for help from the public. "It's pretty simple," said District Attorney Mitch Morrissey. "Walk out into your back yard, look through your Dumpsters, help us find this little girl. She's probably in a black plastic bag or white plastic bag."

Mitch Morrissey was first elected Denver's District Attorney in 2005 and has been consistently reelected since. His office—with 80 lawyers and a staff of 130—handles over 6,000 felony cases and 18,000 misdemeanors every year. By the time the murder trial of Angel Ray was completed in the spring of 2012, he had served as a prosecutor for three decades.

Morrissey is fit and trim and anchorman handsome. His thick silver hair is coiffed perfectly. His face in his fifties is unlined and youthful. His icy blue eyes—warm and sincere one minute, passionate and hot the next, cold and sharp the very next—have held many a juror in thrall.

Born in Denver and a graduate of the University of Colorado and University of Denver School of Law, Morrissey is a nationally known expert in the use of DNA technology in criminal prosecutions and has worked throughout his career to ensure that DNA evidence is made admissible in criminal cases.

His web site says he "is an aggressive prosecutor and an advocate of prevention and intervention initiatives. He makes victims a priority and is dedicated to providing victims a strong voice in the justice system through a number of efforts."

After years in the public eye, both in court and in the media, and as an elected official, Morrissey chooses his words carefully, though he speaks in a fluid, candid voice. He later recalled issuing his "disturbing plea" to the community for help: "We really needed to make a community-wide, a metropolitan-wide request for people to help us find this body."

The case of five-year old Ashley Gray—raped and murdered in 1995—inspired him. In that case a man was driving to his business near Coors Field in Lower Downtown when he heard a little girl had gone missing in that area and may have been killed. People were asked to look for her body. When he arrived at his business, the man—"an older gentleman"—walked the borders of his property and lifted the lid on his Dumpster. Sure enough, little Ashley was there, her body jammed inside.

"My hope," said Morrissey, was something similar would happen. So he went on camera and asked: "If you just take a few minutes, walk back and look in your Dumpster. And if you see anything like that, give us a call." Still Neveah's body was not found.

By Saturday night the search expanded. The police asked the Denver Fire Department to search the Platte River between Sixth Avenue and Interstate 70, a long stretch. The ground search encompassed an area between Sixth Avenue on the south and 20th Avenue on the north, from Downing to Speer Boulevard. This area now went well beyond the Capitol Hill vicinity.

"We need to re-create what these two"—Angel Ray and Miriam—"did yesterday prior to the disappearance of the three-year-old girl," Police Chief Gerry Whitman told the media.

But the next day came. The body was still missing.

Neveah's family was beside itself.

Time was stripping the corpse of precious evidence. The intensity increased another notch. "On Sunday," Denver's media reported, "about 200 volunteers and police officers canvassed downtown ... Using search dogs, volunteers searched since 4 a.m. looking into Dumpsters and around the Cherry Creek and South Platte River for any sign of Neveah Gallegos."

Morrissey later described his memories from that morning, "just looking out into the audience of people there [who came to help with the search]. We were kind of saying, this is what we're going to do; we're going to break up into teams. The people who are not, you know, law enforcement, you're going to have a law enforcement person with you, so if you find the person, if you see something, you get them over there, don't disturb anything. Obviously do not do this without gloves on, without protecting yourself. And I remember John Costigan— who I have known for 30 years, who had retired from the Denver Police Department—was standing there in the audience ... And he's done. His career is over. But he's standing there, going out on the street to look for this little girl."

Morrissey shook his head: "And it was people like that— that were there, that you've known for years, people from my office, investigators, lawyers, people from all different parts of our community: Over 200 people. But I just distinctly remember John, because John, when he ended his career, was the longest-serving detective in the Denver Police Department. So he had the #1 detective badge. And he was a great detective. He had been kind of a generalist-type. And he was standing there. And I just went up to him and said, 'John, what are you doing here?' And ..." the retired detective just shrugged.

The case had powerful appeal. Among those who volunteered from Morrissey's office was Michelle Amico, the sharp senior prosecutor who would later lead the charge against Angel Ray, and who after that would be appointed to the bench.

She, like all the others that long weekend, pulled plastic gloves over her hands and went through the garbage.

And of course Janet and Vera, two-thirds of Neveah's triumvirate, joined in the search. One news report quoted a neighbor who observed how distraught Janet appeared and how frantic was her search.

Vera later recalled asking Janet, "What do you feel? Do you feel anything?"

And Janet said, "I just know that she's in water somewhere." Or "there's water somewhere."

Still despite all the support from the community, the searchers failed to find Neveah. Sunday bled into Monday. Then *something* told the police to look somewhere entirely different, somewhere miles from Miriam's apartment.

And for years—indeed, until now—that something has remained a mystery.

* * *

What was the *something* that happened that Monday?

What sent Detective Crider and the Denver police to a location three miles west of Miriam's apartment to look for Neveah's body?

During all the legal proceedings that followed, including the eventual trial of Angel Ray in the spring of 2012, there was no mention—before the jury or the public—of the reason why the police so quickly shifted their focus from the greater downtown, Capitol Hill, and Platte River areas to that different location. The subject was not discussed at trial and immediately after it, when the jury and others asked Detective Crider for an answer, he refused to give them one.

He insisted: "That I can't talk about ... We can't discuss that ... To my knowledge we will never be able to discuss that."

He was most emphatic and unwavering.

Yet he did concede: "We got there"—to the new location—"for a reason … Something led us there." And he admitted the issue created a curious gap in the narrative.

By early 2013—months after the trial of Angel Ray was completed, and his case had gone to the appeals court—the gap could finally be filled. The real story could be told.

Mitch Morrissey would choose to tell it himself, leading with the punch line: The information about where to find Neveah's body came from Angel Ray himself!

Here is how it came about, according to Morrissey:

"We were … approached by his lawyers, indicating that they would like to have him show us where the body was, if we would take the death penalty off the table." Since Angel Ray was looking at a potential first degree murder charge—involving the intentional death of a child, which is an aggravating factor under Colorado law—Morrissey said, "The death penalty would be considered, at least, by my office … So they came to us and indicated that if we would take the death penalty off the table, they would have—their client would be willing to show us where he disposed of the little girl's body. It was about three days after, we were called."

Morrissey clarified: "The individual that contacted us was Michael Vallejos, not Holly Lucas [who would serve as public defender for Angel Ray in court]. Michael Vallejos was the head of the Denver Public Defender's Office. That's who contacted us about this situation of recovering the body in exchange for us taking the death penalty off the table … But if you think about this situation I'm in, we don't have a body … and this is a body that we know is being exposed to environmental insults that could lead, you know, to the very issue we ended up with," difficulty in showing cause of death.

"It was the amount of time we were losing, the days we were losing, and I specifically talked to Lt. John Priest about this and he and I both had the same concern, that the longer we wait …

with the temperature, with the time, with her being in the environment, that we were going to lose evidence, that we were going to lose potentially things that we could use to show what happened to her just before she was killed. So as far as the death penalty goes, it was a no-brainer. I mean, it was like, we don't have a body, we don't have a homicide."

So the District Attorney took the deal. And on the afternoon of Monday, September 27, the search shifted to a location in Lakewood, roughly three miles west of Miriam's apartment.

* * *

Back then Lakewood/Dry Gulch Park was little more than an overgrown drainage ditch that flowed into the South Platte River. Today a light rail station borders the park and walking and bike trails have transformed it into a glorified drainage ditch.

Forming the northern border of the Villa Park neighborhood, the park runs east-to-west between Perry and Sheridan Streets, roughly parallel to West 11th and 13th Avenues. It is part of a T-shaped park system that brings together three small creeks: Lakewood Gulch, Dry Gulch, and Weir Gulch. The Villa Park neighborhood is hilly and poor, about 80% low-income Latino.

The Set Free Church of Denver sits at 10th and Perry, overlooking the gulch and infusing its aging biker congregants with spiritual direction. The areas next to the creeks are riparian. They are dense and green even in September after the dry summers have turned the tall grasses yellow and the thick bushes brown just a few steps away. Giant electrical towers spew wires across the sky, spoiling the pretense of a natural environment.

Angel Ray was taken by the police to this location. As soon as they had learned about the deal the District Attorney had made, they knew they had to move fast. They wanted to avoid the media that soon would notice the massing of law enforcement vehicles near 11th and Perry.

Detective Crider, leading the investigation, was especially worried Janet would hear the news on TV, before he had a chance to break it to her. On the way to the gulch he did not yet know, but soon he would learn: he would be the one who would personally discover Neveah's body, stuffed in a white garbage bag, a short distance west of Perry, down by the trickling waters, buried under a tire, some rocks, and some sort of log, with her pink princess shoes sticking out.

He later recalled: "It was an overcast day. It had been warmer earlier in the week. It had started raining a bit later. [Dry Gulch Park] is just a huge field, slopes down, really very wooded down by the creek, pretty sharp embankment on the way down. Her body was close to the creek. It was horrible, even thinking now, five years later ... you can see it still bothers me ... I guess the hardest part for me is being a father and seeing that child, you know, thrown out like the trash and nobody deserves that ... a three-year old girl. And that was hard. It's still hard to this day. I'm a pretty emotional guy."

He paused to wipe the tears gathering in his eyes.

"There's certain things," he said, "you picture in your mind and it just triggers these tears. And that'll probably be for twenty more years. Just thrown out like the trash—by her own mother ... Just incredible."

At the time, Detective Crider could not pause to reflect: "We found the body [and] we called the coroner. One of the most important things ... to me was to call Janet before she saw it on the TV ... because ... we had been pretty honest with her, and let her know we thought Neveah was dead, we're looking for the body ... because the media was all over this."

So he pulled out his cell phone and hit her number. But he couldn't complete the call.

He was too overcome to tell Janet himself.

"Actually," he said, choking a bit on the words, "I gave the phone to Detective Joe Delmonico."

Soon Mitch Morrissey joined them, with Verna Carpenter, the head of his family violence unit. Morrissey later recalled: "The detectives were already there." They had already found the body. Angel Ray had stood "up the hill. He was [still] up the hill when I was there [and] the media wasn't there [yet]. When I got there, he had been brought from the jail to the location in the gulch where we found her body. Her body was down a slope, down near a ditch that runs through the slope, and he was up the hill and had pointed down to where we would find her."

Morrissey, Carpenter, Crider, and several others went down into the gulch. "Crider," said Morrissey "was pointing out to me what they had found. She was under a number of items. I remember a tire, some rocks, some tree-type … vegetation-type material. You could see her little pink tennis shoes. I bent down and I saw those little shoes and I knew we had found her body because I knew what she had been wearing. At some point the defendant was taken back to jail. He never was actually down where we recovered her. He had just described where she would be and had pointed down in that direction."

Morrissey had seen enough. "I knew she was there. I knew she was in good hands."

He knew as well the process of documenting the recovery of the body, taking the photos at every step along the way, the whole routine. He had seen it so many times before. He decided to leave this time without watching.

Detective Crider stayed. "And the crime scene guys came out," he said. They photographed and documented everything. Dr. Amy Martin from the coroner's office arrived in her van and together they started slowly removing each of the items—all the debris—from the body.

The prosecutors were glad they had found the body because without it, they knew, this case would be very difficult to prosecute. But for Detective Crider, "that was secondary. We wanted to find this little girl."

He watched as Dr. Martin—short chestnut hair, spectacles, yellow top, black-and-white hooded jacket—placed Neveah's body in a white plastic bag and lifted her up.

"It was just odd," he said, "because you had Detective Delmonico and I, we find the body, we see Neveah, we see her pink princess shoes"—sure to pluck the heartstrings of any father of two young daughters—"Doc Martin gets there, puts her in a body bag … I just saw Doc Martin carrying this bag … it was almost the right thing to do was, 'Hey, doc, let me help you,' not thinking it's … not just thinking: *The body*. It's just here's a female carrying something heavy. So 'Hey, doc, let me give you a hand with that.' And for me, it was like … half-way up that hill, you realize what you're carrying. Not that you forgot it was a body, but it just clicks, it hits. That's for me, I won't say lose it, but that's when it became really emotional for me. At that point, when it's like, you're carrying this girl's body up this hill. It was just kind of odd."

For Detective Crider, that odd feeling remains "one of the strangest things about that case." By the time he reached the top of the ravine, holding the body in its white plastic body bag across his chest, his hands sheathed in plastic gloves, the media were waiting. They captured the moment: Dr. Amy Martin in her black-and-white hooded jacket and Detective Crider in his usual uniform, except for the dark blue windbreaker that had replaced the dark blue suit jacket that overcast afternoon.

His expression is grim. The side door to the coroner's plain white Ford Explorer is swung wide open. The police and prosecutors had achieved the first real breakthrough in the case: recovering Neveah's body before further decomposition would have made it impossible to determine the cause of death.

But it had taken its toll. After carrying the child's lifeless body out of the ravine, Detective Crider later remembered "going home, taking a shower"—and much like the lawyer in the parking lot—"just crying for that little girl."

FIVE: THE AUTOPSY and the LOVE BIRDS

Over the weekend, while everyone was looking for Neveah's body, Vera received a dozen phone calls from Miriam in jail. When Detective Crider later interviewed Vera, she described those phone calls in detail. While their contents contained hearsay that likely could not be used in a court of law, they could be used for investigative purposes. And, in context, these calls —soon after Miriam's arrest and before the body was found— support the conclusions later reached by the experts, the jury, and the community at large.

Miriam was miserable in jail. She called Vera "maybe three, four times a day," sounding frantic and distraught. She told Vera that she had been given some sort of sedative to calm her down and she was isolated because, "they're worried that … I might do something to myself." She was crying a lot and bemoaning, "It's awful in here. I hate it in here … I don't know what's gonna happen to me."

During these calls Miriam also talked to Vera about what she had seen when she arrived at her apartment on Logan Street on Friday afternoon. These were the words Vera recalled Miriam uttering, repeatedly: "It's terrible what happened … it was horrible, horrible what happened … When I got home it was horrible what he did to her. It was horrible what I saw …when I got home from work … what he did to her. It was terrible."

Vera told Miriam she would stand behind her "as long as she did the right thing." She said: "You don't need to describe the details of what he did to her [to me] but you need to do the right thing by her."

And Miriam said, "I will. I will. I will, Auntie."

"Well then," said Vera, "you have to tell the truth and you need to make him pay for what he did to her."

Silence from Miriam.

Vera pressed: "Why did you leave her alone with him?"

Miriam replied: "Because he loved her."

Vera insisted: "You should have never left her ... left the baby with him."

Those, then, were the first conversations Vera had with Miriam shortly after her arrest. Clicking off her phone, Vera couldn't help but wonder: what did that monster do to Neveah?

Once her body was found on Monday afternoon, all attention turned to the autopsy.

* * *

Dr. Amy Martin began the autopsy at 9:10 the next morning. A board-certified forensic pathologist, Dr. Martin joined the Office of the Medical Examiner in 1992 and became the Chief Medical Examiner and Coroner for Denver in December of 2007, only months after conducting the postmortem examination that Tuesday. She has performed many autopsies on victims of child abuse and testified as an expert witness in over 150 cases in Ohio, Colorado, Kentucky and Indiana. She frequently serves on child death review teams throughout Colorado.

Present were Detectives Crider and Delmonico, and Sergeant Kukuris, from the Homicide Unit, Detectives Gabel and Baruch from the Denver Crime Laboratory, and Dr. Kathryn Wells from the Family Crisis Center.

The Autopsy Report was 12 pages long, mostly single spaced. In it Dr. Martin narrated the opening of the body bag and the examination of the corpse:

When the seal is opened, the decedent is in a white plastic trash bag with the tie ends down near the feet ... There are several holes in the trash bag, the largest partially exposing the decedent's face. When the bag is removed, the outside of the clothing is largely clean, except for areas ... exposed by the tear in the bag ... In the front of the crotch area of the pants there is a wet area that is starting to dry, and it dries with a little bit of a lighter ring. The decedent is wearing a pair of multicolor-print underpants. There is some urine staining in the crotch of the pants, but no blood.

Next Dr. Martin removed the child's clothes: the red sweat shirt and sweat pants, those pink princess shoes, which Vera says Neveah picked out for herself at J.C. Penney. Then Dr. Martin proceeded with the EXTERNAL EXAMINATION. It began with a general description of the body—including a notation that the "hymenal opening is somewhat irregular and dilated, but there are no definite tears or scars"—and it cataloged, under the heading TRAUMA, the following:

HEAD: There are faint bruises on the right side and mid side of the forehead that are somewhat brownish in color. The most prominent bruise above the right eyebrow is approximately 4 cm. A fainter possible bruise on the mid forehead ... Another bruise in the right temple area ... a dry abrasion-like pattern on much of the right side of the face around the eye and cheek ... a scabbed abrasion on the right side of the jaw ... some faint purple bruising ... on the left cheek. There is an ovoid bruise more on the lower and left side of this cluster of bruises ... There might be a bruise on the left side of the forehead ... There are two reddish spots, almost like large petechial hemorrhages, on the top of the pinna of the right ear ...

EXTREMITIES: There is sort of purplish-brown bruising on the ... right forearm ... Some punctuate, almost scabbed-appearing abrasion is observed in the center of this. On the inside of the wrist there are some punctuate abrasions and some faint bruising ... In addition, there appears to be some sort of purplish bruising below the right elbow ... The abrasion almost appears to have some drying or a crust. There is also a little bit of brownish bruising on the upper arm ... A band of deep purple-gray bruising on the ... right thigh ... There is some faint bruising clustered around the right knee ... some other sort of ovoid bruises on the inside of the right lower leg ... a cluster of scabbed abrasions above this more later injury ... a faint bruise just above the back of the left wrist ... another sort of healing bruise-like area ... medial to the left elbow.

TRUNK: There is some dark purple-red bruising on the left buttock ... A vertical faint scabbed scratch on the left lateral flank area ... a cluster of scabbed abrasions over the mid back ...

As for INTERNAL EVIDENCE OF INJURY, Dr. Martin found hemorrhages under the scalp, a hemorrhage corresponding to the bruises on the mid back and left buttock, and a "moderate hemorrhage in the root of the small bowel mesentery," the membrane that attaches the intestines to the walls of the abdomen.

When she dissected the child's neck, Dr. Martin discovered "extravasated blood" on the left side, "some hemorrhage deeper right over the thyroid gland on the left," and "extravasations of blood bilaterally along the upper cervical spine."

During the INTERNAL EXAMINATION that came next, Dr. Martin noted "extravasations of blood similar to those in the neck muscle, seen in the chest wall muscle on the left."

And in the microscopic examination of the biopsies and samples she took, she observed "definite extensive recent hemorrhage" in the left cheek, a "recent hemorrhage" of the chin, some hemorrhaging under the scalp and: "There is extensive recent hemorrhage with a well-developed acute inflammatory response" to the root of the small bowel mesentery.

In other words, someone had beaten Neveah Gallegos—as Detective Crider later said—"to a pulp." Someone had punched her in the belly and someone had applied considerable pressure to her neck.

Dr. Martin's DIAGNOSIS, on the cover page of the Autopsy Report, included bruises of varying ages and this key finding: "Evidence of recent blunt force trauma to the abdomen with apparent hemorrhage, root of small bowel mesentery."

Nevertheless, all of this evidence of trauma—some recent and some not-so-recent—was not enough for Dr. Martin to determine definitively the cause of Neveah's death. Accordingly she would have to wait, as a good professional should, for the results of the toxicology and other laboratory analysis of the samples and biopsies she had taken from the body on that morning of September 25. She could not issue her final report and opinion until then.

* * *

On the same morning, the *Rocky Mountain News* ran a story next to its account of the discovery in the ravine. Titled "Previous case bears similarity," the story made public a lot of information that later would be excluded from Angel Ray's trial. It reported on the alleged sexual assault of Neveah by Angel Ray in July of 2006. It also stated Angel Ray had been a "sex offender since he was a juvenile," had violated his probation, had been ordered to serve 270 days in jail, and had served some but not all of that time in a case the jury would later hear about:

> The [case] was a 4-year-old boy who was left in his care two years ago ... The boy told his mother in January 2005 that Montoya tried to choke him "because the suspect was mad," detectives wrote in their affidavit. The boy was taken to a hospital and treated for bruises on his face, throat, shoulder, arms, feet, and wrists ... In an interview with a forensics expert, the child said Montoya ... had hooked him up "on the wall with a tie" and tied his legs together ... Montoya, now 22, eventually pleaded guilty to misdemeanor child abuse and was sentenced to 18 months of probation.

The details of Angel Ray's career as a sex offender were not revealed, but it appeared from the tone of the story to be more than a casual violation. The admissibility of this history, and information about the incident with Neveah in 2006, would later be contested.

But at the time, without actually naming "the boy" in the 2005 incident, the media had inserted—right there, alongside the mug shot of Angel Ray with his wispy mustache, fuzzy chin, and cold eyes like a shark's—the tale of little Jesus Perez. The courage of that "boy" would later become another breakthrough in the case against Angel Ray.

* * *

The Set Free Church of Denver ministers to aging bikers seeking religion: the kind that hold prayer meetings in Sturgis. Their black leather jackets and well-worn chaps, and their braided pigtails and blue tattoos and big silver mustaches, are common throughout the Villa Park neighborhood. Snorts from their hogs—invariably Harleys—echo off the rolling hills.

The building that houses the church is a modest red brick affair with welcoming white doors. Its parking lot is unpaved. Together they occupy the plot of land at 10th and Perry immediately south of the ravine where Angel Ray dumped Neveah's body. Large granite stones placed loosely in a line separate the parking lot from the park.

On the day after Dr. Martin conducted her post-mortem examination on Neveah's body, searching for a cause of her death, the Set Free Church of Denver held a "praise and prayer vigil" to honor her life. Simple flyers with Neveah's picture on the left and a drawing of a child angel on the right announced the time—7:00 p.m.—and asked:

"Please join us as we seek God's face in ministering to family, friends, and community left behind."

A memorial sprang up at the site overlooking the spot where the body was found. A 4-foot statue of a cherub playing a harp soon appeared among the flowers, though later it was removed due to park regulations. Five years after the slaying, dried flowers and a scattering of mementos still mark the place.

On Monday, October 1, Neveah's funeral—a Mass of Christian Burial—was held at 2:00 p.m. at the Archdiocese of Denver Mortuary Chapel. Father Lawrence Kaiser, the Pastor of the Guardian Angels Catholic Church, presided. The red-cushioned pews were less than half filled but there were plenty of flowers, good words, and tears to send Neveah on her way.

It was a week since her body had been found, and her remains rested in a closed white coffin. A bunch of balloons—including one with Elmo's smiling face and one that said "To Cheer You"—fluttered to the right of the casket. Wearing black for mourning, Janet, Vera, and their mother sat alone in the first row, their family and friends arrayed behind. Attire was casual, no fancy suits and ties for the men.

The burial took place at Mt. Olivet Cemetery. The sky was clear, bright, and sunny. The foothills to the west appeared blue and purple. Family photos show a small group of loved ones holding hands around the grave. A red-white-and-blue balloon with a small basket underneath was ready to lift Neveah's spirit to heaven. Indeed, "Neveah" is only a minor transposition away from "Nevaeh," or "Heaven" spelled backwards. Some say "Nevaeh is the secret word to enter paradise." The name used to be rare, but became popular after 9/11.

The family feasted afterwards, as families in so many cultures do. Photos show they gathered in a small unadorned hall with a few white-covered tables. They did their best to muster smiles for the camera but often the gesture looks forced. And whatever smiles there were on their faces quickly turned to frowns when they learned what had happened while they were busy burying Neveah.

***

The media pounced on it. Photos and videos captured the images; words printed and spoken were delivered with dismay:

Angel Ray and Miriam had been set free!

The *Rocky Mountain News* ran a photo of the love birds leaving jail, hand in hand, with Miriam in her light-colored T-shirt and dark pants looking plump and grim on the right, and with Angel Ray in his gym shorts and dark T-shirt, bulging a bit around the waist, tattoo visible on his forearm, looking damn pleased to be free, on the left. The *News* reported:

Suspects in girl's death free for now
Denver DA delays filing charges until autopsy done

The mother and boyfriend suspected in the death of a 3-year-old girl whose body was dumped in a ravine are now free, following their release from jail Monday afternoon.

Prosecutors and police are waiting for the official autopsy report on Neveah Gallegos, which might take several weeks, before deciding whether to file charges against the pair, district attorney spokeswoman Lynn Kimbrough said …
"[S]uspects cannot be held in custody indefinitely," Kimbrough said …

After they left the jail, the couple darted across the train tracks along Smith Road hand in hand to catch a city bus …
The couple didn't speak to the horde of news media outside the Denver County Jail. Sources said that Montoya was so rattled by the media attention that he initially refused to leave jail …

"A decision on filing criminal charges cannot be made until we have all the facts, including the final results from the medical examiner that won't be back for several weeks," District Attorney Mitch Morrissey said.

Montoya is a registered sex offender who, as a juvenile, was picked up at least three times between 1999 and 2002 for indecent exposure. His juvenile records remain sealed.

Pundits and court-watchers got the message: there was no obvious cause of death, such as stabbing injuries or gunshot wounds. The case was not going to be a slam-dunk, after all.

When Vera saw the news, she also got the message. Despite all of her promises, Miriam was not going to do the right thing. She was siding with Angel Ray, not Neveah.

Detective Crider studied many of the photos that were taken of the pair as they left custody. One of them in particular sticks with him, much like an echo of the one that sticks with him from that Friday afternoon in the parking lot at 10th and Cherokee. In this one, Miriam is not looking grim and she is not holding something alongside her face to block the camera.

In this one, she has that same smart snicker on her face.

* * *

Finally, the results from the samples and biopsies taken on the day of the autopsy came back from the laboratories. It was time for Dr. Martin to finalize her report. On November 11, 2007, she signed this OPINION:

Death is due to undetermined causes. There is evidence of trauma of varying ages, including a blunt impact to the abdomen, which are likely from non-accidental (abusive) trauma. However, there is no evidence of hemoperitoneum or peritonitis related to the abdominal injury. An asphyxia mechanism in the death (suffocation or strangulation) has not been ruled out. Additional information through continuing investigation may yield a more definitive cause of death. The manner of death is undetermined.

This, of course, came as a blow to those seeking justice for Neveah. The prosecutors realized their case against Angel Ray had suffered a mighty setback. And the police were left wondering where to go next.

Detective Crider later described his presence at the autopsy and his reactions to the report issued by Dr. Martin. He emphasized that, for a homicide cop, attending autopsies is simply "part of the job." It's essential to properly and fully document and photograph everything that happens for investigative, prosecutorial, and evidentiary purposes. He said this is something you have to get used to, something that becomes "almost" routine. But Detective Crider was also quick to note that, for him, "Children are different." For whatever reason they simply tug at your heartstrings.

Imagine, then, the feelings he had to suppress as he heard the pathologist's cataloging of the bruises, as he watched her scalpel slicing open that tender flesh, as they carefully studied what was revealed inside, searching, searching for a cause of death. Then imagine his disappointment when their study—their search— proved fruitless. Even though he "understood at the time," Detective Crider was distressed: "I understood where Dr. Martin was coming from. But it was still disappointing. We felt we had the guy who killed this little girl. And we would not be able to proceed because we couldn't determine how he killed her. So, yeah, it was tough; it was hard."

Without a cause of death, prosecution for the most serious charges could not go forward. Still the police and prosecutors were not about to end their quest for justice. Not so soon! Neveah had just been buried!

They would just have to clear this roadblock—this setback— and it would take some time. But they were determined to wipe that smirk off Miriam's face.

And, what's more, they were determined to put Angel Ray in a place where he could no longer harm children.

SIX: FAILURES and ALTERNATIVES

Even before Miriam and Angel Ray scooted past reporters on the day of Neveah's funeral, the media cried foul. The death of the 3-year-old girl came only months after the death of 7-year-old Chandler Grafner. And while many important differences distinguished the two cases, the media—and soon the Denver community—quickly lumped them together.

That was because they had "one disturbing thing in common," according to the *Rocky Mountain News*:

Critics say signs were there in kids' deaths

… Child welfare agencies were aware of strong indications of abuse with both children and did not take aggressive protective action.

… In Chandler's case, the boy's school reported to authorities in January that he had bruises on his neck and ear, allegedly caused by his stepfather, Jon Phillips. When Chandler's own story about the bruises changed three days later – matching Phillips' claim that he had slipped in the shower – DHS [the Department of Human Services] – dismissed the report.

In April the school reported that Chandler had not been in school for five weeks. DHS dismissed that report, too.

On May 6, 19 days later, police found Chandler's emaciated body in Phillips' south Denver home. Phillips, 27, and his common-law-wife, Sarah Berry, 22, have been charged with murder, accused of locking the boy in the closet and starving him.

Both cases are drawing sharp criticism from some child welfare experts, who say the breakdowns in the DHS response are all too common.

The rest of the 4-column story focused on Chandler's case. Maybe that was because Neveah's case was so new. Maybe it was because the alleged perpetrators were already in jail. Or maybe it was simply because a lot less was known at the time about her death. Either way, Neveah and Chandler came together as symbols for the need to reform DHS.

* * *

The tragic story of Chandler Grafner could fill its own volume. Starting when he was four, in January of 2004, and stretching until he was seven, in January of 2007, Chandler and his younger half-brother Dominick were the subjects of repeated "referrals" for possible abuse and neglect to the Departments of Human Services for Arapahoe, Denver and Jefferson Counties. These referrals led to judicial proceedings which initially transferred temporary custody of the children from their mother Christina Grafner to Jon Phillips—the biological father of Dominick and so-called "psychological father" of Chandler— and later granted an "Allocation of Parental Responsibility" to Phillips and his common-law wife, Sarah Berry.

Less than a week after full parental rights were awarded to Phillips, a Denver public school, as mentioned in the *News* story, made yet another referral to DHS based on bruises seen on Chandler's ear and neck. The child first said he had been hit by Phillips but later changed his account—he had slipped in the shower instead—and the case was not pursued. Like the referral of Neveah due to possible sex abuse by Angel Ray the year before her death, the allegations in Chandler's case were determined to be "unfounded" rather than "unproved."

Three months later, on April 17, a final referral was made because Chandler had withdrawn from school, but again no action was taken, this time because there were no specific allegations of abuse or neglect.

Chandler died on May 6 of cardiac arrest resulting from starvation, dehydration, and abuse. He weighed 34 pounds at the time of his death, barely "skin and bones." He had been locked for long periods in a tiny closet with a cat litter box to use as a toilet and an air mattress to sleep on. His final trip to the closet came on May 4, as punishment for taking food from the kitchen.

Phillips and Berry were arrested and charged with murder and child abuse resulting in death. With only hours to go before her trial was scheduled to start in August of 2008, Berry pleaded guilty to second-degree murder in exchange for a sentence of 48 years. With time off for good behavior, she could be released after 32 years. She would be 55 at the time.

The case against Phillips went to trial early that same August of 2008. It lasted two weeks. Little Dominick, according to testimony given by his mental-health therapist, told her all about the horrible closet and the abusive conditions at home. He told her how Chandler would scream and beg to get out of the closet. He told her he and Chandler didn't like fish, so Phillips would force them to eat fish when they were bad.

Dominick said, "I hate fish. I'd like to kick the fish in the face. Fish makes me puke. My mommy and daddy make me eat the puke."

The jury reeled when the air mattress, stinking of feces and urine, was unboxed in court. Some held their noses, some fanned their faces. Eyes moistened when Dr. Nancy Krebs of Children's Hospital described the effects of extreme starvation and dehydration on Chandler. She testified, given his condition at death, it must have taken one to two weeks without drinking any or very little fluids for him to have died. She said the level of Vitamin C deficiency in his body had caused his fingernail beds to bleed, and the level of Vitamin B3 deficiency in his body had caused lesions and flaking of his skin. She could not say if he was ambulatory at the time of his death, but if he was, he couldn't walk far or fast due to the muscle loss in his legs.

"His hands and feet would have been cold because his body was trying to conserve energy."

The prosecutor, Verna Carpenter—who had been with Morrissey and Crider in the gulch where Neveah's body was found—broke down during closing arguments. The jury took only three hours to convict Phillips. The judge sentenced him to life in prison without parole for the murder, and, consecutively, 48 more years for child abuse resulting in death.

* * *

The Colorado Department of Human Services issued its Child Fatality Review of Chandler's death on August 27, 2007, four months after he lost his life, a year before the conviction of Phillips for his murder, and one month before the death of Neveah. The DHS report dispassionately detailed the failures, large and small, of the county agencies in Chandler's case: dropping the ball, not following-up, ignoring the warning signs.

These failures were fresh in the minds of the media and the community in the days following Neveah's death. Warning signs had been ignored in her case as well. People wanted answers: Was the problem with DHS systemic? What could be done to solve the problem?

On Friday, September 28, 2007—a week after Neveah's death—the *Rocky Mountain News* announced on page 4 that an investigation of Denver DHS and its failures to intervene in the cases of Chandler and Neveah would be conducted by the Annie E. Casey Foundation and the Kempe Foundation for the Prevention and Treatment of Child Abuse and Neglect, as well as the Colorado DHS. On page 42 the *News* ran a scathing editorial on the blunders that contributed to the children's deaths, adding it was "not entirely reassured that the state"—which also appeared to be culpable—"will be among those conducting the review of Denver's practices."

By mid-October the Kempe Foundation bowed out "to avoid even the slight appearance of conflict of interest." Having received over $3 million in contracts from the city over the prior six years and having participated extensively in personnel training and consulting in particular cases, the fear of the Foundation was well placed. However, that left the Annie E. Casey Foundation as the only independent participant on the review panel. The state could hardly be seen as neutral.

In April of 2008, the Colorado DHS issued both its Child Fatality Review of Neveah's death and its Child Maltreatment Fatality Report for 2007, into which the investigation had morphed. The web site for local Channel 9 News reported:

> A Department of Human Services investigation into child deaths found caseworkers in several counties broke state laws, failed to investigate complaints and did not share findings with other agencies around the state. The review was prompted by several high-profile child abuse deaths in 2007, including Chandler Grafner, Neveah Gallegos, and Zoe Garcia.
>
> In nine of the 13 cases studied, the Colorado Department of Human Services (CDHS) found violations of state law by county agencies … In one case, an investigator took the word of an alleged abuser that he was out of state at the time of reported abuse against his daughter. That claim was never verified and the child died of abuse within a month.
>
> In other cases, investigators failed to interview key witnesses to potential abuse, including accused perpetrators.

The report itself is 52 pages long. It is filled with statistics, charts, graphs, and abstract, impersonal social science jargon. The Executive Summary states:

In response to the increase in child maltreatment fatalities where the victim and families were previously known to Child Protective Services (CPS) agencies, the Executive Director of the Colorado Department of Human Services ordered a review of child maltreatment fatalities focused on identifying any commonalities and making recommendations for improvements in the system based upon those findings. This review specifically examined 13 recent child maltreatment fatalities that occurred in Colorado where CPS had prior involvement in the last five years. In order to determine systemic issues, information from these 13 reviews was then combined with data regarding all child maltreatment fatalities occurring in Colorado over the past five years, as well as data at a national level and from research conducted within the child welfare field. Findings were categorized across four major areas and are summarized here by each category.

1. Child Characteristics

The majority of child maltreatment fatality victims in Colorado over the past five years tend to be Caucasian (ranging from 34% to 51%), with a large percentage claiming Hispanic ethnicity (ranging from 27% to 39%).

2. Parent Characteristics

Parents of victims tend to have their own history of prior involvement with CPS. They also tend to be younger. For example, most parents were in their early 20's at the time of birth and death of the victim.

3. Environmental/Situational Characteristics

Overall, almost 70% of the families in this fatality review had some history of identified Domestic Violence, while 54% had experienced Substance Abuse issues.

4. Systemic Characteristics

Data integrity within the Statewide Automated Child Welfare Information System, known as Trails, as well as Colorado's process for tracking child fatalities, were found to be inconsistent.

Lack of communication between agencies was the systemic factor. This includes communication between county agencies when families move and responsibility for service provision and safety management shift to a new county, and communication on new rules, policies, and oversight from the Division of Child Welfare to the county agencies …

A number of … regulations were found to be incomplete, inconsistent with other policies, or simply lacking definitions of key concepts. In addition, numerous areas of practice were identified where … regulations were not being applied accurately or consistently across county departments.

5. Recommendations

This report concludes with a list of recommendations intended to address many of the issues identified. Specifically, the list is broken into short-term recommendations … and long-term recommendations that will require more time to study and craft.

The recommendations covered things like clarification of existing regulations, better communication and collaboration among state and county agencies, better state oversight, better training for personnel, and a deep analysis of workloads of such personnel.

Meanwhile, the Child Fatality Review in Neveah's case noted two violations of DHS standards, while the Child Fatality Review in Chandler's case noted six violations.

By 2009 people were patting each other on the back for getting so serious about child abuse. Local ABC affiliate Channel 7 won a Peabody Award in April of 2009 for its series titled "Failing the Children: Deadly Mistakes," which followed the stories of Chandler and Neveah, and the resulting investigations and reports, for over a year. And in November of the same year the Annie E. Casey Foundation proudly announced that "significant progress" had been made to address the concerns raised in the 2008 reports.

Yet all this verbiage made one thing clear: the success of any improvements depended upon adequate funding and Denver was facing big budget problems. The economy was crashing and state and local services were on the chopping block.

Would lack of funding scuttle the effort?

In November of 2012, the *Denver Post* and local NBC affiliate Channel 9 ran a huge 8-part investigative series called "Failed to Death," which probed the ongoing crisis at DHS. Its lead-in suggested that little had changed:

"Since 2007, 175 children in Colorado have died of abuse and neglect – beaten, starved, suffocated and burned. Deepening the tragedy is that the families or caregivers of 72 of them were known to caseworkers whose job was to protect them."

Chandler's case and Neveah's case were prominently featured, as were Janet's tears. But the two biggest take-aways from this excellent expose were these: first, the most important and most substantive reforms proposed since 2007 have been tied-up in petty political wrangling—what former Governor Bill Ritter called a "turf issue"—between state and local welfare agencies. And second, at a time when "funding inequities have plagued Colorado's child welfare system," the solutions to the problems facing DHS would require both "political will and often money."

Still budget appropriations to DHS have been decreasing. Something is badly out of whack when it comes to our priorities.

Billions are spent waging wars over the lives of the unborn. But once they are born, many who seek so zealously to protect their lives before they enter the world now abandon them to a system that systematically fails to protect them from abuse.

* * *

The failures of the system in the case of Chandler Grafner became the subject of civil litigation. In December of 2011, U.S. District Judge William Martinez ruled that state and local agencies were immune from wrongful death and civil rights actions brought by Chandler's natural parents, Christina Grafner and Joshua Norris, on behalf of themselves and his estate. But, he also ruled, the claims asserted by the parents against two of the employees of the agencies could go forward.

Judge Martinez held the two were not entitled to immunity because, under the circumstances, their repeated failures to act on Chandler's behalf "shocked the conscience" and violated the child's civil rights. The employees promptly appealed. In late 2012 the U.S. Court of Appeals for the Tenth Circuit upheld the trial court's ruling that allowed the case to proceed against the two employees. Even so, the case is no slam dunk.

The U.S. Supreme Court has made it extremely difficult for private parties—even those with standing, those with custody, those with legally recognized parental rights—to recover damages against state and local government agencies and their employees on Federal claims resulting from their failure to prevent child abuse.

DeShaney v. Winnebago County Department of Social Services was a 1989 case where the guardian of four-year-old Joshua DeShaney sued his local Department of Social Services for not responding to child abuse complaints about him and his father over 2-year period that ended when his father beat him so badly he suffered irreversible brain damage.

The Supreme Court ruled against Joshua on his constitutional and civil rights claims—without ruling on state tort claims—in an opinion written by Chief Justice Rehnquist. The Chief Justice explained that typically the Constitution prohibits the government from acting under certain circumstances; it does not require the government to act. In other words, according to *DeShaney*, the state does not have an affirmative duty to prevent child abuse even when it is known to the agency that has undertaken to prevent child abuse. The opinion does, however, create two exceptions: first, the government does have a duty to protect those it has taken into its custody; and second, the government must provide protection if it is responsible for creating the danger.

This second exception has given rise to competing lines of cases in the lower courts that seek to determine when the government is responsible for creating the danger. As the distinguished Constitutional Law scholar Erwin Chemerinsky has said: "There is no series of cases that are more consistently depressing than the state-created danger decisions. The litigation typically arises because of a terrible tragedy."

Cases from the Tenth Circuit Court of Appeals—which includes Colorado—have been relatively pro-plaintiff in their application of the exceptions to *DeShaney*. For example, in 2001 the Tenth Circuit found a social worker liable for transferring custody of a child from the mother to the father, who later killed the child. Unlike *DeShaney*, the child in this case, according to the court, "would not have been exposed to the dangers from their father but for the affirmative acts of the state."

This is the precedent that will govern the litigation over Chandler Grafner's death. Unfortunately for him, the state removed him from a painfully neglectful home and placed him in a fatally abusive home. And all those reforms made by state and local agencies since his death and the death of Neveah—and the deaths of all those other children—have come too late for them.

* * *

Look at it from the standpoint of Janet and Vera. They knew little about the legal ins and outs of the child welfare system. What could they have done differently? It's a question they ask themselves often. It's a question that haunts Janet in particular.

And rather than responding with a knee-jerk reaction—oh, you did everything you could have to prevent Neveah's death— let's take the question seriously:

With more education about the alternatives available to those who seek to prevent child abuse against their neighbors and loved ones, what else could have been done?

Christine Thornton is a lawyer who serves as a *guardian at litem*—the legal representative of the child—in cases brought by DHS. In Colorado and many other states a guardian ad litem must be a licensed attorney. Thornton graduated from the University of Denver School of Law in 2007 and serves under contract with the Colorado Office of the Child Representative. She is slender and attractive, in her mid-thirties, the mother of a son nearing kindergarten age, practical, independent, and level-headed. She also bakes one helluva cake.

Though the child welfare system varies greatly from state to state, Thornton's experience with the Colorado version is typical. A native of Denver, who bounced around with her family before returning to the city in 1997, Thornton found herself nearing thirty and working at the Jefferson County Public Library.

A call for volunteers for the local victim advocate program went out among the county's employees and she responded, spending three years volunteering with the Jefferson County Sheriff. She dealt with a lot of cases involving children and realized that counseling and police work were not right for her, but the guardian ad litem (GAL) program was a really good fit. It was proactive and focused on the human side of the dramas it dealt with.

Thornton started working with lawyers who served in the GAL program while she was still in law school. She has an uncanny ability to cut through the haze and confusion that face those who try to learn about—and pursue—the legal alternatives available to them when it comes to stopping specific cases of child abuse. She's clear about what she can and cannot do under Colorado's statutory scheme. She is appointed by the court and can only represent the child and the child's best interests when there is an actual or perceived conflict of interest between the child and the parents in cases initiated by one of the DHS agencies. That means virtually all dependency, neglect, and abuse cases brought by the county-level family service agencies.

The Child Fatality Review of Neveah's death— issued by DHS in April of 2008—noted that a case had indeed been opened for her in July of 2006, but a guardian ad litem was never sought for her, nor were court proceedings ever initiated, mostly because Miriam and Janet cooperated in the agency's proposed child safety plan.

According to Thornton, when DHS decides not to proceed at all, and when DHS decides to close a case and she as the GAL disagrees with that decision, she is authorized to file the proper petitions in court and proceed with an evidentiary hearing without DHS. So one avenue open to those seeking to prevent child abuse—in the real world—is to pester the GAL to proceed even when DHS refuses to do so. But that, of course, presumes there is a case in which a GAL has been appointed.

What if—as in Neveah's case—there is no formal court case, and no GAL is ever appointed? What, then, are the alternatives? Thornton explains there are basically four: the first is simply to *keep reporting incidents of suspected abuse* to the schools, doctors, and others who are required by law to report to DHS.

The more referrals—in the real world—the more likely DHS will open the case and do the right thing, especially in the wake of the Grafner and Gallegos tragedies.

But assume DHS—the family service agencies—do not act, for whatever reason, and there is no time or practical opportunity for repeated entreaties. What then? The second alternative is to *take your concerns directly to the police*. Their Child Abuse Units can investigate allegations of child abuse and initiate criminal proceedings in court, with or without the involvement of DHS. Thornton says this approach can be surprisingly effective, especially when the complaints come from people who have intimate knowledge about the family involved.

She is cautious to note, however, that all of the alternatives she is listing can quickly become "technical" and "legal" because, after all, it is "not easy" for the state to come in and take a child from a parent. And it shouldn't be easy. Parents have rights under both the U.S. Constitution and the laws of every state. But they don't have the right to neglect, abuse, or kill their children.

So what is left if the child welfare agencies and the police do nothing? The third and fourth alternatives, under Colorado law, are *petitioning the probate court for the appointment of a "guardian for a minor"—which is not the same as a GAL—or petitioning the district court for an "allocation of parental rights."* The term "custody" is no longer used in Colorado.

Under both of these alternatives, the concerned person takes his or her concerns directly to the court. In proper circumstances the court may appoint a GAL for purposes of the proceedings. User-friendly forms for those who wish to file "pro se"—by themselves without using a lawyer —are available online, and they state in simple terms the statutory requirements for seeking a guardian for a minor or an allocation of parental rights. However, while these proceedings can be initiated "pro se," the technicalities and legalities demand competent legal assistance. If the concerned person cannot afford to pay a lawyer, then legal aid clinics—some devoted entirely to helping children—are often available to provide assistance free of charge.

Thus, section 15-14-204 of the state's Probate Code states:

(1) A minor or a person interested in the welfare of a minor may petition [the court] for appointment of a guardian.

(2) The court may appoint a guardian for a minor if the court finds the appointment is in the minor's best interest, and ...

(c) The parents are unwilling or unable to exercise their parental rights

And, section 14-10-123 of the state's Domestic Relations Code provides:

(1) A proceeding concerning the allocation of parental responsibilities is commenced in the district court or as otherwise provided by law ...

(b) By a person other than a parent, by filing a petition seeking the allocation of parental responsibilities for the child in the county where the child is permanently resident or where the child is found, but only if the child is not in the physical care of one of the child's parents;[or]

(c) By a person other than a parent who has had the physical care of a child for a period of one hundred eighty-two days or more, if such action is commenced within one hundred eighty-two days after the termination of such physical care.

Under both statutes, the "best interests" of the child become the critical issue, and that term is defined for purposes of the allocation statute in the next section. CRS 14-10-124 lists a wide array of factors the district court should consider, specifically including "[w]hether one of the parties has been a perpetrator of child abuse or neglect under [Colorado law] or under the law of any state, which factor shall be supported by credible evidence."

In Neveah's case, the interpretation and application of these state statutes would, of course, have been left to the court. But at least Janet and Vera would have had a chance to articulate their concerns, present their evidence, and argue for the best interests of the child.

Still the message should be clear. Alternatives do exist for those who are frustrated by the failures of the family service agencies. However well-intentioned they may be, children slip through the cracks. We can help fill those cracks by pursuing the available alternatives.

That's why Christine Thornton wants you to know:

There is a vehicle into the system.

* * *

And that's why Mitch Morrissey wants you to know:

Even more help is on the way.

He and a group of civic leaders have joined forces to build the Rose Andom Center, named for the Denver entrepreneur who donated the first $1 million to the project. The 46,000 square foot facility will "create a 'wrap-around' service delivery model to provide victims with one central location for coordinated services involving 25 distinct agencies, including resource providers from both community-based organizations and the criminal justice system." It is patterned on similar facilities in 70 other communities. Located near police headquarters and the offices of the District Attorney and City Attorney, its logo includes this motto: "One Place. Immeasurable Hope."

No longer will it be a mystery or a challenge, where to go in cases of domestic violence and child abuse. If you are in Denver, you will be able to go to the Rose Andom Center. People will be there to help you. And if you live somewhere that doesn't have a place like the Rose Andom Center:

Build one, and surely they will come.

SEVEN: THE PROSECUTORS and the EXPERTS

While the Denver media and Colorado welfare agencies were pursuing their own agendas, the police, the prosecutors, and the family of Neveah Gallegos were pursuing justice. The police "were very confident that Angel Ray Montoya killed Neveah," according to Detective Crider. "The undetermined status of the cause of death was just an obstacle we had to get over."

Although they were disappointed with the outcome of Dr. Martin's autopsy report, the police and the prosecutors pressed forward with their investigation. Experts in DNA and fingerprint analysis were turned loose on the evidence at hand. And within "a month or so" after the autopsy report was issued, a critical meeting led to the second breakthrough in the case.

The meeting was attended by Denver DA Mitch Morrissey, Detective Crider, Dr. Amy Martin, and Verna Carpenter, the Chief Deputy District Attorney who was initially assigned to the case—and who had been down in the gulch with the same people on the afternoon Neveah's body was found.

A seasoned prosecutor who did volunteer work with the elderly, Carpenter was a graduate of the Creighton University School of Law in Omaha. She had straight blond hair, clear blue eyes, a long nose, and a strong chin. Her years of service earned her an appointment to the bench of the Jefferson County Court in 2008. She accepted her judicial appointment immediately after successfully prosecuting Jon Phillips for the murder of Chandler Grafner in August of that year.

Morrissey later recalled the meeting.

First the group reviewed Neveah's autopsy in depth.

Morrissey listened.

When Dr. Martin was finished, he said to her, "Well, okay, Amy, you know I've got a question I've got to ask you. You know I have to ask you this. Is there somebody out there that has the credentials or wherewithal in this area ..."

Morrissey paused to comment: "When you're talking about cause of death with kids, it's different ... there's a lot of issues there ... kids die of all kinds of different things. You really need somebody who has an expertise in that area." And despite her many years of experience, which included many autopsies of children, Morrissey felt Dr. Martin was more of a generalist.

So he asked her: "Is there somebody out there—somebody who you would recommend to us—somebody you could work with? Who is the best? Who should we get?"

Dr. Martin wanted to avoid "hired gun" and "media" types. So she gave Detective Crider, Morrissey and Carpenter the names of several experts.

According to Detective Crider, "Dr. Mary Case was at the top of the list."

The detective later added his recollections of the meeting:

"We respected Doc Martin during the entire process. No one was upset with Doctor Martin. Nobody tried to change her mind. It was never like that. It was, 'Okay, Doc, we understand your opinion.' And, it was kind of delicate, asking her, basically, 'We would like to, you know, have someone review this. Who would you recommend?' And, you know, she wasn't offended by that. She may have been and just didn't show it to us," but that, Detective Crider agreed, "was part of being a professional."

After the meeting Verna Carpenter contacted Dr. Case, who agreed to review the evidence. She was sent copies of every relevant shred: the police report, the autopsy report complete with photos, specimens and slides taken during the autopsy— everything but the body of the child. It would take Dr. Case months to review it all. The long wait for her analysis began.

* * *

Who is Dr. Mary E. Schmidt Case?

She is a Professor of Pathology at the St. Louis University Health Sciences Center and the Chief Medical Examiner for St. Charles, St. Louis, Jefferson, and Franklin Counties in Missouri. Born in 1943, she earned her BA in 1965 from the University of Missouri in Columbia and her MD in 1969 from the St. Louis University School of Medicine.

If Mark Crider is a detective's detective, then Mary Case is an expert's expert. As of late 2011 her Curriculum Vitae listed not only her degrees and her jobs and her many professional associations over her long career as a forensic pathologist and nationally-known expert on child abuse and the causes of death resulting from child abuse. It also listed her 6 grants, 10 honors, 30 workshops attended, 24 published papers, 13 book chapters, 1 entire book, 35 abstracts of formal presentations given to academic societies, and 380 invited talks and lectures.

Dr. Case's expertise combines subspecialties in anatomic, forensic, and neuropathology. She is known especially for her work on "shaken baby syndrome" and has testified in many cases across the country regarding her analysis of the evidence in criminal cases involving the deaths of children. She once described what it was like for her to perform an autopsy:

"When I perform an autopsy, I'm dressed in a scrub suit and operating gown covered with a plastic apron, double-gloved, head covered with mask and goggles, and shoe covers—it can be very hot if the autopsy suite is not really cool, like 65 degrees. Better to be cool than hot. If the case [goes] several hours, it can be physically exhausting; I sometimes liken it to digging a ditch. Being bent over the body to look for bullets can be backbreaking. The autopsies that are long and exhausting are the multiple gunshot wounds, multiple stab wounds or beatings, or cases where I have to do extensive dissection of vertebrae or other bones.

"Then there are the decomposed bodies, where the special effects of smell, insects or larval forms, and putrefaction of tissues challenge all the senses. How do you get used to the smell? You don't. The face coverings make it less daunting by throwing up at least a psychological shield against the bad stuff.

"[But] an autopsy is not the emotional experience people think it is. I don't pick up a heart and think, 'Who's broken this heart?' I look into the body to see why we die. It's like solving a puzzle. I don't think of the brain or the heart as body pieces. It's a body with organs that were all working together."

The clinical detachment displayed in these words does not dehumanize the doctor. No one could be as deeply involved in "solving the puzzle" of so many children's deaths without feeling deeply about her subject matter.

At seventy, Dr. Case still appears vital, fit and strong, with a well-sculpted head of silver-blond hair, eyes that miss nothing, and a no-nonsense manner. It's that manner and the evident confidence of the highly-experienced expert—both in academic and real world terms—that perhaps impresses some people as arrogance.

A few of the jurors in the eventual trial of Angel Ray felt that Dr. Case did seem arrogant on the stand. Most of them, however, simply felt she displayed her confidence by stating her opinions clearly and not wavering under cross-examination. What all of them agreed upon was this: her opinion was authoritative. She certainly knew what she was talking about.

And so it was with great anticipation that the police and the prosecutors pressed forward with their investigation while waiting, waiting, waiting, for the expert opinion of Dr. Case.

* * *

Janet wasn't sleeping. And when she did, she would dream.

"Come get me!" Neveah would call to Janet in the dreams—the nightmares—she began having during the long wait for the expert's report.

Janet in 2013 says she still has those dreams, still hears that voice, as if it's become natural to her, something familiar, part of the burden she carries.

Those months of waiting were, for Janet and Vera and Cathy—Neveah's triumvirate—less a time of anticipation and more a time of anxiety, frustration, and deep guilt. According to Vera, Cathy became "like an ostrich." She would keep her head down low and, whenever Neveah would come up, all she would say was, "I let her go back to her mother that night ... I will always feel guilty about that."

For Janet and Vera, the feelings of guilt were likewise inescapable. They kept wondering what more they could have done. They, too, had let Miriam take Neveah that very last time.

Their frustration came from not knowing the cause of Neveah's death and not being able to proceed against the man whom everyone "knew" committed the crime. It troubled Janet when Cindy Torres—the DA's victim advocate who was assigned to the family—called and told her the coroner, Dr. Amy Martin, "had not put a cause of death on the death certificate."

Janet didn't want Neveah's death certificate to say her cause of death was "undetermined." She wanted it to say "murder."

The anxiety came from not knowing where Miriam and Angel Ray were living. The anxiety was especially intense for Janet, since it was her own daughter Miriam who had caused this tragedy and Miriam wasn't there to help the family deal with it. She wasn't there physically. She wasn't there emotionally. She simply wasn't there. But Detective Crider was there.

At first during this period, Vera and Janet were wary of those in authority. And they were suffering fiercely. Later, they talked about feeling attacked by Dr. Amy Martin when they went to the morgue near Denver Health to identify Neveah's body.

According to Vera and Janet, Dr. Martin was somewhat rude to them. She peppered them with questions:

Who-what-when-where and how?

Tell us what happened to this child! Tell us what you know!

Recall, this was only days after Neveah's death and very soon after the discovery of her remains in the ravine in Lakewood. Tensions and emotions ran high all around.

Still it was Detective Crider who overcame the family's wariness. He kept them informed. After Miriam and Angel Ray were released—on the day of Neveah's funeral—he told Janet and Vera that initially the love birds had gone to a hotel paid for by their lawyers. The police did not know where, however. Did they know?

No, they said, they did not, though Vera added that on the day she was released, Miriam had left a voice mail message on her cell phone that said, "I'm out, Auntie, and I'm just calling to let you know I'm doing fine."

Also, added Janet, one of Miriam's friends had called and told her that Miriam had been in touch with her. So armed with this knowledge the police were able to trace phone calls made to and from the hotel where Miriam and Angel Ray were staying. Not much was happening there, except they had no food, so Miriam left and went to visit a nearby friend to get some.

After the love birds left the hotel, Janet and Vera did not know where they went. At times they thought Miriam was living on the streets, more often they suspected she was living with Angel Ray's mother, cousin or brother. They really didn't know.

Still during this time Detective Crider would stop by Janet's little house on Lipan Street and keep them up to date as best he could. He would come by once a month or so.

He was the one who told Janet that the prosecutors were seeking a second opinion from a "coroner from out of state"— Dr. Mary Case from St. Louis—to determine the cause of death, and it would take awhile to get her report. He was also the one who let them know that most of the time the police were able to hold Angel Ray in custody due to his persistent and continuing failure to register as a sex offender.

Still the wait continued and Janet's heart ached. Once, Miriam stopped by the house on Lipan Street unexpectedly, just to say hello to Janet and show her mother she was alive.

Janet said to her, "Are you okay? We worry about you."

Miriam responded, "I can't come home. I can make do."

Miriam also asked where Neveah was buried, but Janet refused to tell her. So Miriam turned to Vera. She had, after all, a better relationship with her aunt than with her mother. In fact, Miriam called Vera perhaps once a month during this time just to let her know she was still doing okay.

Sometimes Vera would ask where Miriam was living and if she was living with Angel Ray, but Miriam would refuse to say. Sometimes Miriam would ask Vera where Neveah was buried, but Vera always went along with Janet's wishes. She would say to Miriam, "I can't tell you that. Your mother did a good job." That's all Vera would say.

Now this seems odd from hindsight, since the media had reported on Neveah's funeral and burial at Mt. Olivet Cemetery. It should not have been difficult for Miriam to find out where her daughter was buried. Still the story according to Vera goes quite differently:

"We would go to the grave and there were these little butterflies and little things on the grave and we wondered who was bringing these to the grave."

Vera and Janet were perplexed. They knew Miriam had named her daughter Neveah because she associated, rightly or wrongly, the name with the word "butterfly" in Hebrew or some other exotic language. But how could it have been Miriam?

Much later, Janet and Vera learned that one day Miriam had gone to social services and met a friend of Cathy's there. This friend of Cathy's knew where Neveah was buried and told Miriam. So eventually the mystery was solved: Miriam had been visiting the grave and leaving the butterflies and trinkets. At the time, however, the mystery just added to the anxiety.

So Vera and Janet and Cathy simply took care of each other. It was something they were used to doing.

Since they were all witnesses that hopefully would be called one day to testify against Angel Ray, they had been told by the prosecutors and police to not discuss the case with anyone, including themselves. But how were they supposed to separate "the case" from everything else going on in their lives? Did that mean they couldn't talk to anyone about anything meaningful?

They turned to their spirituality. They had been raised as devout Catholics and their homes, especially Janet's, were filled will sacramental candles and little religious icons. They had been "raised this way," according to Janet. And so they prayed every day.

They had started praying to St. Anthony—the patron saint of lost things—during the painful days when they had searched the trash bins for Neveah's body. Now they prayed to him for justice. And they lit candles to Santo Niño, the patron saint for little children. And they went to masses at St. Francis and talked to the priest at St. Joe's.

Mostly they prayed for the spirit of Neveah.

Later Janet talked about relying so much on her faith. She said she took great comfort in it. She figured Jesus had suffered then and now Neveah had been forced to suffer as well. She had come to terms with her belief it wasn't Jesus' fault.

Still her faith could not erase the anxiety, the grief, the guilt. They became a toxic stew.

Janet was stressed. Janet was anxious.

Janet was having those dreams—"Come get me!"—and she was getting little sleep. She admitted she wasn't taking care of herself "health-wise." It's no wonder while everyone waited for the report from Dr. Case, Janet began feeling ill.

* * *

During the time Dr. Case was evaluating the autopsy report and forensic materials she had been sent—it took nearly a year— Verna Carpenter had to shift her efforts into the prosecution of Jon Phillips for the brutal starvation death of 7-year-old Chandler Grafner. The case against Angel Ray was reassigned to Michelle Amico, another veteran Chief Deputy District Attorney, who would drive the case through trial, years after Carpenter assumed the bench.

Amico earned her law degree from the University of Denver. After clerking for a major law firm and for the U.S. Department of Education's Office for Civil Rights, she had joined the Denver District Attorney's Office and she had risen through the ranks. She had great breadth and depth of experience, having pro- secuted countless cases and having served as the director of the Family Violence Unit, the Gang Unit, the County Court Division, the District Court Division, the Juvenile Division, and the Intake Division of the DA's office. She had acted as a legal advisor to the Denver Police Department and as an instructor at the Denver Police Academy.

A volunteer in the community throughout her career, Amico also served as the President of the Board of Directors for the Denver Center for Crime Victims for over five years. She was deeply committed, hard-working, and sharp: a sharp legal mind inside a head of shoulder-length brown hair streaked light; sharp eyes deeply set; sharp chin under cheerful smile.

Amico had been among the many volunteers from Mitch Morrissey's office who had pulled latex gloves over their hands and searched from Dumpster to Dumpster throughout Capitol Hill on the weekend after Neveah's death, looking for her body. In that sense she had been involved in the case from the very beginning.

As soon as she was introduced to Michelle Amico, Janet Gallegos came away with the clear impression that Amico "was a very caring person ... doing the best for my granddaughter."

Indeed, Amico and Detective Crider and victim advocate Cindy Torres all formed powerful bonds with Neveah's family during the long months of their quest for justice.

After the trial one of the jurors remarked that obviously Amico was "emotionally invested" in the case. That was evident from her opening and closing statements. This juror, like almost all of the others, nevertheless believed that Amico did a "phenomenal job" in the courtroom. In particular she did a "terrific job" of maintaining her professionalism at times when— this juror figured—it must have been really hard to "keep cool." As leader of the prosecution team, Michelle Amico would become one of the key players in Neveah's drama, determined, relentless, and skillful.

The support provided by Amico's "second chair," Christine Washburn, proved invaluable. Washburn earned her JD from the University of Colorado School of Law in 1998, served for a year with the DA in Boulder, then joined the Denver DA's office in 1999. In 2008 she became a Chief Deputy DA. That meant two experienced Chief Deputies would eventually take the case against Angel Ray to trial, assuming a cause of death—meaning a homicide—could be established.

And that meant Mitch Morrissey was willing to devote serious institutional resources to putting the child killer away. Later he insisted that questions of resource allocation were entirely "secondary to getting justice for this little girl." Still he admitted the case would take a lot out of Carpenter, Amico, Washburn and others from his office. But economics were never an issue.

In fact, Morrissey recalled, he took an active role in the case himself. He knew his team would need a lot of support so he would stop by Amico's office often and check in with her. Many times he found himself going from a five-minute "hello" to a forty-minute discussion of strategy, tactics, or some point of law or evidence. He became, he said, "very hands on."

Victim advocate Cindy Torres rounded out the team. Denver's Victim Advocate Program—part of Morrissey's office—assigns a victim advocate to each trial team. The victim advocate is trained to cut through the "difficult and confusing" ins and outs of the criminal court system, and provides "support, information and referrals." One of the most important services provided by a victim advocate is simply communication: keeping the victim or the victim's family up-to-date on the status of their case, interfacing with the prosecution and the police, making hard concepts clear to the uninitiated.

In Neveah's case, Cindy Torres performed all of the functions assigned to her and then some. She provided support to the prosecution team as well as the family. She arranged meetings with many of the witnesses—like the lawyer from the parking lot—and provided a contact point for them and other interested parties throughout the long quest for justice. She was always there, always ready, always willing and able to help. Dark-haired and stout, no-nonsense and sensitive and caring, Torres rendered valuable services not only to the prosecution and the family, but to the community at large.

So the prosecution team was set to push ahead. Still there was no determinable "cause of death."

As 2007 bled into 2008, the waiting became tedious, frustrating—and hard. Life went on and the police and prosecutors continued to gather evidence. But it was hard.

* * *

The summer of 2008 was another hot one in Denver. The thermometer reached 104 on August 1, the day Neveah would have turned four.

It wasn't an easy day for Janet, Vera, Cathy and the rest of the family. Candles were lit, prayers uttered, tears shed. And a child's grave was visited.

Finally, after months of reviewing the autopsy report and forensic samples she had been sent, Dr. Case prepared her report. It was dated September 26, 2008: one year and five days after Neveah's tragic death. In her report, Dr. Case provided the second major breakthrough in the case against Angel Ray. She plugged the hole left by Dr. Martin's autopsy report. There were sighs of relief—and more tears—all around.

For in her report Dr. Case said she could indeed specify the cause of Neveah's death.

It was homicide.

EIGHT: THE GRAND JURY and the INDICTMENTS

Twenty miles west of Central London in the English County of Surrey, the River Thames flows past a scenic meadow. The meadow is called Runnymede. On June 15, 1215, twenty-five rebellious feudal barons gathered upon that meadow and watched as a reluctant King John set his Great Seal upon a document he never actually signed.

It was called Magna Carta—the Great Charter—and it became the font from which sprang the Rule of Law, for it required the Crown to recognize the antecedents to many of the basic, "fundamental" rights found today in the U.S. Constitution. Though not specifically mentioned in Magna Carta, the right to a grand jury was among the rights that traced their origins to a time decades before 1215. It was already part of the landscape.

As an institution the grand jury evolved over time, through the High Middle Ages and the Enlightenment into Modernity, and eventually found its way into the story of Neveah Gallegos and Angel Ray Montoya. For armed with the expert opinion of Dr. Mary Case, the prosecutors in Denver were finally prepared to move ahead. But they faced a strategic decision:

Should they initiate criminal proceedings against Miriam and Angel Ray by simply filing a "Complaint"—also called a "Complaint and Information"—or should they seek "Indictments" from Colorado's version of the grand jury?

The decision was not clear-cut. Grand juries had deep roots but could be awkward. Law professor Mark Kadish once wrote:

> [I]n 1166, King Henry II established a system of local informers (twelve men from every hundred or four men from every village) to tell him who was suspected of "murder, robbery, larceny, or harboring criminals." The king's system … required the twelve men to report all suspects and fined them if they failed to indict any suspect or failed to indict an acceptable number of suspects …

During the reign of Edward III (1312-1377), the twelve men were superseded by twenty-four knights chosen by the county sheriff ... Meanwhile, the twelve men, having lost their original inquisitorial jurisdiction, became known as the petit jury, which had responsibility for rendering a verdict of innocent or guilty in capital crimes ...

The vote by the grand jury in the first proceeding determined whether there was probable cause to believe that the individual accused was guilty of the crime charged; the vote by the petit jury in the second proceeding determined whether there was enough evidence to convict. [At this time] the grand juries began to shift their focus away from mere accusation to considerations of fairness for the individual accused ...

By the fourteenth century ... secrecy [became] a part of the grand jurors' oath ... [G]rand jurors were sworn not to disclose the subjects of the inquiry, the witnesses, or any of the evidence. In addition, grand jurors were sworn not to reveal their own personal knowledge, the knowledge of their fellow jurors, their investigative plans, or their deliberations. The reasons ... were first, to prevent the flight of criminals; second, to find out whether witnesses were biased; third, to be free from judicial oversight; fourth, to catch witnesses in their lies; and fifth, to permit the full development of evidence for a possible indictment ... Secrecy made possible the discovery of truth and protected individuals from malicious or hateful prosecution.

Despite these deepest of roots, the grand jury has had a mixed history under U.S. law. The Fifth Amendment says:

No person shall be held to answer for a capital, or otherwise infamous crime, unless on a presentment or indictment of a Grand Jury, except in cases arising in the land or naval forces, or in the Militia, when in actual service in time of War or public danger.

Accordingly the grand jury is deeply embedded in Federal criminal practice. Like many other Federal constitutional requirements, it has evolved over the past two centuries, but the basics remain the same, today governed by Federal Rules of Criminal Procedure 6 and 7.

However—recall the discussion of "incorporation" in Chapter Three—the Supreme Court in 1884 faced this issue: does the Due Process Clause of the Fourteenth Amendment require grand jury indictment in State as well as Federal courts? The case was *Hurtado v. California*. In a 7-1 decision the Court held the Due Process Clause of the Fourteenth Amendment, which was later the vehicle through which almost all other rights in the Bill of Rights became applicable to the States, did not require an indictment by a state grand jury.

The *Hurtado* case has never been overruled and it became, indeed, the case upon which many states relied in either abandoning altogether or substantially reforming their grand jury practice. Today less than half of the States use grand juries and among those that still have them, almost all allow prosecutions to be initiated by Complaint and Information as an alternative to grand jury Indictment.

Colorado is one of the States that has kept the grand jury. That meant the prosecutors in the office of District Attorney Mitch Morrissey had to be thoroughly familiar with its operation, its advantages, and its disadvantages.

In a statement designed for lay people, the Colorado Judicial Branch in 2004 described grand jury practice under Colorado rules and statutes this way:

> In counties [like Denver] with a population of 100,000 persons or more, according to the latest federal census, a grand jury is drawn and summoned by the court to attend the sitting of the court at the first term of such court in each year.

A grand jury consists of 12 or 23 members in addition to four alternates. At any meeting of a grand jury at least nine grand jurors constitutes a quorum … The court, upon its own motion or at the request of the district attorney, can enter an order to preserve the confidentiality of all information that might identify grand jurors when reasonably necessary to protect the grand jury process or the security of the grand jurors …

Grand juror service is for a term of 12 months unless the court discharges the jurors earlier or enlarges such term upon a finding that the efficient administration of justice so requires; except that in no event shall a grand jury serve for longer than 18 months …

The grand jury hears witnesses called only by the prosecution. It also has the power to subpoena witnesses as it deems appropriate. Witnesses may be accompanied by an attorney. However, that attorney cannot participate in the grand jury process.

A grand jury has the authority to return an indictment (also known as a "true bill" or "presentment"). It also may decline to issue an indictment (a "no true bill") … The district attorney can petition the court [to seal the indictment] and no person may disclose the existence of the indictment until the defendant is in custody or has been admitted to bail except when necessary for the issuance or execution of a warrant …

So, Colorado's grand jury system departs from the ancient rule that excludes altogether the lawyers for witnesses, but it preserves the essential characteristic of grand jury secrecy. And in Neveah's case there was another feature of the grand jury system that would prove to be a powerful tool at the hands of the prosecution team.

Still they had to evaluate all of the pros and cons.

The advantages of proceeding by Complaint and Information were obvious. That route is almost always faster and more efficient in terms of both resource allocation and cost. Even in those States where the grand jury has been retained with some modern variations, the vast majority of criminal cases are initiated by Complaint and Information or similar filings made by the prosecutor's office in the trial court with the proper jurisdiction.

What's more, grand jury proceedings are subject to a wide variety of attacks. There are "facial" challenges to the Indictment for its failure to satisfy statutory requirements. The defense can also move to dismiss the Indictment based on lack of probable cause, which is perhaps the most common type of objection. Then there are attacks grounded in prosecutorial misconduct, conflicts of interest, or violations of the requirements of secrecy. Challenges based on any of these grounds can lead to lengthy and costly "discovery proceedings," adding to the time, cost and effort of launching a criminal case through the grand jury route.

Nevertheless, Colorado rules and cases have respected the role of the grand jury and its secrecy with reasons that echo those dating to the 14th century: preventing the flight of those whose indictment is expected; ensuring freedom to the grand jury in its deliberations and preventing tampering with the grand jurors; preventing subornation of perjury or tampering with witnesses; encouraging free and full disclosure of information about crimes; and protecting the innocent who are exonerated from disclosure of the fact that they have been investigated.

In other words, the grand jury as an institution is still, after all these centuries, widely perceived as a truth-telling mechanism that protects both the State and the accused. Furthermore, its advantages and disadvantages get amplified in cases involving more than one defendant, such as those against Miriam and Angel Ray.

That's because two or more defendants can be treated as "co-defendants" or "co-conspirators." Each participated in his or her own separate crimes, but they also participated together in some of the same crimes. Often, statements made under oath by one can be used against the other, and if the prosecutors played their cards right, their key witness could not avoid answering the questions put to her by hiding behind the Fifth Amendment.

That factor tipped the balance in favor of the grand jury. The decision was made before the end of 2008. Michelle Amico and her team would have to wait until the next Denver grand jury convened in January of 2009 and then stand in line while other cases were heard. Detective Crider later explained: "There were a few people we wanted to get in front of the grand jury ... to make sure we were getting truthful testimony. Or to help us get truthful testimony, I should say. That's one of the benefits of the grand jury, because we're locking them into sworn testimony."

Mitch Morrissey was willing to be even more specific: "Well, sometimes ... you want to make sure what a witness is going to say, and if it's an expert witness, you want to flesh that out with the grand jury. But in this case we had a co-con"—he started to say co-conspirator but paused—"somebody that was working to help this man get away with this horrendous crime. And that was the mother of this little girl. And we could put her on in front of the grand jury, with an agreement not to use her testimony in front of the grand jury against her, by immunizing her ... so we could put her in front of the grand jury, have her testify to what she had to say, and she couldn't use the Fifth Amendment to avoid that testimony."

Wait a minute. Exactly how does this "immunizing" work?

Under modern grand jury practice, a witness who is called to testify before a grand jury cannot refuse to answer questions by asserting his or her privilege against self-incrimination under the Fifth Amendment if there is an agreement to not use that testimony, and any evidence derived from it, against the witness.

Such an agreement can be "voluntary" but statutes and rules allow the court supervising the grand jury to force it on a witness by issuing an order, compelling the witness to testify in exchange for such "immunity."

And because the immunity extends only as far as the testimony itself, and any evidence derived from that testimony, this approach—called "use and derivative" immunity—avoids having to dismiss a potential case against the witness altogether. If other competent evidence can prove the witness participated in the crime—or criminal "transaction" as it is often called—then prosecution of the witness using that other evidence is not prohibited. All this is spelled out in detail, in Colorado, in its Courts and Procedure Code, CRS 13-90-118.

Mitch Morrissey emphasized why, using this powerful prosecutorial tool, he wanted so badly to put Miriam in front of the grand jury: "This is a woman that backed the murderer of her daughter. This is a woman that put her daughter in a situation where he was able to continue to prey on her. We were convinced that he had abused her in the past, that he may well have sexually abused her in the past, and this is a mother who knew that and allowed him to still be the primary caretaker for her when mom was at work."

Shaking his head, Morrissey paused to comment that, during the recent economic downturn, his office had actually seen a drop in homicides and other violent crimes in general, but one crime had unfortunately increased:

"These baby death cases where mom would go to work and her deadbeat boyfriend or husband would kill the baby." Of course some of these mothers had to leave their children for "very good financial reasons ... and to a degree there was some of that here, except that this was a mother that knew that she was leaving her baby at risk every time she left her alone with this monster. And this is a monster—and I call him a monster because he did this to other little kids, and we were able to show that in this case, and I believe he did this to Neveah in the past. So, this is a mom who knew. She had an alliance to this guy that I found totally unacceptable."

Decision made. Strategy set.

The grand jury would hear the prosecutors' case against Miriam and Angel Ray in early 2009.

* * *

Amid the arcane legal mysteries of the grand jury—to lay people like Janet, Vera, and their family—there came mythology as well. The entry titled "Murder of Neveah Gallegos" that appears in the popular web site *Wikipedia* includes the following two sentences:

"Extremely frustrated with the lack of arrest of her own daughter Miriam Gallegos and Angel Montoya, the child's grandmother, Janet Gallegos, reached out to attorney/author Donna Thomas for help in procuring justice for Nevaeh [sp]. Thomas had a grand jury convened."

While it's true the family did experience a lot of frustration during the long wait for the report from Dr. Mary Case, and then during the weeks leading up to the grand jury proceedings, the remainder of the first sentence and the entirety of the second sentence are completely false. People closely connected to the tragedy—including Janet and Detective Crider—will confirm Donna Thomas had nothing whatsoever to do with convening the grand jury in Neveah's case.

A person named Donna Thomas was, however, ordered— "publicly enjoined"—by the Colorado Supreme Court in October of 2009 to cease practicing law without a license in the State of Colorado. The case number was 09SA122.

* * *

Still the family's frustration was real. After Dr. Case issued her report in September of 2008 and before the grand jury proceedings the following spring, the weeks moved slowly. There was anger and confusion over what was happening and not happening in the legal arena. The emotions swept past Janet and Vera and swallowed the family whole.

They, for example, have a sister named Frances, younger than Vera, older than Janet. Frances has a daughter named Janet Belew—named, indeed, after her Aunt Janet, Neveah's grandmother. The younger Janet is called Flower inside the family. The nickname also shows up on her social media pages. Her voice broadens the view from the family's perspective.

Flower was in her mid-thirties when Neveah was murdered. Though her resemblance to her aunts is unmistakable, she is taller and less rounded than their generation. Her hair, nearly blond, is longer and lighter. Her smile is broader and her glasses are hipper. A Denver native, she has worked for nearly two decades, since graduating from Lincoln High, in childhood education, mostly at Mile High Montessori. At the same time she has been earning her bachelor's degree and raising her son, Jesse, who was twelve when Neveah was murdered.

Flower is not married but is in a long-term relationship with a man who is not Jesse's father. They live together as a family and she has had absolutely no concern that Jesse would ever be abused by this man. He, she says, "raised my son."

She describes Neveah's tragedy with words like "horrendous" and the pain comes to her in snapshots and episodes. For her one of the worst times was "the day that we buried Neveah ... walking into my grandmother's room"— Neveah's great-grandmother, the one with the doggie—"and watching her get dressed for her great-granddaughter's funeral ... who was three years old ... It was just awful."

Of course Flower's mother Frances was also "devastated" by the whole ordeal, but like many others in the family they spent a lot of time and energy trying to comfort Vera and Janet, who were the hardest hit and the most engaged with the police and the legal process.

Then there was the time, shortly after the murder, when the wounds were still raw, and Jesse overheard some teachers in the hallway at his school talking about it. According to his mom, Jesse just "fell apart." When the teachers asked him what was wrong, and he told them they were talking about his cousin, they immediately put him in touch with the school counselor. "The school was great," says Flower, "they helped him through it."

Still the wounds went deep. Years later, when the family's quest for justice finally came to an end, Jesse wrote a very touching report for his high school literature class that was titled "Heavenly Ceremony." In it he created a series of rituals meant "to commemorate the life of Neveah and our brief, but valuable time spent with her ... she helped us develop a refined understanding of the most prominent virtues of appreciation and love. The most prominent effect ... emerged in the form of family convergence."

Though she admits Janet and Vera still remain haunted by the death of Neveah, Flower—much like her son Jesse—found some measure of closure when the trial that loomed in the future finally came to an end. She found enough closure, at least, to have a bright red tattoo of a smiling Elmo inked into her forearm in memory of the child the family had lost.

* * *

The Denver County Statutory Grand Jury convened in January of 2009. Its Indictment of Angel Ray came in late April and its Indictment of Miriam came in early May. While the grand jury's proceedings remain secret, what transpired inside the grand jury room may be inferred from the Arrest Warrants issued with the Indictments.

Angel Ray's Arrest Warrant is dated April 22. It includes over six single-spaced pages of factual allegations to support the charges made in the Indictment.

The first 40 paragraphs provide a general background; a complete narrative of the day of Neveah's death, as described in Chapter Three and as provided by Miriam; the discovery of Neveah's body in the gulch in Lakewood; and the beginning of the autopsy by Dr. Amy Martin.

Then it appears Detective Joe Delmonico testified before the grand jury, since the perspective shifts to him for the next few paragraphs:

"Detective Joe Delmonico ... was present for the autopsy and noted multiple visible injuries on Neveah. She had bruises to the right side and the middle of her forehead, bruises on the left forehead, multiple bruises on the left cheek, and one that almost resembled a pattern."

Four more paragraphs talk about the bruises and abrasions Detective Delmonico witnessed during the autopsy, then there is a paragraph about the fresh hemorrhages underneath Neveah's scalp and in the strap muscles and soft tissue in her neck, "and deep paraspinal hemorrhages [that] were fresh [and] extensive."

Next there is a sentence about the extensive hemorrhages in the root of the mesentery. Then, the conclusion:

"Dr. Martin was unable to make a determination regarding the cause and manner of death. However, she provided the name of a top child pathologist in the country, Dr. Mary Case."

Paragraphs 49 and 50 move into the forensics performed by Jeanne Kilmer, the serologist who tested many of the items taken from the Logan Street apartment and the clothing of Neveah and Angel Ray for blood and saliva. Kilmer reported that she had found blood on Neveah's shirt, the left leg of Angel Ray's gym shorts, some towels in the bathroom, some "wipes found in the trash in the kitchen," a sheet found crumpled under the vanity, and "the pillow from Neveah's bed."

Sylvia Thurmond, another forensic serologist, performed DNA testing and reported that the blood on Angel Ray's shorts "was a mixture of DNA from Neveah, Gallegos and Montoya."

The next seven paragraphs—52 through 58—describe an incident from 2005 in which Angel Ray viciously beat and choked another small child. This was the tale of Jesus Perez, mentioned in Chapter Five.

In the publicly-available versions of the Indictment, the name of the child has been redacted. However, his courageous public testimony at trial—seven years after he was nearly killed by Angel Ray—became the third breakthrough in the case, driven by his name and his voice.

Finally the Arrest Warrant devotes eight paragraphs to the report made by Dr. Mary Case. These are critical paragraphs for they fill in the biggest blanks.

The cause and manner of death, undetermined for so long, now became crystal clear—at least for the prosecution:

59. Law enforcement officials provided Dr. Mary Case [various materials, including photos and microscopic slides from the autopsy] for her review. On September 26, 2008, Dr. Case prepared a report regarding the cause and manner of Neveah's death.

60. Dr. Case opined that there was extensive evidence of blunt trauma to the body of Neveah far beyond what would be expected from the normal activity of a child of that age.

61. Dr. Case opined that the cause of Neveah Gallegos' death was asphyxiation. She described it as putting pressure on the muscles of the neck restricting the airway in the neck. The pressure keeps the blood from flowing to the brain and cuts off the oxygen that flows to the brain thus causing her death.

62. Dr. Case indicated that you would not see external signs of injury on the neck but that there would be clear indication of internal injury to the strap muscles in the neck. She opined that the injuries found in Neveah's neck were from pressure to her neck.

63. Dr. Case indicated that it would take approximately 10 to 30 seconds for the child to lose consciousness and about two, three, or four minutes to cause death. Dr. Case also reported that a juvenile will start showing signs of rigor mortis within about 15 to 30 minutes of death, quicker than an adult.

64. Dr. Case also indicated that the injury to Neveah's abdomen, including the extensive hemorrhaging in the mesentery, was clearly caused by blunt force to the area, likely caused by a punch or kick to the abdomen.

65. Dr. Case clarified that the injuries to Neveah found at autopsy were not caused post-mortem. If she sustained injuries from the stump or debris found on her Dr. Case would have seen indentations or different kinds of abrasions. She opined that Neveah's injuries all occurred prior to her death.

66. Dr. Case opined that the manner of Neveah Gallegos' death was homicide.

* * *

So the mystery over the cause and manner of Neveah's death was solved: homicide by asphyxiation.

Based upon these findings and the other evidence presented to the grand jury, Angel Ray was indicted for two felonies: Murder in the First Degree and Child Abuse Resulting in Death. Shortly after, Miriam was indicted for two felonies as well: Child Abuse Resulting in Death and Accessory to Crime.

The *Denver Post* reported on the Indictments on May 7, quoting this tidbit from one of them: "As Montoya left with Neveah in the duffel bag, Gallegos kissed him goodbye and told him she loved him." The *Post* article also revealed how easy it was to locate and re-arrest Angel Ray: "Later in 2007 [after his release on October 1] Montoya was jailed on unrelated charges of failure to register as a sex offender and has remained in the Denver County Jail."

That meant the Angel of Death was already in custody.

As for Miriam: "Police arrested Gallegos on Wednesday," according to the *Post*, "as she walked near West Evans Avenue and South Broadway. She is being held in Denver County Jail on $500,000 bond. 'She was surprised, and when I saw her, she was crying,' Denver Division Chief of Investigations Dave Fisher said at a news conference announcing the indictments."

Finally, after nearly twenty months of investigation and waiting, the community's quest for justice entered an important new phase: preparation for trial.

NINE: ONE PLEA and TWO FALSE STARTS

Miriam did not go down without a fight. She was miserable in jail. She wanted out.

Her court-appointed lawyers—Scott Reisch and Mellissa Trollinger—quickly filed a flurry of motions meant to achieve that result. They filed a Motion to Suppress Evidence that argued Miriam's rights against unreasonable search and seizure under the Fourth Amendment had been violated by the police search of her Logan Street apartment on September 21, 2007. They said Miriam had given Sgt. Zimmerman the key to her apartment for the limited purpose of finding a photo of Neveah in connection with the false kidnapping story she was telling the police back in the parking lot at 1080 Cherokee. Because his search went beyond that limited purpose, everything found during that search, and discovered as a result of it, including Miriam's confessions, had to be excluded from evidence.

If successful, this attack could wreck the prosecution's case against Miriam.   Admittedly, the police search of the apartment went beyond its original purpose. As stated by the defense: "The officers conducted a full searched [sic] Ms. Gallegos' apartment. They observed and collected a paper towel with possible blood stains from the living room; blood drops from the floor of the bathroom; and a towel in the bathroom trashcan which appeared to be covered in vomit and sunflower seeds." They also collected Miriam's Sports Authority ID and a photo collage they showed Stephen Matthews, the neighbor, who identified the man in the picture, Angel Ray Montoya, as the man who had asked to use his phone earlier in the day.

The defense argued that once the photos had been collected, there was no reason to go searching in the bathroom: "Even given the paper towel found on the floor of the living room, the officers were required to obtain a search warrant to continue the search of the apartment."

They conceded the standard for reviewing cases like this was "totality of the circumstances," and at the time the police thought they were dealing with a kidnapping and therefore time was of the essence. An Amber Alert had been issued. The search for Neveah was on. Still, said the defense, because the apartment search went beyond the purpose Miriam had consented to, the evidence found—the blood drops in the bathroom and the towel covered in vomit and sunflower seeds—had to be excluded. So, too, any evidence derived from that evidence, the "fruit of the poisonous tree." That meant the search warrant that was later obtained was no good, according to the defense, and even Miriam's confessions and statements would have to be excluded.

The motion was contested. Miriam lost. The paper towel on the floor of the living room was in plain sight and it gave the officers plenty of reason to look around for more. The evidence against the mother, collected on the day of her daughter's death, was not inadmissible.

Another motion filed by the defense sought to review the issue of "probable cause" as determined by the grand jury, to quash the Indictment that resulted from their proceedings, and to authorize discovery of information relating to the grand jury's proceedings. This challenge of the Indictment based on the alleged lack of probable cause was altogether routine.

Miriam lost this motion as well.

Finally there were battles fought at the outset of the case over the terms of the "gag order" requested by both Miriam's lawyers and Angel Ray's public defenders. Authorization to issue a gag order in order to prevent *pervasive prejudicial pretrial publicity* could be traced to the U.S. Supreme Court's decision in 1966 in *Sheppard v. Maxwell,* the case that inspired the popular TV series *The Fugitive.* In the real life proceedings, the "circus atmosphere" that had surrounded the prosecution of Dr. Sam Sheppard for the murder of his wife had plainly tainted his ability to get a fair trial.

The issue confronting the Court was easy to understand but hard to negotiate: to what extent can a court, to insure a criminal defendant gets a fair trial, issue an order preventing the media from discussing or disclosing information that would cause widespread prejudice against him?

It's an obvious clash between the Sixth Amendment's requirement of a "fair trial" and the protection of a "free press" required by the First Amendment. The Court, in an opinion that should be read by anyone who thinks constitutional rights can be enforced absolutely, recognized the weighty concerns on both sides of the case. Here two equally important rights collided. Absolute enforcement of one right would necessarily infringe on the other. But the need to insure a fair trial for the defendant was deemed so important that the right to a free press would have to yield, though in a very limited way.

Cases interpreting and applying *Sheppard v. Maxwell* are legion. According to the motion filed on behalf of Miriam, her lawyers' "concern about filing a gag order …came as a result of the arrest of Ms. Gallegos and a press conference" held by DA Mitch Morrissey and the Denver police chief, "patting themselves on the back after the Indictment and arrest following their 17 month investigation." The press conference was all over the TV, Internet, and *Denver Post*. Indeed, the case had "been covered in the news for nearly two years." All this resulted in pervasive pretrial prejudice against Ms. Gallegos.

The prosecution filed an extremely detailed response, and quibbled over the terms of the order as it related to necessary disclosures under Colorado's Victim's Rights Amendment. Ultimately, however, the **"People concede[d]** *in substantial part* **the written motion filed by the Defendant, Gallegos, and orally joined by co-defendant Montoya as it relates to information provided to the media."** The bold and italics are in the original brief, which also insisted the prosecution wanted only "to ensure a fair and just process for all parties involved."

Accordingly the trial court did issue a gag order that prohibited extrajudicial statements by the lawyers in both cases to the media if (a) "dissemination would pose a clear and present danger to the fairness of the trial" or if (b) the extrajudicial statements concern "Opinions about the Defendants' character or the Defendants' guilt or innocence ... Admissions, confessions, or the contents of a statement attributed to the Defendants ... References to the results of investigative procedures ... Statements concerning the credibility or anticipated testimony of prospective witnesses ... [or] Opinions concerning evidence or argument in the case."

The gag order further prohibited, in even greater detail, extrajudicial statements by the police. Signed by the judge on May 14, the order came only 8 days after Miriam was indicted.

By June of the following year, she had had enough. Her minor victory on the gag order did not wipe away the wide array of evidence against her, and her substantive motions had failed. It was time to cut a deal, a plea bargain, with the prosecutors.

On June 25, 2010, Miriam signed and initialed every paragraph of the elaborate paperwork that constituted her plea of guilty to the charge of Child Abuse–Negligently Causing Death, a class 3 felony. On the same day, in exchange for Miriam's guilty plea, the prosecution dropped the first two counts, the more serious counts, against her.

The court entered a Minute Order, dated the same day, which stated: "THE SENT IS OPEN; THE DEF AGREES AS PART OF THIS PLEA DISPO TO RESPND TO ANY LAWFUL SUBPOENA & TO PROVIDE TRUTHFUL TESTIMONY IN ANY PROCEEDING INVOLVING THE CHARGED CO DEF ANGEL RAY MONTOYA."

Finally, a little over six months later, on January, 6, 2011, the judge—William D. Robbins, an experienced jurist—closed the sentence. He gave Miriam 12 years in state prison plus 60 months of mandatory parole.

The *Denver Post* reported Judge Robbins said this to Miriam at her sentencing hearing: "Common to every living creature, from mud worms to human beings, is the instinct to protect the young … If you wanted to play house with Mr. Montoya, fine. That's your business. But you had no business bringing Neveah into that situation." What she had done to her child, said Judge Robbins, left him speechless.

Even so, Miriam was not finished fighting. She promptly filed a hand-written request for a reduction of her sentence, citing several reasons, including "no prior felonies" and the family and community support system she had on the outside. Miriam also wrote: "The defendant assisted the D.A. against co-defendant because the actions were wrong against the victim, in which she is very sorry for."

In other words, Miriam had done exactly what she said she would do, nothing more.

Judge Robbins denied Miriam's request and stated the "Defendant fails to produce sufficient reason or evidence to reconsider the sentence. Due to the nature and the facts of this case, including the fact that the victim was Defendant's infant daughter, the Court finds Defendant was appropriately sentenced and reconsideration is not warranted."

* * *

Throughout these proceedings, Michelle Amico was assisted by Kerri Lombardi, rather than Christine Washburn, who would be Amico's "second chair" in the eventual trial of Angel Ray.

And from very early in the case, it was Holly Lucas of the Denver Public Defender's Office who represented Angel Ray. Lucas became yet another key player in the courtroom dramas about to unfold. She's a dark-haired, sturdy-looking woman with a large presence, a small tattoo above her ankle, and a determined, committed air about her.

Every day Holly Lucas performs the valuable public service of representing the indigent in criminal cases against them. She is among the thousands of law school graduates who forsake a more lucrative private practice so she can perform that public service. She is experienced and she is tough, and while some of the jurors and witnesses in the trial of Angel Ray found her manner to be too brusque, too impolite, too aggressive, others knew she was just doing her job.

It was her duty to protect the legal rights of Angel Ray. If that meant she had to make a lot of interruptions, objections, and motions on his behalf, then so be it. She had to be mindful of the effect these tactics might have on the judge and the jury, to be sure, but equally she had to be scrupulous in building a record for a possible appeal if Angel Ray were convicted.

After all, the prosecution still bore the heavy burden of proving murder by legally admissible "proof beyond a reasonable doubt," and Holly Lucas meant to make sure the rules—especially the rules of evidence—were strictly observed. If her courtroom mannerisms and her facial expressions seemed a bit too much to some, to others they were all just part of giving Angel Ray a vigorous defense.

* * *

The murder trial of Angel Ray was set for February of 2011. Pretrial activities were well underway. Witnesses like the lawyer in the parking lot were being prepared to testify. She was given a transcript of the statement she had made to Detective Estrada on September 21, 2007 to review. She also watched the video-tape of the interview from which the transcript was taken and she listened to a recording of her 911 call.

Watching the video, the lawyer found herself wiping tears from her eyes at the exact point where she wiped tears from her eyes on the screen. For her this was surreal.

Like many of the witnesses in the case, she had relived that day many times over the years. Every time the memories were about to fade into background noise, some new development in the case would jar her back to that day in the parking lot and police headquarters. Now it was finally time for the trial to begin and that jarred her back in a big way. The transcript, the tape, the video: they made it all so vivid in her mind.

She was ready to testify, and so were the other witnesses.

Last minutes motions—"motions in limine"—were filed.

Battle stations in lawyer land.

Jury selection began on Valentine's Day, February 14, and emotions were running high.

That's when Janet's health caught up with her. She had been paying less and less attention to the symptoms even as they had worsened. She figured it was all just the stress and guilt and waiting and grief.

Oh, the relentless grief. And those nightmares!

She began having abdominal pain, usually on the right side, after she ate. Over time the pain had become severe. She began eating less and less.

One day in late-mid February, after jury selection had begun, and while she was at work, Janet began having that same abdominal pain, but this time it was terribly severe. She became very weak and was having bad chills.

"I couldn't stop shivering," she recalled.

At last she went to the hospital—St. Anthony's—and luckily, she went just in time.

She had an acute bowel infection, diverticulitis, and soon learned she had diabetes as well. Her doctors said they had to control the infection before they could go in surgically to cut away the blockage or obstruction in her colon, and that meant she had to spend a couple of weeks in the hospital. Even after the surgery, she would be on drugs and painkillers that would disqualify her from testifying for some time.

Vera called Michelle Amico and gave her the bad news: One of her key witnesses would not be available for trial. Amico, Christine Washburn, and victim advocate Cindy Torres went to St. Anthony's before the surgery to visit Janet and give her their support. There was little doubt in anyone's mind the trauma of the past few years had finally overtaken her.

Surgery to remove the obstruction in Janet's bowel was performed on March 23. After a few more days in the hospital, she was sent home with a colostomy bag. On May 2, her surgeon released her to go back to work. By then, of course, the trial of Angel Ray had been rescheduled, this time for August, only a few months down the road.

In between, Janet would have to undergo a second surgery, this time to resection her colon and remove the colostomy. This surgery took place on June 28 and it was estimated by her doctor that recovery would take six weeks. That meant she could return to work on August 9.

* * *

Again just in time. Angel Ray's trial was set to begin the third week of that month.

By Thursday, August 18, the jury had been selected. Michelle Amico delivered the prosecution's opening statement. In it she acknowledged the jury would have to evaluate the credibility of Miriam, one of their key witnesses. True, she had lied to investigators. She had tried to foist the fake kidnapping story onto the authorities. And she had changed her story even after admitting her daughter was dead.

But, said Amico, assuring the jury, "You will get to judge her credibility. You may have a hard time believing a lot of what comes out of her mouth, but what she says is corroborated by all the other evidence."

The opening statement for the defense was delivered by Sarah Welton, one of Angel Ray's public defenders. She warned the jury of the holes they would punch in the prosecution's case.

Christine Washburn for the prosecution called the People's first witness: the lawyer from the parking lot at 1080 Cherokee. The prosecution lawyer walked the real estate lawyer through the events that began at 3:01 p.m. on September 21, 2007. There were many objections made by the defense and many "side bar" discussions among Washburn, Lucas, and Judge Robbins.

These discussions, held to the side of the judge's bench that is furthest away from the jury, are the vehicle for the quick resolution of evidentiary and other disputes, outside the hearing of the jury, the public, and the witnesses. In fact, in Denver District Courts, there are white noise machines that are used to drown out the possibility of these discussions being overheard.

Nevertheless, later transcripts of this testimony included the contents of the side bar discussions. Principally they focused on the evidentiary rules governing statements made by alleged co-conspirators. These rules were triggered by questions asking the lawyer from the parking lot about statements made by Miriam and her impressions of Miriam's demeanor. Defense counsel argued there was no conspiracy, or at least none had been shown to this point. They went around and around, on more than one occasion, until the judge made his ruling, turned off his white noise machine, and sent the lawyers back to the arena.

And so it went for the first week of the trial, which was expected to consume four weeks. Imagine, then, how deeply invested in the case all the players were by then: the lawyers for the prosecution and the defense, the witnesses, the family, the jury, the judge—even the news media—and most especially Angel Ray, who throughout the proceedings sat stoically silent, his face a mask of stone.

For him this was not "Perry Mason."

This was real life.

And in real life, trials tolerate little in the way of surprise. Trials in real life are choreographed events. Their steps and tempos are set beforehand by the judge's pretrial rulings on motions filed by the parties, by the rules of procedure and evidence, and by the disclosures that must be made by each side to the other long before the trial begins. To the lawyers and the judge, at least, this is a dance that is well known.

Surprise deviates from the choreography. It is not favored.

Yet a big surprise was soon to come.

On Wednesday, August 24, Miriam was called to the witness stand. She described Neveah's life and her own failures as a parent. However, as the *Denver Post* reported, "When it came to details that could potentially harm Montoya ... she claimed her memory was fuzzy." She often had to refer to a transcript of the interviews she had given to the police on the day of the killing. She had to admit she had lied to the police.

Miriam's testimony could not be completed in a day. It stretched into Thursday, August 25. She was answering a series of questions about the reasons why Angel Ray had not called the police on the day of Neveah's death. That's when she responded—basically blurting it out—that Angel Ray had said "they were going to look at him being a sex offender."

A bolt of silence stunned the courtroom. Public defender Sarah Welton later said the jury had "appeared mildly bored until those words"—*sex offender*—"came out."

In a blink the defense shot to its feet, objecting.

Legal pandemonium reigned. Miriam, according to the *Post*, "dropped her head into her hands."

Just the day before, in private, Judge Robbins had specifically instructed Miriam about what she could and could not testify about. Angel Ray's history as a sex offender—his conviction for indecent exposure in 2000, his failure to register as a sex offender, even his likely violation of Neveah in July of 2006—all this was strictly off limits.

It was strictly off limits even though the media had previously reported much of it.

The prosecution conceded Angel Ray could not get a fair trial once the jury heard those two magic words: sex offender. Judge Robbins had little choice but to declare a mistrial. He was plainly not happy. He questioned whether Miriam's violation of his clear order was accidental.

She answered, "I forgot."

He said, "This is not a burglary. This is not a car theft or a dope case that was mentioned … Ms. Gallegos appeared to understand the admonitions yesterday. I'm not in a position to say whether she did this on purpose or not."

After the mistrial, according to Mitch Morrissey, there were plenty of tears all around his office. This is when, he believed, his people needed him and his support the most. So much blood, sweat, emotion, time, and energy had gone into the community's pursuit of justice for Neveah! They couldn't believe it had all been scuttled.

The family was in shock. Everyone seemed to be in shock.

The trial of Angel Ray was rescheduled for April of 2012. Another eight-month delay.

* * *

Why did Judge Robbins so clearly order that no mention of Angel Ray's past as a sexual predator could be made in front of the jury? The answer lies in Evidence Rule 404(b).

In general, evidence of prior crimes is not admissible in a later prosecution of the defendant for different crimes. This is "hornbook" or Black Letter Law. Prior convictions may be highly prejudicial on the one hand while having little probative value on the other. They are viewed as legally verboten, not relevant. But like almost all legal rules, there are several significant exceptions.

Colorado Evidence Rule 404(b) says:

Other crimes, wrongs, or acts. Evidence of other crimes, wrongs, or acts is not admissible to prove the character of a person in order to show that he acted in conformity therewith. It may, however, be admissible for other purposes, such as proof of motive, opportunity, intent, preparation, plan, knowledge, identity, or absence of mistake or accident, provided that upon request by the accused, the prosecution in a criminal case shall provide reasonable notice in advance of trial, or during trial if the court excuses pretrial notice on good cause shown, of the general nature of any such evidence it intends to introduce at trial.

In this case, Angel Ray's past as a sex offender didn't really pass muster. No one was saying Neveah had been sexually molested at the time of her death. The autopsy certainly did not establish that. Furthermore, Angel Ray's past offenses were for indecent exposure and failure to register, not for sexual assault upon a child. The initial offense had happened when he was a juvenile in his teens. And he was never arrested, charged or convicted for his suspected penetration of Neveah in 2006.

It was clear. Statements concerning the defendant's history as a sex offender were strictly and absolutely prohibited. Miriam's violation of the rules was severe. It caused a mistrial.

It caused much heartbreak and delay.

But Evidence Rule 404(b) would come into play in a very different way, once the case finally went to trial in April of 2012. And this time it would not cut in favor of the Angel of Death.

TEN: THE JURORS

Angela Kana was born in South Korea twenty-nine years before she served as a juror in *People of the State of Colorado v. Angel Ray Montoya*. She brought a wealth of experience—some might call it baggage, though she had never let it hold her back —to her participation in the jury selection process, the weeks of trial, and the agonizing hours of deliberation. Her story and the stories of the other jurors who sat in judgment of Angel Ray are critical parts of the bigger story, yet seldom are the stories of the jurors told, except in media sound bites, quickly forgotten.

By the time jury selection began, for a third time, in mid-April of 2012, all the pretrial motions and proceedings had long since been resolved. Rulings and orders had been entered. Everyone seemed to be on board. This time the trial would go off without a hitch.

This time there was also a new judge: Sheila Rappaport, fresh off her December 2011 ruling—later reversed—that Colorado's state education law was unconstitutional because it underfunded public schools. Her 183-page opinion had called the state's public education funding system "unconscionable" and she had become mildly controversial as a result.

With this new judge and the new jurors, something else was notable: the dominance of women among the dramatis personae. Except for the police, the DA, two of the four alternate jurors, a few of the witnesses, and of course Angel Ray himself, the major players inside the courtroom were women, from the lawyer in the parking lot to Miriam and Vera and Janet, to Drs. Mary Case and Amy Martin, to both of the prosecutors and both of the public defenders, to the judge and the court reporters, and finally to the jury that was selected, all twelve of whom were women.

It's something Angela Kana noted once the jury settled into its box. She hadn't really wanted to be there, but there she was and now she "wanted to be a part of it."

Angela was one of seven Koreans adopted as infants by a couple in Oklahoma. Her twin brother Andrew was another of the seven. Her last name—pronounced "Kahn-ya"—is Czech; her great-grandfather immigrated to Texas many decades ago; her mother's family was German. With her long straight black hair, cheerful easy smile, and manner of a young professional, Angela was a water engineer with a company in Boulder at the time of the trial of Angel Ray.

She had grown up in a small rural town and attended Oklahoma State University, earning her undergraduate degree in civil engineering and her master's degree in environmental engineering. She was living in Denver with her boyfriend, soon to be her fiancé, when she was called for jury duty in the spring of 2012. She had been called twice before, while in college back in Oklahoma, but she had never had to serve. When she was told the trial of Angel Ray would last three or four weeks, she was wary of being selected. She didn't want to spend so much time away from work.

On the first day of the selection process, a Monday, there were hundreds of people in the jury pool and she didn't think she would be selected. Her friends had told her lawyers don't like having engineers on their juries because they tend to over-analyze things. But then a significant number of those who had been called were released and the rest, still a large number with Angela among them, were herded into a courtroom and told to fill out a detailed questionnaire.

She was nervous. She could tell the questionnaire would not disqualify her: it was not "make or break"—it seemed to her— unless you were involved in social services. That resulted in more dismissals. The pool was shrinking. The potential jurors were sent home. They returned on Wednesday. There were 65 people left. She counted. It was nerve-wracking. Some were called for private interviews and the rest were dismissed and told to come back in two hours.

When Angela returned to the courtroom, the jury pool had shrunk again. That's when the lawyers started their oral examination of the potential jurors, which is called "voir dire."

Angela didn't know what to do. She really didn't want to be picked. She was torn. She felt sympathy for the child who had been killed, but didn't want to miss work. And there was another reason, a very big reason, why she felt conflicted: "Having been an abused child"—yes, hold that thought—"I wanted to be a part of it but I didn't want to be a part of it."

She decided to keep quiet and hope for the best.

The questioning continued.

Soon Angela was called for her one-on-one with the lawyers. It proved uneventful: name, occupation, nothing to disqualify her. There was an exchange about two answers she had given in her questionnaire. She had answered yes when asked if she had any friends or family who had been charged with a felony, gone through the court system, and been incarcerated. And she had also answered yes when asked if she had ever been abused.

The lawyers asked her, in general, emphasizing they did not want her to disclose any details, whether she felt she could be objective in the case against Angel Ray given her life experiences. She said yes, she thought she could be. There was "enough engineering in me," she later recalled, that she honestly believed she could be objective.

Still it seemed strange they didn't ask her for the details. Instead she was sent back to sit with the others while more potential jurors were called for questioning. Angela resolved to keep her mouth shut. The questioning droned on.

Plenty of things were said that she really didn't agree with, but she held her tongue. It wasn't always easy.

Finally, however, almost without thinking, she gave in.

"One girl" said something with which Angela disagreed so very strongly, that she found herself raising her hand to interrupt. The topic was "behavioral patterns" and the issue was simple:

If someone did something in the past, does that reflect on whether he or she did or did not do something similar at some later time? Recall the discussion of Evidence Rule 404(b) at the end of the last chapter.

This was an important issue for the lawyers. The example they gave was something like, if a man rapes 20 women and is in the vicinity of another rape, does his past reflect on whether he committed the 21st rape? The "one girl" insisted the answer was no and Angela couldn't help herself.

Hand aloft, she said: "You've got to be kidding me. There's a certain mental capacity that a person takes on to do a crime like that and to continue doing a crime like that."

Then she caught herself. She figured, great, now the prosecution wants me. But she didn't back away from what she had said, and others soon chimed in, and now the lawyers were eliminating more people from the pool and there were only five places left to be filled and nine people left to fill them—and still she didn't think she'd be chosen—but sure enough, they let four go and took the remaining five and she was one of them.

She was shocked. There she was—an overly analytical engineer who had been abused and who knew someone who had been through the criminal system—and still she had been chosen. Again she wondered why they had never even asked her for the details when she said she could be objective.

For the details were not pretty.

Growing up had been hard, being part of a large family with so many Asian kids in a small town in rural Oklahoma. The dynamic was not comfortable.

Beginning when she was six, escalating in the third grade and again in the sixth grade, and continuing until she was seventeen, Angela's twin brother Andrew had beaten her, oftentimes severely. And she wasn't the only one in the family he had assaulted.

He was a physically violent person. That's all there was to it.

Her parents and her siblings were all aware of Andrew's violence. He was sent to boot camp. They tried to reform him. But they simply couldn't.

He was diagnosed with multiple personality disorders, some chemical in nature, some not. Yet her parents refused to give up on him. He was their son, after all.

And he was Angela's "blood." She often pondered the age-old nature-versus-nurture question and thought: "I'm his twin and I obviously don't do those things!"

They shared the same genetics: it couldn't be that.

Finally one day when she was seventeen, her older sister was visiting at the family home. Andrew pulled a knife and tried to stab Angela and her father. Angela had finally had enough.

Her twin had traumatized her younger brother, herself, her sister, and her parents—enough!

She called 911. Her sister also called 911.

They waited. The police came and took Andrew away.

And while Angela generally does not think highly of this country's prison system, she did feel in the case of her brother it could possibly help: "Sometimes in order to shape up from being a bully you need to be bullied."

Andrew was sentenced to ten years but served only two. Released in 2001, he had a very hard time finding work at first. No one wanted to hire a felon. So he became a welder. He has a daughter but no wife and lives with his parents in Oklahoma.

Until shortly after the four-week trial of Angel Ray in the spring of 2012, Angela tried her best to have some sort of relationship with her parents and with Andrew. But it was simply too toxic for her. After years of trying, she ultimately severed all contact with them. That plus 600 miles keeps her mind off the abuse she suffered for nearly twelve years.

On the day Angela was selected to sit on the jury in the case against Angel Ray, she went home, still in shock, and told her boyfriend, "I don't know if I can do this."

Could she really be objective, as the lawyers had asked her, given the details of what she had gone through? She and her boyfriend talked it through. They came back around to the answer she had given to the lawyers: yes.

Angela felt she was professional enough, enough of an engineer and a scientist, and far enough away from the toxic effects of her brother, that she could go through with it. And so she became "a part of it," the quest to find justice for Neveah.

* * *

Angela didn't have to commute to Boulder while serving on the jury, so she had a little extra time in the morning to prepare "mentally, spiritually, and emotionally" for the day ahead. Often, she would gather with three other jurors in the parking lot near the courthouse before they had to go inside. They would meet, smoke a few cigarettes, and chat about anything other than the case and its gruesome details. Angela bonded with these other jurors while serving with them. They remained friends long after they rendered their verdict.

Ashley Perez was just a few years younger than Angela, twenty-four at the time of the trial. She had straight blond hair, bright eyes behind nondescript glasses, round apple cheeks, and an easy cheerful smile, much like Angela's. Born in Denver and reared in South Carolina, where she went to college, Ashley moved from there to Omaha and eventually back to Denver.

Unlike Angela, Ashley was married and the mother of a daughter aged 6 and a son aged 3. She worked outside the home at a collections agency. Her husband was a stay-at-home dad. And she had no history of abuse.

Ashley had never been called or served on a jury before. She later recalled being ambivalent about wanting to be picked. Though she carried no personal baggage, she was the mother of two young children and was "curious" about the case.

At the same time, she said, it would have been fine with her if she had not been chosen. In fact, she found one demand of being a juror particularly difficult. Once the proceedings really got moving, she found it hard to go home at night and not tell her husband all about them, because, as she later said, "I tell my husband everything."

Still she followed the judge's admonitions not to talk about the case until it was over. And, like Angela, once she was selected to sit on the jury, her ambivalence evaporated. Describing it later, she used the exact same phrase her new friend Angela had used.

Ashley said, ultimately, she "wanted to be a part of it."

* * *

Kristy Skinner was tall and slender. Her dark brown hair was parted down the middle and often tied behind her head. She had dimpled cheeks and a model's fine features. She was born and reared in Lexington, Nebraska, a town of 10,000 just north of I-80 on the Platte River in the south central part of the state. She graduated from the University of Nebraska in Lincoln, 165 miles to the east, where she studied fashion merchandising, then spent seven years in Omaha before moving to Denver.

It was May of 2010 and Kristy was going through a divorce. Her parents no longer lived in Nebraska but she had plenty of family in Denver: a sister with twin boys as well as an aunt and her husband. So, she later said, "I ran away from my life" and moved west to join them.

She hasn't regretted it. She loves living in Denver.

In April of 2012, when called for jury duty—her first time— Kristy was working for a Fortune 500 company. If picked for the jury, she would miss four weeks of work, but her employer told her it would pay for only one of those weeks, and insisted on her working without pay during her off hours to keep up.

Kristy found this unacceptable so she responded positively to a recruitment inquiry from a company that did IT staffing. She actually interviewed for the job while the trial was going on. It was "awful," she later said, "because I wasn't sleeping [and was] drinking a lot of wine." She feared she wasn't at her best.

Nonetheless she landed the job, and by the summer of 2012, as soon as the trial of Angel Ray was finished, she began working for the company that had recruited her, doing sales and business development. She really enjoys the work, she says.

During the jury selection process, she recalled, she filled out that same questionnaire about her personal history. Like Angela, she answered truthfully, disclosing she had been physically and emotionally abused in high school. Again the facts were ugly.

This time the abuser was not a twin brother but a boyfriend, so it was still someone who normally should be trustworthy. The abuse began about a year into the relationship when, Kristy said, her boyfriend began using drugs. And this time the abuse lasted from ages 14 to 16, not the dozen years Angela had endured.

Still it was severe enough that Kristy accessed the courts and obtained a restraining order against her boyfriend, which proved "pretty effective." Looking back on it, she later said she had been "young and stupid" at the time, letting it go on for years, but she had been "really scared."

Like Angela, Kristy thought it was "odd that we would have been allowed through." In fact, she soon learned, at least four of the jurors had been physically or sexually abused at some point in their lives. How common the incidence of abuse had become.

* * *

Samantha Hudson—Sam—no relation to H.D. Hudson, soon to take the stage in the role of the jail house snitch—was the fourth of the young women who hung out in the parking lot near the courthouse, smoking a few cigarettes and bonding.

Sam had long wavy hair, chestnut streaked with blond, blonder at the ends. She favored dark sunglasses even bigger than Kristy's, the fashionista of the group. She wore a tiny silver stud tucked into the crease of her left nostril and she smoked Camel Pink cigarettes. Like her new friends she had a broad, friendly smile when she was smiling.

The youngest of three, Sam was born and raised in Vermont. By the time she graduated from high school, her brother was living in Missouri and her sister was living in Denver. She chose Emporia State University in east-central Kansas so she could be half-way between them. She met her future husband at Emporia, dropped out of school, married him in 1997, and moved around with him to Denver briefly, then to Chicago and Kansas City. They were back in Denver by 1998 and divorced in 2005.

When Sam was called for jury duty in April of 2012, she was thirty-seven years old—the oldest of the four new friends, though she hardly looked her age—and working for the global giant CH2M Hill, headquartered south of Denver in Englewood. She was a regional business analyst, focusing mostly on finance, assigned to the operations and management business group.

Though CH2M Hill is best known for providing water and wastewater services—as well as many other consulting and engineering services—worldwide, Sam's region was mostly the central and western U.S. She would often interact with city officials, helping them make their projects more cost effective.

She laughs when she says as simply as possible: "It's about making money."

Sam had been called once for jury duty in Arapahoe County before she was called in the case against Angel Ray, but she had not been selected. And ironically, she had been called originally for a date earlier than her April date with Angel Ray, but could not comply because her car had broken down. So as fate would have it, she had to make up for her lost appearance by serving on the jury chosen to hear the evidence against the Angel of Death.

Like many in the jury pool, she was torn. Part of her was fascinated by the case as it was described to them, and part of her was concerned about missing work. Her supervisor was a little panicked when Sam told her the trial could last for three-to-five weeks, but Sam reassured her that she would work nights and do her best to keep up. Hers was not the only employer that refused to yield altogether to the demands of jury duty.

As soon as the potential jurors "all got stuffed into the room" where the lawyers would whittle them down, and they began filling out their questionnaires, Sam quickly became worried. She was one of the few among the group who had never heard of the case before. Her sources for news back then were mostly national like MSN.com, as she later recalled.

She figured she might, for this reason, be likely to be picked.

At the same time she found the jury selection process was "playing with my emotions." Sure the case was "fascinating" and she could probably juggle her work-load, but like Angela and Kristy and at least one of her other fellow jurors, Sam had suffered abuse. This time, like in Kristy's case, it was physical abuse perpetrated by her "high school sweetheart, if you will." The abuse took place over several years. "He liked to choke," Sam later recalled, "and he did the head-butt thing."

Because, however, her boyfriend never "close-fisted hit me in the face," she rationalized it—she justified it to herself—by telling herself: "It'll get better, it's okay, he loves me."

Until she got wise and dumped him.

Like Angela and Kristy, Sam also noticed she was not questioned by the lawyers in detail about this personal history. In her case she never even had a one-on-one voir dire discussion with them. And indeed she noticed the questionnaire and oral examinations seemed to focus more on people who had been abused as children and people who were parents.

In any event she was selected. Ready or not, she was about to join the quest for justice for Neveah.

* * *

Angela, Ashley, Kristy and Sam were well aware of the gender gap on the eventual jury. They were all women, ages twenty-ish to fifty-ish, so it was obvious from the start. But soon they came to be aware of other divides among their number. Some were married and some were not. Some had children and some did not. Some—at least four of them—had themselves been abused and some had not.

And some of them had higher education and some did not. This education gap, several of the jurors later remarked, was perhaps their biggest gap. It was reflected in the first decision they made: their election of Karen Gieseker as their foreperson.

Dr. Gieseker was the Director of Global Heath Curriculum at the Center for Global Health at the University of Colorado's School of Public Health, located at the new Anschutz Medical Campus in Aurora, east of Denver. She had an MS and a PhD and became the leader the jurors needed when they needed one.

Some of them wondered whether the education gap—or any of the other divides among their number—would have any impact on their decision. The answer to that question would have to await the end of the trial in four long weeks.

This, for the jury, was just the beginning.

At 9:45 a.m. on Thursday, April 12, 2012, they were escorted from their jury room to Denver District Courtroom 5A in the new Lindsey-Flanigan Courthouse on West Colfax, which opened in 2010. They were seated in two rows in the jury box.

It was a tidy medium-sized courtroom painted light blue over light wood wainscoting: modern, unadorned and considerably less imposing than the majestic courtrooms of yore. No over-sized portraits of bearded jurists glowered down upon them from the light blue walls. No golden flourishes or hand-cut carvings or bronzed legal icons were needed to tell them just how serious were the proceedings that took place in that room.

To their left was the judge's bench, dominating the front of the room, flanked by flags of the U.S. and State of Colorado. Facing the bench, the defense sat on the right and the prosecution sat on the left, so the prosecutors were those closest to the jury. That meant the jury would be facing the defendant, Angel Ray Montoya, throughout the proceedings.

Between the bench and the jury box, the witness stand with its thin microphone stood empty, waiting. Behind the lawyers' bar were several rows of pews for the public and the media: simple, hard wooden benches barely covered with thin cushions. Family, friends, a scattering of police officers, and plenty of reporters packed the pews.

An air of nervous energy filled the courtroom.

Angel Ray was seated next to his counsel. He was dressed in the same sort of garb he would wear throughout the trial, a plain button-down shirt over simple khaki or tan cotton trousers. On that day—the opening day of his trial—the color of his shirt was light blue like the walls.

Sheriffs in dark blue uniforms, with pistols on their hips, hovered close by. Papers shuffled. Lawyers talked to lawyers in lowered voices.

Judge Rappaport was already seated on her raised bench. She turned to the jury and said, "Welcome back, and thank you for your patience … I'm going to go ahead and swear you in and give you some instructions for the trial, so if you would all stand up and raise your right hand."

"Whereupon," as the transcript reports, "the jury panel were duly sworn."

ELEVEN: OPENING STATEMENTS

From 9:04 to 9:45 that Thursday morning, Courtroom 5A hosted a very different sort of ritual. First the courtroom was cleared of the public and media, leaving only Judge Rappaport, her court reporter, the lawyers for both the prosecution and defense, Detective Crider—the designated "advisory witness" for the prosecution, allowed to come and go as his schedule would permit—plus Melissa Trollinger, who was Miriam's lawyer, and Angel Ray, the defendant.

Next Holly Lucas stated formally for the record: "It's my understanding that both counsel and – counsel and the Court are going to be bound by the law of the case." That meant the parties would be required to observe all of the previous rulings made in the case by Judge Robbins in the aborted trial in August of 2011, including "specifically [the] prior evidentiary rulings" made at that time.

Then Miriam was brought into the courtroom and seated in the witness box near the judge. Trollinger stood close to her client so she could answer any questions Miriam might have. The judge told Miriam to pay attention and stop anytime she didn't understand something that was being said to her.

It was clear: the parties and the judge were taking great pains to prevent another mistrial. They didn't want any repeats of Miriam's last performance.

Michelle Amico stood at the podium and began a recitation of all the things that Miriam had been ordered not to talk about in her testimony. There was to be no mention of her prior juvenile or adult criminal history. No mention of "any prior pregnancy that you had before Neveah's birth." And absolutely no mention of the claim she had made at her own sentencing that she had been "sexually abused by a family member."

Amico stopped to make sure Miriam understood.

Miriam said, "Yes, ma'am."

Amico continued, "with respect to the usage of marijuana," that Miriam could talk about her usage when she was younger, and she could talk about her usage during the first trimester of her pregnancy with Neveah, but she could not talk about her usage when she smoked pot with Angel Ray, except:

"Okay, there's one exception to that, and that one exception is the actual night before Neveah's death, so Thursday night, the 20th of September, when" two friends came over to the apartment on Logan Street and smoked pot with her and Angel Ray.

By now the rules and their exceptions, and the exceptions to the exceptions, might have sounded bewildering to a non-lawyer. But they were just getting started.

Amico turned to "some really important things now."

There could be no mention whatsoever that there had been a previous trial. "So the word trial," said Amico, "previous trial, cannot come out of your mouth, do you understand that?"

"Yes, ma'am."

They could talk about testimony she had previously given in other situations as reflected in prior transcripts—like transcripts of interviews with the police—but zero, zip, nada, nothing about a prior trial. And she could say nothing about having been indicted, or Angel Ray having been indicted, by the grand jury.

The hot buttons were glowing, getting hotter and hotter.

Miriam could make no "mention or reference to that incident that took place in July of 2006," when Janet had taken Neveah to Denver Health due to vaginal bleeding, and "there was at least an allegation or suspicion of some form of sexual assault [but] no charges were ever filed against anyone for that particular case."

"Yes, ma'am."

Miriam also could not talk about any affiliation that she, Angel Ray, or his brother may have had with any gang.

"Okay, said Amico, "another area that you cannot talk about is -- let me start with this -- I have told you that you will be permitted to testify about what the defendant said to you about

that prior incident involving another little boy. But any further –
all you can say are what his statements were to you, okay, about
that. You cannot add any additional details ... Does that make
sense? Do you understand that?"

"Yes, ma'am."

"Along the same lines," the prosecutor said, "you cannot talk
about times that Mr. Montoya was in and out of jail"—except for
the times that related directly to the present case.

Then Amico hit the hottest of the hot buttons. Miriam could
say nothing about Angel Ray's past as a sex offender: "And so,
you cannot say at all that Mr. Montoya ever had a case for failing
to register as a sex offender, that he was a registered sex
offender. The words 'sex offender' cannot ever come out of
your mouth during the testimony. Do you understand?"

Miriam said, "Yes, ma'am."

Amico hammered it home. If Miriam ever thinks, while she
is testifying, that she is getting close to saying something she has
been told not to talk about, she should say, "I don't know how to
answer that question," and that will signal the question needs to
be reworded to steer her away from the forbidden disclosures.

Finally Amico gave the last of the instructions: "You cannot
mention anything that you know about how Neveah's body was
recovered. Okay? Who found it, how – how they got there, not
a mention of that, okay?"

"Yes, ma'am."

At shortly before 9:30, Judge Rappaport briefly paused the
proceedings to allow the jury, which had begun congregating in
the hallway, to pass through the courtroom and into the adjacent
jury room. Miriam stepped out, the jury came through, Miriam
stepped back in, and the ritual resumed.

Amico told Miriam there was also an exception to the rule—
"Thou shalt not talk about your prior criminal history"—and that
was in connection with this case. Miriam could talk about her
own conviction and plea bargain.

After Amico was finished, Judge Rappaport essentially repeated all of these same instructions from the bench. When she got to the incident from July of 2006, she said, "What can be talked about is, evidently, while at the hospital you shared with – or at that point with your mother and maybe an aunt, that Mr. Montoya had abused a child in the past, not sexual abuse just physical abuse."

"Yes, ma'am," said Miriam, this time to the judge.

And here the judge repeated the crucial dividing line between what could come in and what must stay out—when talking about Angel Ray's past criminal history: "You can mention physical abuse, nothing about sexual abuse. Sexual abuse in no form or shape comes out at all in any of this."

"Yes, ma'am."

"Nothing sexual, leave that out of your vocabulary entirely."

"Yes, ma'am."

Holly Lucas made her record: "Let's be clear. The child we're talking about is Jesus Perez, no other child at all."

Judge Rappaport agreed, "That's the only child, that's the only time."

Right about then a juror peeked her head out of the door to the jury room and the drill had to stop. Later the judge questioned the juror to insure nothing had been overheard and came away convinced there was no problem.

Then Judge Rappaport repeated how important it was for Miriam to take a break if she got confused. She sounded downright comforting—until she advised Miriam what would happen to her if she failed to comply:

"Now, I want you also to know that if – this is a court order, what I've just said ... It's an order of the Court, I'm entering as an order not to go into these areas that we've talked about. If you do, I will hold you in contempt of court, which means that you could have an additional jail sentence of six months and it will be consecutive ... after what you are serving."

Miriam got the point. She was returned to her holding cell. The judge called a brief recess. At 9:45 the jury entered the courtroom and the judge swore them in.

* * *

After formally swearing in the jury, Judge Rappaport gave them some instructions. She told them the opening statements they were about to hear were not evidence. She reminded them not to talk about the case with each other or anyone else until they had heard all the evidence and their deliberations began.

She said, "I want to remind you that the defendant is presumed to be innocent [and] the prosecution must prove guilt beyond a reasonable doubt."

She covered housekeeping matters like parking and the keeping of notebooks. She told the jurors not to watch any local news or go online. And no electronic communications.

Then she called for opening statements.

Michelle Amico, her features sharp and her eyes blazing, stood at the podium and spoke to the jury: "On August 1st, 2004, a beautiful baby girl was brought into this world by the skilled, trained, careful hands of a doctor in a delivery room. Her name was Neveah Gallegos."

Amico held her own hands before her, creating with her first sentence the theme that would permeate her opening statement, her closing statement, indeed her entire case against Angel Ray.

"Neveah was raised and nurtured by patient protective loving hands, the patient protective loving hands of her grandma Janet, of her young teenage aunt, Cathy, and of her great aunt, her grandmother's sister, Vera.

"She was a little life full of promise for the future; and on September 21, 2007, when Neveah had turned just three years old, her promising little life was ended, ended at the hands of the defendant, Angel Ray Montoya.

"His hands were not careful. His hands were not patient. His hands were anything but protective. And his hands were not loving, his hands were hurtful. His hands caused pain. His hands caused injury, his hands caused bruises, and his hands squeezed the last breath out of her tiny little body.

"And once she was dead he continued to use his hands to cover up his tracks by putting her in a plastic bag and disposing of her, as if she were worth nothing more than a piece of trash."

Next to his counsel, Angel Ray sat stone-faced, eyes blank.

Amico began telling the jury the narrative of Neveah's life, her upbringing by the triumvirate, her mother's rebellions and loss of interest—the outlines of what the evidence would show. When she gestured with her hands, observant eyes may have noticed on one of her wrists a small bracelet with butterfly charms—a duplicate encircled the wrist of her second chair, Christine Washburn—meant to evoke the constant presence of the child whose name supposedly meant butterfly in Hebrew.

Amico talked about Miriam's relationship with Angel Ray, how he made her "feel special, made her feel beautiful, made her feel wanted … They talked about getting married, they referred to each other as husband and wife … They got matching tattoos that had special significance, they had a special song that was theirs called Always and Forever … It became their motto."

By the fall of 2007, Miriam had created the fantasy of living with Angel Ray and Neveah as a family. She took a job at Sports Authority and in September they rented the small studio apartment on Logan Street. "And as soon as that apartment was rented, it was time to make an effort to play house."

So Miriam lied to Janet. She claimed she had several days off from work and was going to pick up Neveah for those days. "What Miriam failed to tell her family is that she was scheduled to work all that week at Sports Authority and that it was the defendant who would be the one caring for, taking care of, watching Neveah in Miriam's absence while she was at work.

"She didn't share any of this fantasy with her family, whatsoever, because if she had, they never would have allowed Neveah to leave from their protective hands."

Amico told the jury how Neveah had cried when she realized Miriam would be taking her to stay with Angel Ray. And how, on Wednesday and Thursday, "various injuries began showing up on Neveah, a bruise on the left cheek, a bump on the forehead, scratch on the back. Oh, Miriam saw them; but she turned a blind eye, because she was living her fantasy that they were now going to be a family."

Then on Thursday night Miriam came home from work and noticed "Neveah seemed sick, maybe like she was getting the flu bug, like something was wrong, she felt warm. She didn't have an appetite at all. She was really thirsty, she even vomited a little bit of water that Miriam tried to give her that night. She was not herself … something was very wrong."

Amico told the jury they would indeed hear the reason why Neveah was feeling that way. Now this information—about the bruises and her illness on Thursday night—began to provide some of the missing details of Neveah's last days, something none of the triumvirate could do. Yet despite all these red flags, the next morning Miriam left for work, clocking in at 9:08.

The prosecutor's narrative skipped to after Neveah's death, the frantic phone call from the neighbor's apartment, Miriam's rush home, the fake kidnapping plan, the dumping of the body:

"He used his hands to lift a rock, he used his hands to lift a big log, he used his hands to pick up a two by four, he used his hands to pick up a tire; and he used his hands to put all those things on top of her body to conceal her … He did such a good job in hiding her that when police finally found her body four days later, all you could see … was a portion of that white plastic trash bag, and that portion … had a little hole. And outside of that little hole you could see a small, pink glimpse of her Disney Princess tennis shoe sticking out of that bag."

Meanwhile Miriam launched her false kidnapping story, confronting the lawyer in the parking lot, though it didn't take long for that story to fall apart. She began telling different and inconsistent versions of what had happened.

Angel Ray was arrested by Detective Ryan, the fruitless search for the body lasted throughout the weekend, and finally on Monday the body was found.

Amico admitted there would not be a single witness who could say, "I saw the defendant strangle Neveah, I saw the defendant hit or kick or punch Neveah, because this is a crime of seclusion, a crime between two." Still the autopsy report would reveal all of the injuries the child had suffered, including the blunt force trauma to her mesentery, which "certainly would have caused her those symptoms her mother was seeing, thirsty, loss of appetite, lethargic, not really herself Thursday night, bruises, not common, not common for a child that age, too many, indicative of abuse. Hemorrhages in the neck, in the left strap muscle, which is the front of the neck, in the paraspinal muscle in the back of the neck."

And of course the jury would hear from Dr. Mary Case, whose expert opinion would identify the cause of Neveah's death as "asphyxiation by neck compression." The jury would hear from a parade of other witnesses—lay people and police and forensic pathologists and family members—and "each one of them will form pieces of a puzzle you will need to make the evidence fit."

Indeed, a trial is much like a jigsaw puzzle, with jagged, hard-to-fit pieces that nevertheless reveal, when enough of them fall into place, a picture of what happened—the truth.

Amico closed, asking for Angel Ray's conviction.

Sarah Welton, second chair for the defense, stood and gave her opening statement. Yes, Neveah was a "delightful child" and her death was a "tragedy" but "don't forget that it's also a tragedy when an innocent man is accused of a horrific crime."

Welton added little more except for some detail about the tiny studio apartment on Logan Street: "They have no phone ... no furniture. They have a couple of lawn chairs and they have a toddler bed. They don't have a bed. They have no sofa. They have no sitting chairs ... they have no food in their house. This is the food they have, they have Pop Tarts, they have peanut butter, they have sunflower seeds."

Welton tried to paint Miriam's relationship with Angel Ray as a "modern romance, she was the breadwinner, he was the homemaker. Their apartment was clean. He was doing the best he could."

She tried to make it sound like Neveah could have gotten hot that Thursday because "they live right next to the boiler room." She tried to make it sound like there was little real evidence to prove that Angel Ray had killed the child: "There is no evidence tying him to any wrongdoing, nothing direct or circumstantial."

She ended: "Mr. Montoya is innocent. Thank you."

By this time the jury had seen for itself: Amico's passion ruled the courtroom. She was plainly "emotionally invested" in the case—two words used by more than one juror when later recalling their immediate impressions.

Yet throughout the trial Amico would tame her passions and present her case as an organized, experienced, and efficient professional. The same jurors also would later use the same word—"phenomenal"—when describing her performance.

Since the opening ceremonies had consumed the morning, Judge Rappaport called the noon recess a few minutes early.

Court adjourned at 11:54.

* * *

Miriam took the stand as the prosecution's first witness a little after 1:00. She must have felt nervous. She must have felt conflicted. She must have felt a degree of shame.

After all, the judge had told her only hours earlier: if she didn't follow her instructions and again spilled the beans about one of the forbidden topics, she would spend additional time incarcerated. And how she hated incarceration.

At the same time she would be testifying against the man she thought she would love "Always and Forever." In addition, she was about to give sworn testimony in public about her own guilt, her own involvement, and her own responsibility for her daughter's death. That she was appearing in court as a prisoner of the state, a convicted felon in handcuffs, only drove the message home.

Amico began her direct examination. Within seconds she asked if Miriam knew Angel Ray and Miriam said yes. Amico asked Miriam to identify him: "What I'd ask you to do, ma'am, is I know you have cuffs there, but if you can point out where he's seated and just describe the color of his shirt that he has on so that our court reporter can take that information down."

Miriam said, "Right there, light blue shirt on."

From there Amico elicited the skeleton of the narrative. Or, to use her metaphor, assembled the initial pieces of the puzzle: the 911 call made from the cell phone of the lawyer in the parking lot, played for the jury to hear; the fake kidnapping; the general outlines of Neveah's short life, including the role of the triumvirate—Janet, Vera and Cathy—as her primary caretakers.

They turned to June of 2007, when Miriam and Angel Ray were living with his mother Sandy, and Miriam started looking for a job. She applied at Sports Authority on June 27, falsely identifying Sandy as her mother-in-law. She got the job.

Miriam worked through the summer and in September she rented the studio apartment on Logan Street with Angel Ray, who did not have a job. It was a six-month lease and Neveah wasn't listed as an occupant because, Miriam testified: "I didn't intend on her staying, living with me … because I couldn't financially provide for her."

Though air conditioned, the apartment was barely furnished. Lawn chairs passed for seating. On a table from Sandy's house sat a TV, VCR, Nintendo 64, radio with speaker, and Xbox that held the love birds' music. Photos of the place were entered into evidence and circulated among the jurors.

Finally Amico reached the week of Neveah's death, and here Miriam began to layer flesh upon the bone. She admitted that when she called Janet to say she had a few days off and wanted to take Neveah, she knew she was scheduled to work all week. She lied because the triumvirate didn't like Angel Ray and she couldn't bring herself to tell them Neveah would be left alone with him for many hours for three days.

Miriam clocked out of the Sportscastle at 9:23 p.m. on Tuesday and took a ride with a co-worker to her mother's house on Lipan Street to pick up Neveah. No one was there so they drove around the block to the North Lincoln Projects where her sister Cathy had a friend named JD. There they found Cathy and Neveah, who was happy to see her mother until she realized Miriam was taking her away.

And what's worse, Miriam's co-worker didn't have a car seat so Neveah had to sit between her mother and Angel Ray, who was also in the car, all the way to Logan Street. She cried the whole time.

Yet Miriam agreed: Neveah was in perfect health when she arrived at the studio apartment that Tuesday night. She went to sleep on the bed used by Angel Ray's niece and nephew when they visited the apartment, and the love birds slept on the floor.

Amico shifted to the items in the back pack Neveah had brought with her. Miriam freely admitted the money was more important to her than her mother's note about medical insurance and "being careful."

The next morning she clocked into the Sportscastle at 9:10. She described how she had "snuck out" of the little apartment to avoid getting Neveah upset about being left with Angel Ray.

Miriam clocked out at 4:47 that afternoon and met up with Angel Ray and Neveah to get something to eat at the Arby's on Broadway. While they were walking there, Angel Ray told Miriam that Neveah "was walking down the stairs, she fell, scraped her back and hit her forehead."

Amico showed the jury photos of the stairs at the apartment house on Logan Street. She dwelled on the incident, the first time Neveah showed any signs of injury that week. Miriam told the jury she could not see anything, "but you could feel a bump on her forehead."

"And how could you feel that?" asked Amico. "Show the members of the jury what you did to Neveah's forehead and where you felt something."

"I just rubbed her forehead, checked where he said she might have hit it; and then it just felt like a knot was starting to form there …"

"Did you take a look at her back?"

"Yes, ma'am."

"And what did you see?"

"Scrape, like right down the middle of her back," near the lower portion of her spine. Still they went into Arby's where Neveah ate about half of a roast beef sandwich.

Back at the apartment, Miriam noticed a bruise "on the top part of her cheek, and it was like an outline of a circle." It was clearly visible. Still they all went to sleep and in the morning Miriam took Neveah with her on the bus to run some errands.

Miriam said, "She kept asking for water that day. She was really thirsty for some reason … she wasn't hungry, either."

So they stopped at Wendy's where Miriam got her some water then proceeded with their errands. On the way back to the apartment, Neveah started acting odd: "She's normally this bubbly goofy, you know, hyper-kind of girl; and she just kind of wasn't – she was very relaxed, I guess you could say, she wasn't very jumpy."

Miriam noted the change. It seemed out of character. Still Miriam went to work and clocked in at 2:22, leaving Neveah once more alone with Angel Ray. Clocking back out at 9:05, Miriam returned to the apartment to find Angel Ray's niece and nephew there, playing and watching TV.

Neveah was not playing, however. She did not leap up to greet her mother as she usually would do. Instead, Miriam said, she was "just kind of sitting there. She didn't look too good." She looked "like flushed. It was hot in the apartment. She just didn't look like she felt good."

The air conditioner was running. Angel Ray was cooking "some chicken croissant roll things." Miriam asked him how Neveah had been that day, what she had eaten, that sort of thing. He said she had eaten a Go-Tart and some Ramen noodles. But she had continued to be thirsty all day, asking for water.

Around 11:00 Sandy arrived to pick up Angel Ray's niece and nephew. Shortly before she came, Neveah asked for water. Miriam said, "I went to get her some water. She drank it pretty fast and within not even a minute she – it came right back up, she couldn't hold it down." It had just been half of a small child's cup, but she just "chugged it down, really really fast, and then within a minute she was throwing it back up."

Miriam gave Neveah some Pepto-Bismol and a little more water and "she held it down." After Sandy left with the other two children, some friends named Lorenzo and Juliann came over with a box of pizza and some marijuana. They stayed for about half an hour. Angel Ray and Miriam ate some of the pizza and "smoked marijuana together" with them.

Amico asked, "Where was Neveah while everybody is in that living room area smoking the marijuana?"

"Laying in the bed," said Miriam.

"Was she still awake?"

"I don't recall." But Miriam did recall Neveah was still acting out of character so she put a cool cloth on her head.

The next morning Miriam got up around 8:30. Neveah had wet her bed. Miriam stripped off the sheet and tossed it in her laundry basket. She asked Angel Ray to give Neveah a bath then left for work, never to see her daughter alive again.

Miriam must have been concerned. Neveah had shown the first signs of fresh injuries on Wednesday and had shown even more dramatic signs all day Thursday and that night. Still the wayward mother clocked in dutifully at the Sportscastle at 9:08 a.m. after once more leaving Neveah alone with Angel Ray.

A little while later Miriam used the Sports Authority phone to call her sister Cathy to ask if she knew anything about the bruise on Neveah's cheek. Cathy said she did not. Miriam was so concerned about her mother's expected reaction upon seeing the bruise that she asked Cathy to go later in the day to the Logan Street apartment to look at Neveah and see the bruise for herself. It was a favor Cathy never had a chance to fulfill.

Early that afternoon, working in the stock area, Miriam was told she had a phone call. She went upstairs to the office area to take it. Angel Ray was on the other end of the line.

Miriam said, "He was hysterical, he just kept repeating for me to come home, that I needed to come home." She clocked out at 1:22 and ran home. Angel Ray opened the door and stood between Miriam and the apartment. "Always and Forever" was playing on the Xbox. He was crying and looked upset. He kept saying over and over, "Wait, babe, please just listen."

Miriam rushed past him and found Neveah on the bed, covered with a blanket. She moved it aside and saw her daughter's "eyes were still open, just staring. She was gone."

Miriam cried. She tried CPR. Neveah felt cold.

Angel Ray told Miriam "he got her ready to take her out to the library because it was stuffy in the apartment … He said she was thirsty, she asked for water … After she drank the water she began like gasping – gasping for air, like she couldn't breathe, and then collapsed on the floor."

Miriam tried to close Neveah's eyes but they wouldn't close. The bruise on her cheek looked "more distinctive."

At this point a bench conference was held among the four attorneys and Judge Rappaport to set the next day's schedule. The lawyers complained about the clacking from the computer of the Channel 7 reporter, which was so loud it was getting distracting. The judge said she'd do something about it.

Back on the record, late afternoon, she reminded the jurors to avoid all media while the case was going on—and especially not to talk about the case with anyone, even among themselves. Then she adjourned for the night.

Miriam testified all the next day.

Holly Lucas had all weekend to refine her cross-examination of the prosecution's key foundation witness. On Monday afternoon she tore into Miriam's credibility: "Not one word of anything you said to police officers was true. You couldn't even stand the county jail. It was miserable ... You would have done anything to get out of there."

Attack, attack: there was little else the defense could do.

* * *

For the next six days of trial, the prosecution brought a parade of witnesses before the jury, layering flesh upon the bone, adding pieces to the puzzle. The lawyer from the parking lot testified though for a shorter period than during the earlier trial, for the prosecution had learned from those earlier proceedings how to present some of what she had to say more efficiently.

The jury felt deep sympathy for the family when they heard the testimony of Janet, Vera, and Cathy, all of whom showed great emotion on the witness stand. The jury listened carefully as Detective Crider described in detail the police investigation that opened the door for the forensic experts to testify about blood samples and DNA.

The detective choked up on the stand when he described the recovery of the child's body, though later the jurors would describe his performance as outstanding and professional.

Next, more cops and forensics. Then Dr. Amy Martin walked the jury through the autopsy and her report. And just as it was predictable the defense would attack Miriam's credibility, it was entirely predictable it would pounce on Dr. Martin's inability to fix the cause of death.

According to some jurors, the cross-examination by the defense of Dr. Martin went on for so long it became ineffective. And for them it was marred by the use of a life-sized plastic doll. The defense lawyer made the coroner associate photos from the autopsy with places on the doll, even though they plainly were not in close proportion to each other. This was a ploy that did not play well for several of the jurors.

And throughout these proceedings Angel Ray sat virtually motionless, like a rock, his face devoid of expression, his eyes cold and blank. Sometimes he wore glasses; sometimes not. Some of the jurors later said he appeared to tear up and show some emotion when photos of the recovery of the body and photos from the autopsy were shown. Others said they saw no such deviation from Angel Ray's stone-faced demeanor.

The trial lurched forward. It was not until the end of the second week that the prosecution introduced its heaviest hitters. By then the outlines of the story had been told, there was plenty of flesh put on the bone, the puzzle was pieced together enough that the jury was getting the picture.

What the jury had not yet heard was the testimony of three key witnesses who, some later recalled, would make the biggest impressions on them:

The child, the expert, and the jail house snitch.

TWELVE: THE TESTIMONY of JESUS PEREZ

Saline dripped into the arm of the four-year old boy in the hospital bed. It was the evening of January 6, 2005, and the name of the boy was Jesus Perez Martinez. He had been brought by his mother Andrea to the pediatric urgent care clinic at the Denver Health complex at 8th and Bannock Street.

As Dr. John Ogle, the director of pediatrics, later testified: "The primary concern of the medical staff was an altered mental status or altered level of consciousness. He was not acting and interacting in a normal manner. His state of arousal was not appropriate to a boy of that age. And the child wouldn't respond, so that with certain medical procedures, he would become more alert, but he generally was not very responsive at the time period that he was there. He – it was described that his eyes had rolled back in his head," though he wasn't seizing.

Vital signs were taken, and they were within normal limits. A CT scan on the head, a spinal tap, and a urinalysis all failed to yield an explanation. But the child's blood chemistry was off: his potassium level was high and his sodium level was so low that "most children and adults where their level is that low may have neurologic signs and symptoms from that." Occasionally seizures result.

When Andrea had given Jesus' history to the medical staff, she said he had been healthy until he threw up and complained of abdominal pain. She also said he had a cousin who had died of Addison's disease, another name for adrenal insufficiency. The adrenal gland produces several important hormones, the absence of which can cause serious or critical illness. Over time the condition can be fatal.

The child's abnormal blood chemistry and family history of adrenal insufficiency were both consistent with his symptoms. The medical staff acted on suspicion, without a formal diagnosis, assuming the worst case.

Jesus was treated "in an emergent manner." He was given intravenous fluids that contained sodium to raise the level of sodium in his blood and two medications that would provide the hormones missing in an Addison's scenario.

It worked. Jesus improved rapidly. He regained normal interactions with his family and the medical staff. After an overnight stay, he was released with instructions to follow-up with an endocrinologist.

But sixteen days later, on January 22, little Jesus was back, this time with some of the same symptoms—and a host of new bruises on his body. One was a fresh hematoma, a raised bruise, on his forehead.

At roughly 7:00 that morning Andrea had left Jesus asleep in her apartment, in the care of her boyfriend, Angel Ray Montoya. She had to attend a class that day at the preschool where she worked. Angel Ray was barely twenty at the time and Jesus later remembered him as wearing glasses and having pimples.

When Jesus awoke and saw his mother was gone, he cried. Angel Ray told him not to. Jesus did not cooperate. Angel Ray got mad. Jesus later said Angel Ray tied his feet together and used a necktie to hook him up to the wall. Angel Ray admitted hitting the boy several times. Consistent throughout, in every telling and retelling of the events, with all their variations, Jesus insisted Angel Ray had tried to choke him. And that Angel Ray had broken his favorite Power Rangers DVD.

At noon Andrea returned to her apartment and immediately noticed Jesus was acting lethargic, sleepy—sick—and he had bruises all over his body and face. She confronted Angel Ray, demanding to know what had happened. He claimed Jesus had tried to hurt himself by banging his head on the floor.

Andrea pressed Angel Ray. He acted nervous.

She said she was going to call 911. He gathered his things and left the apartment. The police said he "fled."

Andrea took Jesus back to Denver Health.

Because he had an injury to his forehead, they did another CT scan but it showed no brain damage. Again his vital signs were basically normal, as was his blood chemistry, with two curious exceptions. This time his sodium level was high and his potassium level was low—exactly the opposite of before.

The medical staff was perplexed. And of greater concern were all those bruises: on Jesus' forehead, his cheeks, his neck, his chin, his shoulders, his wrists, his thighs, his legs, his feet, and his toes. So many bruises in so many places could not be explained by a single accident, such as a fall into a table.

One of the doctors prepared a drawing that diagramed all the bruises. Their size and position were carefully recorded. The medical staff suspected "non-accidental trauma," or child abuse. As a "mandatory reporting party," they called the police.

Officer Christen Drennan responded. She interviewed Andrea in the hallway of the urgent care clinic. She observed Jesus and tried to question him, but he was, as she later testified, "so sleepy that he could barely keep his eyes open." Since the child was wearing a hospital gown, she was able to see his body and the bruises that covered it. She photographed them.

Then Officer Drennan got as much information as she could about Angel Ray and "issued a request" for Andrea and Jesus to appear at the Family Crisis Center for a follow-up interview.

Jesus was stabilized, treated for dehydration, and transferred to the pediatrics ward, where he would stay for several days so the doctors could monitor his level of consciousness and his interactions with others.

That evening Dr. Ogle was notified by telephone that Jesus had returned to the hospital. He visited the child and his mother the next morning. He examined Jesus personally, observing all the bruises for himself.

Jesus recovered and left the hospital. On February 14, Andrea took him to the Family Crisis Center, as the police had requested, for a follow-up interview.

Karen Blackwell was the adolescent forensic interviewer who met with Jesus. He was hyper throughout his time with her, flitting about and drawing pictures. Eventually he grew anxious when the subject of death came up and she decided to stop the interview.

Angel Ray was arrested and charged. He pled guilty to misdemeanor child abuse and was sentenced to 18 months of probation. He was on probation when he later became involved with Miriam. And he was on probation in the summer of 2006 when Janet and Vera took Neveah to the same urgent care clinic at Denver Health, bleeding from her vagina.

* * *

Imagine how badly the prosecution in 2012 wanted to tell the story of Jesus to the jury. This time, however, the rules of evidence were not the problem. What those rules took with one hand they gave with the other. Evidence Rule 404(b) took the prosecution's ability to introduce evidence of Angel Ray's history as a sexual predator. But it gave the prosecution the ability to introduce evidence that he had abused and choked another child in a similar setting.

That's because the rule that forbids introducing evidence of a previous crime or wrongful act to prove the defendant's guilt in the present case allows that such evidence "may, however, be admissible for other purposes, such as proof of motive, opportunity, intent, preparation, plan, knowledge, identity, or absence of mistake or accident."

So the problem wasn't the rules. The problem was finding Jesus and persuading him to testify. DA Mitch Morrissey later recalled both the problem and its solution:

"Well, what we were able to do—one was because of good work—we were able to find him. And ... I distinctly remember Michelle and Christine coming. 'We found him.' And initially his mother wanted nothing to do with us, wanted nothing to do with this guy. She had acted completely appropriately. When she found that he was abusing her little boy she said, 'Boom! Done!' She acted like a mother is supposed to act, completely the opposite of Miriam. So then when we approached her … basically she told us, 'Listen, my little boy is recovering. I don't want [him] to go through this again.' She was reluctant."

Andrea's reluctance was understandable. She had taken Jesus and moved out of state to get away from Angel Ray and what he had done. She had started a new life for them.

Still the prosecutors went to her and spoke with her and eventually she agreed to let Jesus be interviewed and testify. Morrissey later recalled:

"He was very good about what had happened to him. And what had happened to him was similar enough—same kind of setting, same kind of relative age—all of those things that allow us to use the prior transactions against him. So it's like when we have a serial rapist, it's like when we have a serial murderer, there is a rule of evidence that allows us to bring in other acts of misconduct, not to prove that he actually committed the act we're trying him for, but to show things like it wasn't an accident or it wasn't a mistake … there's *modus operendi*, which is the pattern. This is the way he kills kids … If you remember, the big issue in this case was [according to the defense] that she wasn't killed. We couldn't say what the cause of death was. He's just getting rid of a body, a girl that died on him. And he's afraid—because he's a registered sex—or unregistered sex offender—that no one's going to believe him and he's going to be tried for murder. So the attack on the other little boy, or the other child, becomes part of our proof to overcome what he's claiming. It's not to prove that he did it in accordance with the way he behaves, it was to prove a specific issue in the case, and that is, this baby didn't just die on him. So it helped us with the critical issue in the case, which was cause of death."

Locating Jesus and getting him to testify became the third major breakthrough in the prosecution's case against Angel Ray, after discovering Neveah's body and determining the cause and manner of her death. The expert testimony of Dr. Mary Case, soon to come, would persuade the jury that Neveah did indeed die from asphyxiation. First, however, they would hear from Jesus himself, and several corroborating witnesses, about what had happened to him. In other words, they would hear about Angel Ray's M-O of choking little kids.

Before hearing that testimony, the jury was given repeatedly —before each of the witnesses took the stand—what is often called a "limiting instruction." This instruction was delivered by Judge Rappaport as follows:

"Certain evidence of actual transactions in this case is being admitted for the limited purpose of showing the defendant's identity and/or the absence of mistake or accident. At this time – at this time the evidence is being admitted, you are admonished that it cannot be considered by you for any purpose other than the limited purpose for which it is admitted. You are instructed that you must not consider it for any purpose other than the limited purpose for which it is admitted. For that limited purpose, you may give it such weight as you think it is entitled. The defendant cannot be tried or convicted of any act not charged in this case."

Indeed, the very fact that Angel Ray had pled guilty to misdemeanor child abuse in the case of Jesus Perez could not be told to the jury. Throughout the prosecution's presentation of the story of Jesus, they had to assiduously avoid that revelation. And, as it turned out, the efforts of both the prosecution and the defense to avoid revealing the legal outcome of the case proved to be grounds for plenty of argumentation.

But in the meantime, there was a child named Jesus who had a story to tell.

* * *

Judge Rappaport gave her limiting instruction to the jury at 9:06 a.m. on Wednesday, April 25, the last day of the second week of trial. The eleven-year old boy who took the stand was thin, dark-haired, and—as Detective Crider later recalled— plainly afraid of seeing Angel Ray in court.

Jesus had a low voice and a charming smile when he smiled. He was in the sixth grade and his favorite subject was science. He helped take care of his three-month old half-brother and he liked to play football, basketball and tennis in his spare time. The Green Bay Packers were his favorite NFL team, and he did not particularly like the Broncos, which did not go over well with his family in Denver.

Many were the questions put to Jesus by Washburn for the prosecution and Lucas for the defense to which he answered he simply did not remember. Much was made of the fact that seven years had passed since the events about which he was testifying. And several questions were meant to confirm Jesus knew the difference between telling the truth and lying, between what was real and what was made-up.

Still Washburn got to the point early in his testimony: "Was there anyone that your mom had as a boyfriend at that time?"

Jesus answered: "Ray."

"Okay," said Washburn. "Do you remember anything about what Ray looked like?"

"He did wear glasses."

"And do you remember anything about the color of his hair?"

"No, I do not."

"Do you remember anything about his face?"

"No, I do not."

"Was there ever a time that Ray watched you when your mom wasn't there?"

"I do not remember."

"Do you remember getting hurt at a time when you were with Ray?"

"Yes, I do."

"I know this was a long time ago," said Washburn, "but I want you to tell the people here in the courtroom everything you can remember about that."

Lucas objected; the question called for narrative. The judge overruled her objection. Washburn said to Jesus: "You can answer that. Tell us everything you remember about that."

Jesus said, "The only thing I remembered what Ray did to me was choke me. Only thing I remember."

"Okay. When you say he choked you, what part of his body did he use?"

"His hands."

"And what part of your body did he choke?"

"My neck."

"Was it the front of your neck, the back of your neck, or something else?"

"I think it was my front of the neck."

A few questions later, Washburn drove the message home: "How did it feel when he choked you?"

"It didn't feel good," answered Jesus.

Then Washburn asked a series of questions about whether Jesus remembered saying a variety of things, at the time, about the incident. For example, she asked, "Do you remember saying that he"—Ray—"said to you, 'Don't say bye to your mom.'?"

"Yes, I do."

But he did not remember saying a lot of other things, like Ray smacked him on the butt, or Ray "flipped" his "pee-pee." He did not recall saying Ray had poured hot water on his toes. He did not recall saying Ray had actually hooked him up on a wall with a tie.

Yet some of his memories were clear and precise.

Washburn asked, "Do you remember, Jesus, whether or not you had a favorite DVD?"

"Yes," said Jesus. "I do."

"And what was the DVD?"

"The DVD was Power Rangers."

"And was it a particular Power Rangers DVD?"

"Yeah, it was a Power Rangers Dino Thunder."

"And do you remember Ray doing anything to that DVD?"

"He broke it."

"Was that the same time when he choked you?"

"Yes, it was."

Washburn had no further questions. Holly Lucas began her cross-examination. Her tone was friendly, less belligerent than normal for her. She was downright gentle with the boy, something a number of the jurors recalled favorably. Still she had a job to do and that job meant trying to show Jesus had too many problems with his memory to be fully credible.

Lucas, like Washburn, went through a litany of questions about whether Jesus remembered saying this thing or that thing about the incident. In many cases, he said he did not remember. She focused a number of these questions on statements Jesus had made to Karen Blackwell, the forensic interviewer with whom Jesus had met a couple of weeks after the incident.

She asked, "Do you remember her asking you about the tie that you said you were hooked up with, if it was on your arm and you saying, 'No'? Do you remember that or not?"

"No, I do not remember."

"Do you remember showing her how long the tie was?"

"No."

More questions with no memories until Lucas asked Jesus: "And do you remember telling her he choked you and he said, 'Don't say bye to my mom'?"

"Yes, I do," he said. This was a detail that stuck as firmly in his mind as the name of the Power Rangers DVD.

Finally, perhaps realizing she wasn't scoring any points, Lucas wrapped her cross-examination: "Were there any words I used that you didn't understand?"

"No."

"Okay. Were there any questions that were confusing for you?"

"No."

And with that, Lucas turned the witness over to the prosecution for redirect examination. Washburn kept it simple: "I just have one question, Jesus."

"Okay."

"Did Ray actually choke you?"

"Yes."

"That's all I have. Thank you."

Lucas asked a few half-hearted questions on re-cross, but the message had been sent and the damage had been done. Jesus was excused from the witness stand.

* * *

Because so many details were left incomplete about the choking incident in 2005, the prosecution called a number of witnesses to flesh-out the story and make it even more damaging for the Angel of Death. In fact, Jesus spent far less time on the witness stand than most of the witnesses in the case.

Yet his testimony had a big impact on the jury. According to several of the jurors, what proved to be persuasive to them were the very weaknesses in his story that Lucas had tried to exploit. True, there were many things he admitted he did not remember, but that seemed to indicate he was telling the truth, not that he had been coached to say what he was saying. And despite the many things he could not recall, he had very specific memories on critical details: Ray had broken his favorite DVD; Ray had told him not to say bye to his mom; Ray had choked him.

Still the prosecution wanted to buttress the child's testimony. First they brought forth the police officer who had responded to Denver Health when Jesus was admitted for the second time. Judge Rappaport read the jury its limiting instruction and Christen Drennan, now a detective, took the stand.

She testified about her introduction to Andrea in the hallway of the hospital and what Andrea had told her. Washburn asked her if Andrea had told her where Angel Ray had gone.

Detective Drennan answered: "I asked her where he was, and she said that – when she started asking him about this, he fled the apartment and he was really nervous and she didn't know where he went from there."

"Let me ask you about her demeanor when you were talking to her. How was she acting?"

"She was panicked. You could tell that this – she was really worried about her son. She cared for him deeply."

Lucas jumped in: "Objection, speculation. Motion to strike."

Judge Rappaport ruled: "That last part is stricken. Not the panicked part, but the reason for it is stricken."

Washburn asked, "Was she crying at all?"

"Yes," answered the witness.

"Was she cooperative with giving you information?"

"Very cooperative … She had told me that [Jesus] was recently diagnosed with Addison's disease. I wasn't very familiar with that, obviously. She basically told me that it had something to do with the lethargic behavior, that that was somewhat normal, but that she couldn't ignore the bruises."

At that point the police officer went into the room and saw Jesus lying in the hospital bed. He was sleepy and "could barely keep his eyes open" but he did acknowledge her presence. "Really lethargic, very sleepy, and very sad-looking" was how she described him.

Upon objection, the judge struck the "the sad part."

Washburn shifted to the bruises all over the child's body.

Detective Drennan described them, at one point referring to "marks on his wrists that looked like ligatures." The lawyers quibbled over the word "ligature" and the judge had Washburn rephrase her question so the answer became "a circular bruise around the wrist." Then Washburn and Detective Drennan ran through the photos she had taken that day in the hospital room.

Next she described her efforts to question Jesus: "His mom had told me what he said to her, but I wanted to ask as well, so I asked him – kind of sat him up and tried to get him to wake up a little bit to talk to me. I asked him what had happened, and he said that his dad got mad at him and tried to choke him … He was so quiet that I had to literally put my face next to his mouth to hear him talk. It was as if it took every bit of energy he had."

Soon Washburn ended and Lucas took over. Her cross was uneventful—clarifications here, a little push there—until she questioned the detective about her conversations with Andrea. Lucas got the witness to admit the word "fled" was used by her in her report but was not actually used by Andrea when she described Angel Ray's departure from the apartment.

It was, in fact, "a police word." Okay, point taken.

Then Lucas asked a question she had little reason to ask: "And when you asked Jesus what happened, what he said was that Ray tried to strangle him – choke him, correct?"

"Yes." There was little more to add.

A few more questions and Detective Drennan was dismissed, to be replaced on the witness stand—after another limiting instruction—by Karen Blackwell, the adolescent forensic interviewer, who by the time of trial had moved to the FBI.

Blackwell explained that the goal when interviewing a child was to "gather a statement or elicit a narrative, whichever way you like to say it, in a developmentally sensitive and unbiased, also legally defensible manner." She described her experience —13 years, over 2000 interviews of children, 295 of them with the FBI—and the "phased interview" process she used.

Then she described her interview with Jesus three weeks after the incident. It was recorded through a two-way mirror built into the special interview rooms at the Family Crisis Center at 10th and Federal.

She talked about always having some paper and markers or crayons so the kids can draw during the interview. "It can be both a comfort thing and also very good tool for them to be able to show us about things that have happened to them."

The interview was conducted without Andrea's presence. Blackwell assured Jesus he was not in trouble. She gave him drawing tools and he used them throughout the interview, which lasted roughly a half hour. Jesus was "extremely active" and "anxious at times." He moved around a lot and jumped from topic to topic. He was not the lethargic kid in the hospital bed.

Blackwell had to simplify her language with him. He told her what had happened. It's on the video recording. Finally, "when I was with Jesus, he appeared to be growing more and more anxious, and when he started describing the death of a – you know, someone that he knew, I knew that we had gotten into a place where he was not emotionally okay."

The interview ended as did Blackwell's testimony. After the noon recess and yet another limiting instruction, the last witness for the day took the stand. It was Dr. John Ogle, the head of pediatrics at Denver Health. His testimony was preceded by a lengthy and intense side bar argument between the lawyers over the limits they had to observe with him.

Welton insisted the court's prior rulings under Rule 404(b) limited the prosecution to questions about bruising and choking. She was concerned Washburn was going to question Dr. Ogle about the medical staff's notation in the records of the January 6 visitation that "Jesus might have an abdominal injury." If that were brought up, it might suggest to the jury that it was a mesentery injury, like the one Neveah had suffered, bolstering the similarities between the two cases.

Washburn responded that possible abdominal injuries had not been ruled out. Rather, further tests were not run because the symptoms resolved themselves. If she steered away from any hint of mesentery injuries, and kept it specific to the doctor's evaluation of Jesus, she should be able to bring it up.

Judge Rappaport split the baby. Washburn could raise the issue of abdominal injuries, but only if she kept it specific to how Jesus "presented and how the doctor analyzed his injuries, not that they are similar, the same, or consistent with Neveah."

Finally the direct examination began. Washburn elicited the background of the witness—his education, his awards, his role as the director of pediatrics at Denver Health for 20 years—then she offered Dr. Ogle to the court as an expert in pediatrics. With no objection from the defense, the judge accepted and Washburn moved into some questions about the pediatrics department and emergency rooms at the Denver Health complex.

Next Dr. Ogle testified about the first time Andrea brought Jesus to the clinic. Then he compared the concern of the medical staff on the second visit: "Well, the concerns with regard to medical staff were now different, because the blood chemistry was in a different direction. The – we felt that this was not a reflection of Addison's disease at the time period, that he was in fact dehydrated at the time period that he came in and needed intravenous fluids in order to support dehydration."

And of course "the Emergency Room physicians again were concerned with regard to the bruises that there's not an explanation for. The – when we have injuries or signs of an injury on a child, we inquire as to the nature of those injuries. Where there has been an accident that's been witnessed or where there has been an event that has occurred that has resulted in an injury, then we would say, you know, there's a traumatic injury, and we understand the accident that occurred, child fell and his knee is bruised, for example. In other sorts of circumstances, the – we don't have an understanding of where the injuries came from, or there may be no story or no explanation or the pattern of injuries may be one that would be uncommon for a simple fall or accident, and then the terminology that might be used is 'non-accidental trauma.' The child ... was dramatically injured, but in a pattern that is not considered to be accidental."

The medical staff was especially concerned about the hematoma on Jesus' forehead but a CT scan showed nothing untoward. Dr. Ogle emphasized, however, that an "intracranial injury or closed-head injury" can be very "subtle" to detect. A person can be knocked unconscious and still have a normal scan.

The questions shifted to Dr. Ogle's meeting with Andrea and Jesus the morning after he was brought in for the second time. Dr. Ogle said Andrea was "obviously upset." Welton objected and the question was rephrased. Dr. Ogle answered: "The – you know, we meet a lot of families in difficult circumstances, and I would say that she appeared upset."

And why not? There were bruises all over her son's body.

The prosecutor led the doctor through all those bruises, referring often to People's Exhibit 236, the drawing of the bruises prepared by the medical staff. They went into detail on the bruises around the chin, neck and shoulders, reflecting upon the proximity of the bruises to the neck in relation to the trachea.

Dr. Ogle opined: "It would be very difficult to imagine how a single injury or fall would result in this pattern of injuries."

"Do you," asked Washburn, "have an opinion as to whether or not these injuries on Jesus were the result of non-accidental trauma?"

"Yes."

"What is that opinion?"

"They were."

Washburn then moved onto the thin ice the lawyers had argued about: the possibility of abdominal injuries. Immediately Welton objected. More jousting ensued. Back on the record, questions rephrased, another objection, another side bar.

Welton asked for a mistrial. Judge Rappaport denied it, and everyone took a break. At 2:52, back on the record, more questions and more objections, then finally Dr. Ogle testified: "Our diagnosis for Jesus was non-accidental trauma."

The cross-examination by Welton seemed entirely routine: more details and clarifications, including a long detour into the drugs that were given to Jesus on his first visit to the hospital and their possible side effects. There were digressions and a few word games, but it seemed to go smoothly enough.

When it came time for her redirect, Washburn called for a side bar conference. She argued: "Judge, it's my position that Ms. Welton opened the door to this doctor testifying about what Andrea Martinez told doctors on January 6, 2005, when they came in, that she came home from work, he was in the care of her boyfriend, and she found him in the condition he's in. The reason I say this is because Ms. Welton specifically elicited from this doctor that Jesus had a bruise on his mouth and a bruise on his back. I purposely did not elicit that information because of this Court's ruling about the January 6, 2005, incident and any suggestion that there was abuse. Now they've opened the door that there was potential abuse by pointing out those bruises, and so I think it is only fair that he be able to give a complete picture of what was said with regard to that."

Judge Rappaport was not about to hand the prosecution such a stunning victory. Consider the impact on the jury if they learned Angel Ray might, just might, have been involved in two abusive incidents with Jesus, just as he might have been involved in two, or at least two, with Neveah.

The judge denied Washburn's request. There wasn't much left for her redirect. Soon Dr. Ogle was off the witness stand. And though Washburn had lost a critical skirmish, she had won a major battle. The jury had heard loud and clear what Angel Ray had done to Jesus.

He seemed to like choking children.

* * *

At the end of the day, the prosecutors joined brave Jesus and his mother in their "war room" deep in the basement of the Lindsey-Flanigan Courthouse. It had been a long day.

The war room was one of several Spartan conference rooms inside a suite of windowless offices kept by the prosecutors under the building where they tried their cases. On the wall there was a large white board on which Amico and Washburn kept a tally of their days in trial, seeking justice for Neveah. That day they let Jesus make the mark on the tally.

Then, just to the right of the words "Montoya Count-Down," he drew a little smiley face. For him, the ordeal of returning to Denver to confront his abuser was over.

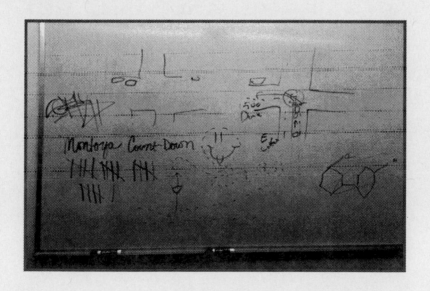

THIRTEEN: THE TESTIMONY of DR. CASE

At 9:06 a.m. on Thursday, April 26—the day after Jesus testified and two weeks after the trial began—Dr. Mary Case took the stand. Nearly seventy and sharp as a tack, she had a strong presence that made a strong impression: silver-blond hair, sparkling eyes, confident manner, authoritative bearing.

Michelle Amico began by "qualifying" her as an expert. They went over her education, professional achievements, teaching activities, publications and awards. She described her work as a forensic pathologist, her specialty in neuro-pathology, the 11,000 autopsies she had performed and the many thousands more she had supervised, and how she became interested in child abuse early in her career: "Because I am a neuropathologist I like to see all the brain cases ... what I found was there were many, many cases of child abuse. Many of them were head injuries."

As an expert in the deaths of children caused by their abuse, Dr. Case had helped the State of Missouri develop legislation to govern the review of child deaths. She was an internationally-recognized expert on what is called "shaken baby syndrome," which Dr. Case preferred to call "abusive head trauma."

And she had conducted many workshops for forensic pathologists on the Investigation of Child Deaths. In them she taught the importance of looking beyond the autopsy to "all of the additional kinds of information that we need to consider when we are looking at the death of a child ... information dealing with medical records, dealing with police reports, dealing with – with information that comes from the department of family services, from the juvenile court, from the death scene investigation itself."

Amico moved to admit Dr. Case's curriculum vitae as a formal exhibit. Defense lawyer Welton objected, arguing the exhibit was cumulative, and it gave the "impression" Dr. Case knew what she was doing more than Dr. Martin.

The judge admitted the C.V. along with Dr. Martin's. Amico didn't take the time to go over the document in detail; instead she asked Dr. Case: "Have you specifically presented on the topic of neck injury in child abuse?"

"Yes," answered the witness. "When we deal with the neck of a young child it's very different ... than it is in middle childhood or an adult. Under the age of nine the bones are very cartilaginous ... you can injure the neck in ways in a young child that you can't injure it later in life. For example, we have what we call SCIWORA, spinal cord injury without radiological injury. You can't see it on an x-ray, but you can deform the spine enough to get spinal cord injury ... And this occurs in young children."

After asking about the "hundreds" of times she had testified as an expert, Amico moved "to qualify Dr. Case as an expert witness in the area of forensic pathology, including her expertise in child abuse and conducting autopsies on children with the focus on how that expertise pertains to her opinions that she rendered as related to the death of Neveah Gallegos."

Welton did not object.

"All right," ruled the judge. "She'll be accepted as an expert in the area as proffered by the Prosecution."

A few questions later, Amico asked: "Do you as the forensic pathologist determine cause and manner of death?"

"Well, yes," said Dr. Case. "Part of the law specifically addresses that the two driving issues in the activity of the death investigation is to determine the cause of death and the manner of death. The cause of death, for example, would be like a gunshot wound to the head. The manner of death refers to how did the cause of death come into being? So a gunshot wound to the head could be a homicide, it could be a suicide, it could be an accident ... you have to examine a great deal of the circumstances ... An autopsy may be totally negative and yet if we go back to the scene and we understand how the position of the body was ... that will tell us something about why the individual died."

Welton objected. In the side bar she insisted, "Your Honor, Ms. Case is not certified as a crime scene investigator. That is what she is testifying to right now."

Judge Rappaport disagreed. The witness was simply saying the scene of death is a factor she considers; she was not saying she is an expert on crime scene investigation.

Objection overruled.

This led to a series of questions about the importance of "nonanatomical findings" in rendering an opinion on cause and manner of death. Dr. Case distinguished, for example, between a true case of sudden infant death syndrome and a case of suffocating in a "microenvironment of rebreathing" created by breathing into a pillow or blanket. Though the autopsy might be negative in both, an examination of the scene of death might tell you which condition caused death.

"Is it," asked Amico, "actually generally accepted in the field of forensic pathology that all surrounding facts and circumstances of death should be taken into account in conjunction with true medical findings when determining cause and manner of death?"

Welton objected: "Calls for speculation."

Judge Rappaport responded: "Overruled."

Dr. Case answered yes, her explanation interrupted by another objection, again overruled.

Amico asked, "And when you teach about this do you use a quote about having to look at the surrounding circumstances that kind of ... hits this point home?"

"I do ... It's not my quote, but it's a quote [from] a very wise man, Dr. Charles Hirsch, who is currently the medical examiner, and has been for a long time, in New York City ... And he has a saying that ..."

"Objection," said Welton, "hearsay."

"Overruled," said the judge.

"… goes like this," continued Dr. Case: "If you fail to look at all of the circumstances surrounding how an individual has died, that kind of thinking is denial of reality for the sake of objectivity. In trying to be objective, you deny the reality of the situation, where the reality is that the circumstances may well tell you why an individual has died. So that was maybe the most valuable piece of information that I ever had in terms of good thinking about how to approach cases."

More back-and-forth; more objections; then finally:

"Is it even more important in the death of a child to look at what you've described as all the surrounding facts and circumstances in addition to the anatomical findings?"

"In the death of a child," answered Dr. Case, "it's even more important because children are very vulnerable, much more vulnerable than at later ages in life. But young children can be killed in very subtle forms of ways that leave no indication in anatomical finding … So they can be killed in ways that you couldn't kill an adult. For example, you can take a child and put it in a plastic bag and then …"

"Objection," said Welton, "relevance."

"Overruled."

"Motion to strike."

"Overruled."

The witness finished her answer.

Then Amico asked, "Dr. Case, you've talked about looking at the totality of the circumstances in the death of a child. Did you in fact review the death of 3-year-old Neveah Gallegos?"

"I did, yes."

"Were you able to determine her cause of death?"

"Yes."

"And did you render an expert opinion as to the cause of death?"

"I did."

"What was that expert opinion?"

"My opinion is that Neveah's death is a homicidal death. It's an asphyxial death. And by asphyxiation I'm talking about something that prevented her from getting oxygen, from uptaking oxygen or bringing oxygen into the body, and it is by a homicidal means. So the manner of death is also homicide."

"Any doubt, Dr. Case, in your mind based upon your review about cause and manner of death in the opinion you render in this particular case?"

"My opinion," answered the witness, "is to a reasonable degree of medical certainty."

At 10:21 the judge called a break.

Back on the record at 10:38, Amico moved into the process by which Dr. Case formed her expert opinion. First they covered the materials the doctor had reviewed in forming her opinion, all the reports and slides and specimens sent to her.

After many of these documents and photographs were "authenticated," admitted into evidence, and "published" to the jury, sometimes over the objection of the defense, Amico and Dr. Case reviewed the bruises, contusions, and abrasions all over Neveah's body at the time of her death.

Dr. Case confirmed these were not injuries that could have incurred after death. They paused when they got to the child's left cheek. It had a "fresh hemorrhage in the subcutaneous fat with early neutrophillic infiltration and that a few of the neutrophils are disintegrating … So fresh means it's early, it hasn't been there very long."

Amico asked Dr. Case to tell the jury what she meant by "neutrophillic infiltration."

"Sure," she replied. "When the body is injured in any way, by trauma, by an infectious agent or disease, whatever is damaging tissue, the body has a process that responds to that, and we call that the inflammatory response. It is going to take care of – if it's a dead piece of tissue it will carry the dead tissue away … And the first thing that happens in the inflammatory process is kind of influx of blood into blood vessels, and it carries with it a type of inflammatory cell called neutrophil. So, this is a type of white blood cell … that appears sometimes as early as 20 minutes after the injury, but it may take 12 to 18 hours for it to appear. And it will stay for several days and then it will die. As it is beginning to die it has the appearance of disintegrating, and I have indicated that. So, that tells you that these neutrophils have been there for a period of time, probably greater than 24 hours. So, it tells us something about the aging [of the injury] and it tells us that there is a response of the body to this injury …"

Next they covered the injury to Neveah's chin, identified as a "focal acute hemorrhage … That means that it's very early. It didn't occur very long before the child died. So it's a very early hemorrhage because it does not yet have any inflammatory response."

Asked to compare the injury to the chin with the injury to the cheek, Dr. Case said, "The injury to the left cheek occurred probably the day before, maybe a little bit before that, before the child died. At the time you die all of that reaction stops. So the chin has injury that occurred shortly before or at the time that the child" died.

Similarly, Neveah's right parietal scalp—"kind of the top of your head and slightly behind the ear"—showed recent injury: "So it's like a scalp bruise. So there's some kind of an impact there that has caused bleeding. It's very fresh. It has not caused any inflammatory response … this is blunt trauma."

The many bruises on Neveah's body, and the timing of their infliction, showed she had been hit, beaten, struck or smacked at least a day or two before she died. That squared with Miriam's account of when she started seeing bruises on Neveah. But those were just the bruises.

Amico moved to the injuries to the child's belly.

Referring to a photo admitted into evidence, Dr. Case said: "It is an area where you can see loops of small bowel, and then there is dark red. That is the portion of what we call the mesentery, which is kind of a flap of fat that the blood vessels that carry blood back and forth from the intestine pass through … So that – all of the dark red color is blunt force trauma. So, that's hemorrhage in there … And it's a very large area in terms of – meaning it's a very significant injury … So it is a common area where impact to the abdomen goes right through, there's nothing to – the wall of the child's abdomen does not in any way stop the force. The force goes right through and forces everything back to the spine. And in this case there's a lot of bruising in the soft tissue of the mesentery. So this is a very significant injury. In this case it has not caused tearing of the bowel, but it's quite a significant injury."

"And explain what you mean by quite a significant injury."

"All right," said Dr. Case. "There is a literature that has looked at abdominal injuries in children."

Objection. Side bar. Question rephrased.

Objection. Side bar. Seeking to stop this entire line of questions, Welton cited *People v. Martinez*, a Colorado case that talked about "not how much force but basically how little force needs to be applied in order to show that it's blunt force trauma."

Hiding her delight, Amico quickly replied, "Well, first of all, I'm familiar intimately with the case of People versus Stephen Martinez 'cause I happened to be the trial prosecutor on People versus Stephen Martinez. It was a very different scenario."

In detail Amico distinguished the two cases.

Judge Rappaport overruled the objection.

Dr. Case said: "This kind of injury is consistent with – for example, I could do this with my fist to a young child of this age. I could do it with my foot. I don't need a ball bat. I don't need an instrument to do this. But this is a very significant injury. It covers a great deal of mesentery."

"And what amount of force might be necessary to cause that significant of an injury to the mesentery?"

"This is what I would consider a large amount of force. This is – I have seen 20 to 30 of this type of injuries and usually they were accompanied by tearing of the bowel or ... bleeding into the abdominal cavity. So the child is actually dying from this injury. When a fatal injury occurs in this area, the amount of hemorrhage in the mesentery does not look any different than it looks here ..."

Another objection; overruled. Another question, this time slightly rephrased; then yet another objection.

In the side bar Welton said: "Your Honor, I have to renew my objection. This is exactly what *Martinez* talks about. The level of force is imputed to knowledge ... The other thing I would ask is that the jurors are rolling their eyes and ..."

The judge asked: "What do you mean rolling their eyes?"

"They're rolling their eyes and sighing when I'm objecting, and I would like the Court to instruct the jurors that it's appropriate to object and they should not hold that against the Defense."

Judge Rappaport overruled the objection, once again, but did remind the jurors "that both sides have an obligation to object when they feel evidence is perhaps inadmissible ... you shouldn't hold it against whatever side makes the objection."

Allowed to proceed, Dr. Case explained the injury to the mesentery was not the sort of injury that would occur simply by falling on something in the house or by over-eager efforts to resuscitate her. This was an abusive trauma, a non-accidental trauma, "an inflicted injury."

But how could she possibly see this type of internal injury with no bruising on the abdomen to suggest it exists?

The witness answered: "Well, the nature of the abdomen in a young child is very different than your abdomen. The rib cage is very widely flared so that a large surface area of the abdomen is exposed. It consists of just mainly soft tissue. There's no muscle. A small child does not have a reflex. If you strike it, it does not have that reflex to tighten its abdominal wall. So if you strike a child in the abdomen, the force goes right through, and it goes all the way through until you strike the backbone … the great majority of impacts that create very significant injury inside do not leave any mark at all. Because there's so little soft tissue in that abdominal wall, the force just goes right through it. It does not register in the soft tissue."

In Neveah's case, there was "extensive fresh hemorrhage with well developed neutrophillic response with some beginning to disintegrate." This meant the injury had occurred "somewhere around 24 hours or more before the child died."

"And can you tell us then, Dr. Case, what might be some typical symptoms that a child might exhibit if she had this particular injury with – in 24 hours or [so] before death?"

"Sure," she said. "It would be painful. It would be painful at the time. It would continue to be painful. There could be nausea and vomiting. The child might not want to eat but would drink water, so would want fluids … They would want water because the reaction here is kind of seeping out some fluid. They're losing – there's fluid being lost in the soft tissue, so the child would want to drink."

That explained the mystery surrounding Neveah's notable loss of energy, her lethargic manner, and especially her thirst— all as described by Miriam—throughout the day before she died. The child had been suffering from the injury to her mesentery.

Finally, Amico turned to the injuries to Neveah's neck. Tensions began rising in the courtroom. Amico knew this was where she had to deliver the goods to the jury.

She started with the paraspinal area, "the back of the neck just below the skull," and referred often to the parade of photos entered as exhibits and displayed to the jury on the court's large flat-screen TV monitor.

Here Dr. Case found very extensive fresh hemorrhaging that extended down into the cervical and thoracic regions. She was convinced, given the position of the body when it was found, this "is not lividity" and the early neutrophil response told her "the individual was living for a short time with this particular injury."

They paused to focus on the subject of lividity and the reasons why Dr. Case did not believe the blood in Neveah's neck came from post-mortem settling. She explained decomposition had been delayed due to the relative coolness of the place where her body was found—shaded and near running water.

Welton objected occasionally. Sometimes a question was rephrased; sometimes a few words were stricken from the record; sometimes the objection was overruled.

Amico shifted gears: "I want to start in terms of your expert opinion that Neveah's death was the result of asphyxiation by neck compression. Can you, first of all, please tell the members of the jury what asphyxia or asphyxiation is?"

"Sure," said Dr. Case. "Asphyxiation refers to a mechanism of death whereby oxygen is going to be excluded from reaching the body, or at the cellular level interfered with from being uptaken. So asphyxiation would include things like suffocation, smothering, strangulation, compression of the chest, anything that is going to interfere with breathing or the ability of the body to take in freely oxygen in the air."

"And when you say that this is asphyxiation by neck compression, are you saying this is indeed strangulation, or what do you mean by that?"

"I'm not saying that it's strangulation, or I would have said strangulation. I said neck compression. There has been pressure placed on the neck and there is hemorrhaging in muscles that are internally present in there. That can be done in a number of ways. It can be done by something pushing against the neck. It could have been done by placing a hand on it ... It could have been a forearm ..."

Usually, she continued, loss of consciousness occurs during the first ten seconds of compression, certainly within the first minute; irreversible brain damage occurs after 3 or 4 minutes; death occurs after 4 or 5 minutes.

"Can someone," asked Amico, "suffer asphyxia by neck compression and there be absolutely no external signs at the time of autopsy?"

"Yes. In children under about the age of 6 or 7 years, unfortunately you can kill children by asphyxiation by neck pressure without any kind of stigma or anatomical or pathological change internally or externally on the body ... because the airway is very soft. It's soft enough that with my two fingers I can actually collapse the airway of a child. That is very different than later in childhood or in an adult ... In a child I can cut off the airway with pressure from my fingers and that's not even a pound of pressure ... It doesn't produce petechial hemorrhage in the eyelids or in the eyes or on the face. And these are changes that we commonly see in adults when we strangle them or cause some kind of asphyxiation. So children are just very vulnerable. We are able to cause them to die from asphyxial means and nothing may show up. You can do the same thing with suffocation. But neck compression is particularly likely not to show any kind of injury."

Nevertheless, asked Amico, didn't she actually find "internal signs of neck compression here in Neveah's case?"

"In Neveah," answered the witness, "she was actually hemorrhaging. Had that not been there I would have the same opinion that this child had been asphyxiated. I might not have said neck compression. Homicidal death by asphyxiation. But because there is neck hemorrhaging there I go farther and say there is evidence that there has been pressure on the neck. But it's an asphyxial death."

Amico had saved some of her most potent stuff for last. She turned to the strap muscles on the front of the neck. Here there was a "deep hemorrhage over the thyroid gland on the left" and some blood on the nearby bones.

At this point Dr. Case left the witness stand and stood next to the TV monitor, pointing at the screen as she guided the jury through several photos of the insides of the neck. When she was finished she went back to the witness stand.

Amico asked, "What did the microscopic examination of the tissue here in the left strap muscle of the neck reveal or indicate?"

"The left strap muscle showed that there was fresh hemorrhage with no inflammation."

"So what does that tell you with respect to your expert opinion?"

"That the injury had not been present long enough to develop neutrophils coming in. So it's a very fresh injury."

Was she sure this was not lividity? She was sure.

A few more questions; more objections; more answers. Then came a discussion about a study that showed children who had been killed in homicides often "had many, many, many marks in addition to whatever the fatal injury was."

This was consistent with the many bruises of different ages found on Neveah and with the injury to her mesentery. Dr. Case emphasized there was no "explanation for that other than some form of very significant abusive injury."

So, yes, she had indeed considered all of these things—all of the surrounding facts and circumstances—when she was forming her expert opinion. More objections came, this time sustained, when she referred to the child being "hidden away in what you could call a shallow grave."

Still the bottom line was clear: "For me to render my opinion as to the cause and manner of this death I took all of these circumstances into consideration. And it was my consideration that this is not any kind of natural death. This is a homicidal death ... In this case there is actually indication of neck compression. So it's my opinion this child is dying as a result of asphyxiation by neck compression as a means of homicide."

Letting that statement hang in the air, Amico ended her direct examination. The judge called a recess for lunch.

At 1:31 Welton began her cross-examination.

First she questioned whether Dr. Case had gone to the scene of the recovery of the body and what materials she had reviewed in rendering her opinion. No, the doctor said, she had not gone to the scene; and no, she had not reviewed any videos of interviews with Miriam or from the autopsy. The suggestion might have been that Dr. Case could not have looked at all the facts and circumstances if she had not done these things. But the message was lost in verbiage.

Next Welton spent a lot of time questioning Dr. Case about "shaken baby syndrome," which—again—the doctor preferred to call "abusive head trauma." They went over all the work and lecturing she had done on the topic. The suggestion might have been that Dr. Case was biased due to her focus on the topic, even though no one had ever alleged Neveah had died from abusive head trauma.

What about the fees she charged for all this testifying and lecturing all over the world? Didn't that suggest bias? And what about the good doctor's methods: did they really follow the scientific method?

Sometimes Dr. Case answered with a simple yes or no; sometimes with more elaborate explanations. Her choice of words danced around the insinuations. She had been down these roads many times before.

But then the suggestions started getting more specific and more personal: "Have you heard of cognitive bias?"

"Yes, I have," said Dr. Case.

"Have you heard of unconscious bias?"

"Yes."

"Do you believe they can be willed away?"

"I don't even know what you are talking about."

After a few questions concerning "the tendency to test [a] hypothesis by looking for instances that confirm it," the focus shifted to the real issue Welton was trying to raise: whether the non-forensic information Dr. Case considered showed she was biased against Angel Ray.

After all, she knew the last names of both Angel Ray and Miriam; she knew Neveah's body had been concealed; she knew Miriam had told conflicting stories. And she knew race, poverty, and other socio-economic conditions were risk factors in cases of child abuse. Still Dr. Case resisted any suggestion she had been biased in reaching her opinion.

Often she replied: "I'm not sure what you mean."

Welton doubled down: "But you had a notion of what an abuser looks like before you even opened the evidence in this kit. Am I correct about that?"

"I beg to differ with you," insisted Dr. Case. "You never have a notion. First of all, when I'm putting forward a cause and manner of death, I'm not indicating who the individual is that is doing this abuse."

"Well, let me just ask you. You knew Mr. Montoya fit your criteria before you even opened the evidence kit. Am I correct about that?"

"I would say those are not criterial for a child abuser. That is epidemiological information, that if you look at who is it that is abusing children, this is what the data shows. I'm just putting that forward. I'm not saying well, if you just look at these factors you can pick out who does this. That's not at all what that means."

But hadn't the doctor admitted she would rule this death a homicide even without evidence of neck injury? And hadn't she admitted she would call it an asphyxial death even without evidence of pressure on the neck?

"So even if no evidence, he still did it, correct?"

Dr. Case answered with great precision: "I have nothing to say about him. I'm saying that someone killed this child. But I am not saying who did that."

These words stuck with the jury. To them the witness had just demonstrated her lack of bias. Still the defense insisted on more questions challenging her objectivity, her association of bruising with cause of death, her work on abusive head trauma, on and on. This drew a rare interruption by Amico: "I'm going to object at this point in terms of what is the relevance of this line of questioning?"

After a side bar, Judge Rappaport allowed a few more questions about the surrounding facts and circumstances.

Dr. Case took the opportunity to drive this message home: "I have never had a child that was for some reason dying and then the body was concealed for other than the fact that someone had killed that child."

There was simply no other explanation in this case.

Welton returned to the injuries to the mesentery, to lividity, to the possibility Neveah had some genetic disorder. She went from topic to topic, hoping to shake this unshakable witness. There was sparring over questions based on lecture notes.

Finally Welton asked: "Would it be irresponsible to form an opinion based on your own biases?"

And Dr. Case answered: "I think that depending on what your biases were. For example, if your bias was always to be truthful and use every bit of your knowledge, if that is your bias then I don't think it would be irresponsible. But if your bias was I'm going to see how far I can stretch the truth, then obviously that would be irresponsible. So depending on what the bias is."

Welton had no more questions. A recess was called at 3:09 and nineteen minutes later court reconvened.

Amico declared: "The People see no need for redirect examination." That ended the testimony of Dr. Mary Case.

FOURTEEN: THE TESTIMONY of H.D. HUDSON

On Monday, April 30 at 3:04 in the afternoon, Amico called to the stand a 34-year-old man named Hudson Dawson Hudson. Now here was a witness who could not only corroborate much of Miriam's testimony but who had his own story to tell.

And while some might say his story didn't tell the police or prosecutors anything they didn't already know—a position later taken by Detective Crider—it did tell the jury a lot of things they would not otherwise have learned. For H.D. was the jail house snitch whose letters to the police and prosecutors provided the fourth and final breakthrough in the case, after the discovery of Neveah's body, the determination of the cause of death, and the testimony of little Jesus Perez.

H.D. was born in Denver in 1978. His mother nicknamed him Doug but later everyone took to calling him H.D. He went to West High School but dropped out, though later he did earn his high school diploma. He had worked as a printer, worked at Discount Tires, worked at a few restaurants—and at the time of his testimony he was working in "the food industry" and living at a "halfway house," serving a six-year community corrections sentence for his latest felony convictions.

H.D. had a prodigious career as a criminal and an even more prodigious career as a snitch. He answered the questions put to him in a forthright, nearly cheerful manner.

The jury lapped it up. They welcomed the levity H.D. lent to the proceedings—and the break from the gruesome details. After Amico led him through several questions about the restrictions imposed on him while living in the halfway house, she turned to the summer of 2009.

H.D. had been arrested for one of his crimes, taken to the city jail and transferred to the county jail, located back then on East Smith Road, off I-70. He was housed in Building 6, Tier D, Cell 10, sharing the cell with his friend Ray Wright.

For an hour each day they could leave their cell and interact with other inmates. They could use the phone, take a shower, or just walk around, mostly inside the building, but every few days outside in the yard, enclosed by a high fence and home to a basketball court. It was during one of those hours of free time in the yard that Ray Wright introduced H.D. to Angel Ray.

Amico asked H.D. to identify Angel Ray for the jury, and he responded, "Sitting right next to me in a red shirt."

Turned out H.D.'s girlfriend Demetria had a sister called Brownie who was friends with Miriam, "and that's what started our conversation off, period."

What's more, Demetria just happened to be in jail with Miriam at the time, which was shortly after the re-arrest of her and Angel Ray following their indictments by the grand jury.

Soon Wright was transferred from jail to prison, leaving H.D. alone in his cell. And soon after—in August—Angel Ray was transferred to Tier D, Cell 9, right next to H.D. By then H.D. had become a tier clerk, who was allowed out of his cell more often to serve food, mop floors, and "wipe off the phones."

He and Angel Ray started talking in more detail.

Amico asked, "Okay. Can you explain for the members of the jury how it is that you are able to communicate with one another between cells?"

"We have walls in between the cells, and from where the walls are, where the walls end, to where the walls are to the bars there's about an inch in between, so you probably see about this side of his face over, and you can sit there and talk."

"Okay. And for the record, Mr. Hudson, you were showing from about the nose to the right side of your face would be the amount that you could actually see each other?"

"Yeah, or the left side, depending on what side."

At first the two inmates just talked in general, "about life, you know," but then Angel Ray began telling H.D. things about what happened to Neveah.

The details trickled out over time.

"I mean, you know, it wasn't all day every day we talked about Neveah. We'd go maybe two or three days without actually taking about Neveah, you know."

As Angel Ray's story emerged, H.D. realized he was hearing things that might become useful to him. He grabbed his pencil and paper and began taking notes, "so I could remember what it was that he had said to me about certain things."

H.D. also began listening carefully for details. He'd been around this track before. Details were valuable.

And yes, the exhibits now being introduced by Amico were his actual physical notes. In fact there were two sets of notes, one made by H.D. while he was actually talking with Angel Ray and a second made by H.D. after the fact: "It's just the notes I had tooken [sic] on the prior one written out so that they're readable and nicer."

And no, Angel Ray could not see H.D. was taking notes at the time. So what did Angel Ray say had happened to Neveah?

"He told me that Neveah was coming out of the kitchen, and she just fell and started hyperventilating ... breathing crazy and that she just fell and was kind of – couldn't breathe, but her heart was still beating, you know, but she was – pretty much just fell."

Angel Ray said he "freaked out" and went to a neighbor's apartment to call Miriam. He told H.D. that Neveah was already dead when he made the call.

Miriam rushed home. She was the one who wanted to hide the child's body. H.D.'s notes read like this: "Miriam told him to get rid of the body, 'cause she lost her baby; she wasn't going to lose him, too."

"Okay," asked Amico, "did he tell you about whether or not he did anything after Neveah collapsed and wasn't breathing?"

"He said that he tried to give her CPR."

"Okay. Did he explain to you how he tried to give her CPR?"

"The way he explained it was he was on her straddling her as if a girl is riding you, is how it was said."

"Okay. What do you mean, 'as if a girl is riding you?' What's the position?"

Welton objected. She knew the image that was coming. Judge Rappaport overruled her, "if he knows."

H.D. replied, "Legs on the side of you, you know, sitting on top of you."

His notes said, "Tried CPR, straddled like a girl riding you."

Welton's instincts had been right on: the image was one that stuck with the jury. And it wasn't a flattering image.

Amico asked if Angel Ray had told H.D. anything about the night before Neveah died. The answer: "Hisself and he told me two friends, two of his friends ... I believe one was Face, and the other one was – can't recall. I believe Julian ... They were at the house [the apartment on Logan Street] smoking weed."

H.D.'s scratchy contemporaneous notes said, "Smoke weed night before, blew smoke at baby." The more refined version of his notes said, "Night before he was smoking weed with friends Julian and Face, and he was blowing smoke in Neveah's face and she was high."

"Do you," asked Amico, "remember anything about his demeanor when he was telling you about the fact that he was blowing smoke in Neveah's face?"

"I remember right, it was like of a giggling, funny thing."

Welton objected. The judge overruled. Another image that could only damage the defendant was free to sink into the jury's collective mind. And just to hammer it home: "He was acting like as if it was – you know, like it was funny, like she was high, they were high, like having little giggles about it."

This despite the fact Angel Ray said Neveah was sick and wouldn't eat during those few days. He even said he had tried to take her to the doctor but was turned away for lack of insurance. And this despite the fact that his mother was a nurse.

Amico returned to the afternoon of Neveah's death. She led H.D. through the disclosures Angel Ray had made: "Wrapped baby in plastic bag, then put her in brother's duffle bag," according to H.D.'s scratchy notes. Then Amico asked whether Angel Ray had said where he went.

H.D. answered, "He went to Colfax and got on the 16, took it down to Broadway and Colfax and transferred to the 15 and took it up to Perry and Colfax to the McDonald's." While he was at the McDonald's—two to three hours—he kept Neveah's body in the duffle bag on the floor next to him. He told H.D. he had spent his time crying at the restaurant. Then:

"He said he took her down – he left McDonald's and walked down Perry and then got to the river – or the river down there and that he took her over by a log and took her out of the duffle bag, covered her up if – I believe he said a cover – pulled the log over to her and then covered her with a tire so he would know where she was."

Now this got the jury's attention. Here were details they had not heard, details never published in the media, details only Angel Ray could know. They were being admitted as evidence only because the rules banning hearsay have an important exception for admissions against interest. And it certainly was not in Angel Ray's interest to be telling these details to anyone, let alone a jail house snitch.

Next came another detail that only Angel Ray could know: he had decided to remove the body from the duffle bag and had taken the duffle with him because it had his brother's name on it. He told H.D. that he "didn't want to throw her in the dumpster. He said that she wasn't trash." And—yet more details never previously published in the media—after being released from jail on the day of Neveah's burial, he and Miriam had initially stayed at the Days Inn motel at 6th and Federal; later he had stayed with his cousin "Coach" Montoya.

Amico then used H.D.'s notes to support his recollections.

One entry read: "Father figure. Mad 'cause baby acted scared. He was only nice."

H.D. elaborated: because Neveah did not have a father, Angel Ray "wanted to be that father figure, but he would get upset because the baby would act scared of him and would stick by Miriam, and he didn't understand why because he was always nice to her." Good old Daddy Ray.

A shift in gears, and Amico asked whether Angel Ray and Miriam had been communicating with each other while in county jail. Yes, they would write poems back and forth to each other in the *County Times*, the jail house newsletter.

Amico began tying it all together. In September of 2009, about a month after Angel Ray started spilling his guts, H.D. was still in custody for his latest charge of criminal trespass. He had a long record that included criminal menacing and burglary. And he had something in particular he wanted from the system, something that wouldn't come out fully until cross-examination.

So H.D. decided to use his notes to his advantage. He sent letters to the District Attorney and Denver Police Department, saying he had information about Angel Ray. As a result, Detective Crider interviewed him, with his attorney present.

Amico asked: "What's that called, Mr. Hudson, when one inmate gets information from another and then provides that information in terms – in turn – to law enforcement."

H.D. answered, "That's called snitching."

Amico asked whether he had met her briefly on the day of the interview and H.D. agreed he had. She asked, "Okay. Did I, Mr. Hudson, on that particular day make you in any way, shape, or form, any promises or guarantees about anything you had to say or anything you had pending in the court system?"

"No you didn't … There was no deal on the table. The understanding was just give you what I had and see what happens from there." What happened was H.D. delivered his notes to the police and was interviewed a second time in October.

He also provided the police and prosecutors some letters from Miriam to Angel Ray, which Angel Ray had given to H.D. and which H.D. had kept when Angel Ray was moved to a different cell. Even after all this—two interviews, the letters, and both sets of notes—no plea deal was reached immediately. One was, however, eventually reached.

Amico went over the deal with H.D. He had pled guilty to a reduced charge, a Class 6 felony, criminal attempt to commit first-degree criminal trespass. He had also pled guilty to criminal mischief, a Class 1 misdemeanor. They worked out a deal for his parole violations as well. They provided for years of intense supervision after his release and capped his sentence to 18 months in the County Jail.

H.D. also had to pay restitution and "to provide truthful testimony in any criminal proceeding" against Angel Ray.

Amico asked, "Okay. Have you provided truthful testimony here today, Mr. Hudson, in terms of the conversations you had with the defendant, Angel Montoya?"

"Yes."

Still, sure enough, after all his plea deals, once H.D. was released he "got in trouble again." He asked Amico for help.

She asked, "Did I ever do anything to assist you with what happened after you pled guilty and made this plea bargain with me on those other cases?"

"No, you didn't."

Amico announced, "I don't have anything further for you. Thank you, Mr. Hudson."

It was almost 4:50 p.m. Judge Rappaport adjourned.

The next morning, May 1, after a few housekeeping matters were resolved, H.D. again took the stand. Welton began her cross-examination of him with a series of questions about the various aliases he had used over the years. Then she moved into "some of the crimes that you've been convicted of," hoping this testimony would impeach his credibility.

She asked, "The first time that you were convicted as an adult was in 1997, correct?"

"Yes," answered H.D.

"And that is because you broke into someone's home?"

Amico objected. A lengthy side bar ensued. She insisted, "You cannot elicit the facts of a prior felony conviction."

The lawyers hurled precedent at each other, trying to get the edge in their argument over how deeply the defense could delve. After considerable haggling, the issues were settled by the court.

Welton could ask about prior felony convictions—there were at least seven—and she could ask about the elements of the crimes that were the subjects of such convictions, such as burglary meaning breaking and entering. She could also ask whether H.D. had pled guilty in those cases.

But Welton could not ask about the facts underlying the convictions, nor could she ask about arrests that did not lead to convictions, nor could she ask whether H.D. had pled to reduced charges in the cases where he was convicted. In essence, she could not get into the original charges or the facts.

The argument was anything but theoretical. Welton meant to show that, through his repeated exposure to the criminal justice system, H.D. had "learned a pattern of snitching. He's a career snitch. He has offered to give up, in my count, 14, 15 people just since the letters were written in this case."

Amico agreed Welton could ask about his history as a snitch and if he had gotten any benefit from snitching. But she could not ask if specific charges were dismissed or reduced as a result.

Back on the record, Welton questioned H.D. about his six-year sentence for burglary back in 1997. She asked about the harsh restrictions placed on him while he was in prison—DOC—Department of Corrections. She asked about his early release and probation in community corrections. She asked about his return to jail for violating the conditions of his probation.

On and on Welton probed until she tripped another wire.

Amico objected again and the lawyers approached the bench once again. Recall, during all of these side bar conferences, white noise was spilling from the courtroom's speakers, drowning out the arguments and likely fatiguing all who heard.

Again the argument was over what the defense could and could not ask. Amico again insisted, "You don't get to discuss or go into sentences that were served in those prior cases, only as related to the plea deal ... I gave some leeway to ask what happened," but Welton had crossed the line.

The defense lawyer replied: "Your Honor, again, he wasn't [just] facing one year. He was facing 12, and he was bitchable and actually facing 36 years ... and it's relevant because this is where he learned to snitch."

Bitchable is slang for being eligible to be charged as a habitual criminal with attendant tripling of sentence.

"... it goes to his credibility, Your Honor. He learned to be a career snitch. Not only that, but he learned certain snitching techniques. Namely, note-taking."

The argument raged. The judge ruled, again setting limits for the defense. Back in open court, Welton returned to H.D.'s history of snitching. She hammered away, emphasizing the promises he had broken and the lies he had uttered over the years, telling the court "I'm not going to commit any crimes," and telling his mother "I'm going to change."

When Welton asked about the blame he had tried to place on his brother in his menacing case, Amico objected once more. Yet another side bar interrupted the proceedings. How far could Welton go into this matter of blame without getting into the specific facts? The limits placed on her cross-examination were, admittedly, not always easy to observe.

Next she began asking H.D. about his more recent crimes. By the summer of 2009, he was in big trouble. He was looking at his fourth felony conviction and possibly being charged as a habitual criminal.

And he certainly did not want to go back to DOC. Snitches don't fare well in prison. So H.D. found himself writing letters to the police and prosecutors about Angel Ray. Welton quoted snippets from the letters. In them H.D. emphasized he had been a snitch and a witness in other cases, his girlfriend Demetria "was over there with Miriam Gallegos," and he could get her to talk if necessary. In exchange, H.D. wanted out in time for him to have a place for Demetria to land when she got out of jail.

These letters got the response he wanted. The dance began. A deal was cut. On October 20, H.D. pled guilty to attempt to commit first-degree criminal trespass; he was put on probation; he bonded out—and nine days later he was back in jail on new felony charges, again eligible to be treated as a habitual criminal. That would mean he would go back to prison for sure.

He was desperate. On November 6 he wrote Amico:

"Hello. I know you're shaking your head because I'm sitting in jail again ... Please, city jail instead of county ... I'll do everything to help you." In subsequent letters he begged: "Please let me do county time ... I accept my sentence, but just cannot accept DOC. I can't be in Seg ... I agree to county time, no matter how much."

Welton led H.D. through the oppressive conditions he would face in "Segregation, when you're locked down 23 hours a day."

And with this, the pieces of his puzzle fell into place.

H.D. would be put in Seg—or Ad-Seg—because he had snitched on his uncle in a murder case. For his own protection, he would be eating and recreating and sleeping all alone. Training and education would be only by video. He would have no contact with others. Telephone privileges would be tight.

But rather than following up immediately on this line of questioning, Welton began a meandering review of H.D.'s later exploits. She led up to a letter he wrote to Amico the next May.

The judge called a recess. Everyone took a break.

Welton picked up her narrative.

She hammered at H.D. that he was, by this time, "facing up to 24 years … If they filed bitch charges on you. And bitch charges are habitual criminal charges, correct?" So H.D. kept writing letters, offering to snitch in even more cases.

The questions shifted to a survey of how H.D. had learned, through his prior stints in jail and prison, how to communicate with others. Welton said, "There is lots of ways for an inmate to gather information; wouldn't you agree to that?"

"Correct."

"And you had access to television and newspapers, right?"

"Yes."

Then Welton asked about Demetria, the woman who at the time was H.D.'s girlfriend—he called her his wife—and her friendship with Miriam. In June of 2009, when he was out of jail but Demetria was in, she was in with Miriam. They were close. The woman called herself "Neveah's godmother" and posted photos of Neveah on her MySpace page. So it was only natural Demetria would communicate with Miriam.

And it was only natural she would communicate with H.D. One of her letters to him described in lurid detail the sex acts she was going to perform on him when she got out. The point was: H.D. knew Miriam had confided things to Demetria. In one letter to the police and prosecutors he said, "And my wife told me what Miriam had told her."

Welton began pouncing: H.D. was a liar. He had broken many promises. Was he really telling the truth? She reviewed some of the statements he had made, information he claimed he had gotten from Angel Ray. She questioned him about the letters Angel Ray had given him. She suggested he was in community corrections at the time because, even though he wasn't eligible, a district attorney had gone to bat for him.

Welton wrapped up her cross-examination by trying to leave two impressions: first, H.D. lacked credibility due to his criminal history and the deals he had made with the prosecutors.

And second: maybe, just maybe, H.D. had gotten his information from someone other than Angel Ray, someone like his girlfriend, or from some newspaper or TV coverage. It was this second impression that prompted Amico to spring the trap Welton had set for herself.

Amico requested a side bar. White noise filled the room. The lawyers approached the bench. This time their arguments were anything but routine. Amico contended the implication that H.D. could have gotten his information from Miriam, via his girlfriend Demetria, or from reports in the media, had opened the door for Amico's re-direct to counter that implication.

She said, "Mr. Hudson has a detail that has never been published in TV or newspapers ... And so I'm asking the Court to make a ruling about the door being opened to a detail he has that has never been anywhere and is protected by a gag order ... I don't know why Ms. Welton would ask if [he] had access to TV and newspapers, knowing that that is the one detail that has never been released in the media, and the one detail that has been protected [from] newspapers, that Mr. Hudson got directly from his conversation with Angel Ray Montoya."

Judge Rappaport thought at first Amico was arguing over the details about where Angel Ray and Miriam had stayed after their initial release and who had paid for their motel. But no, that was not what Amico cared about. Those details, all agreed, could be dealt with according to a joint stipulation. Instead, Amico was talking about the deal Angel Ray had made with the prosecutors.

The judge said, "That's not a fact we have ... that Miriam passed along to anybody that the defendant led the police to the body in exchange for not seeking the death penalty."

The lawyers quibbled over what was known by whom. Welton argued, "It's in the Supp Report."

Amico replied, "But not in exchange for the death penalty. That's the specific detail Mr. Hudson wrote on his note. Nobody had that information."

Welton insisted the issue was not the gag orders entered by Judge Robbins, "but a contractual obligation that was made between the parties. And I think that is a totally different matter to opening the door, or not opening the door."

Amico responded, "Well, then, he violated his end of the contract by saying it to H.D. Hudson ... I have the original notes ... regarding how the police were led to the body in exchange for no death penalty."

The judge ruled: "But arguably, it could have been from another source. I don't think the door's been opened. I think it's too nebulous, given their relationship."

Amico was forced to abandon her effort to introduce that most damaging of details: that Angel Ray had led the police to the body "in exchange for no death penalty." What, after all, could be more probative of his guilt?

Or, from the standpoint of the defense, more prejudicial?

So instead Amico focused her re-direct examination on only a few select issues. She asked, "Okay. Did you ... Mr. Hudson, have a specific reason why you did not want to return to the Department of Corrections?"

"Yes, I did," said H.D.

Back and forth, they spelled it out. He had snitched in a number of high-profile cases, including the first-degree murder case against his uncle. She asked, "Have you personally been threatened ever since you testified in your uncle's case?"

"Yes, I have."

"If you were to return to the Department of Corrections, what label or jacket would you be wearing?"

"Snitch jacket."

"How," asked the prosecutor, "are snitches treated in the Department of Corrections?"

"Their lives are taken from them."

"What do you mean by that?"

"They are murdered."

"And if you are a snitch or in danger when you go to the Department of Corrections, is that one manner in which you might be placed into Seg or administrative segregation?"

"Yes, ma'am. I would automatically be."

"Is that for protective custody?"

"Yes."

Amico made it clear that all the letters H.D. had written were intended to keep him out of DOC. He had never asked her for a flat-out dismissal of any charges or probation. He just couldn't face going back to prison where he would be a marked man.

Next Amico squarely faced the implication that H.D. might have gotten his information from a source other than Angel Ray: "Is the information that you wrote on those notes ... based on information from Demetria or Miriam? Or is it based on information from your own personal conversations with the defendant, Angel Ray Montoya."

"It's only from conversations between me and Angel."

Finally Amico began wrapping up. She knew not to wander at this critical point. She asked: "Despite the risks that you are now serving a six-year sentence in Community Corrections, that if you violated in [any] way, shape or form you could go to the Department of Corrections, did you still come here to testify in front of the members of the jury?"

"Yes, I did."

"We've heard about the benefits that you received after you gave information to Detective Crider and the plea disposition that you got after you gave information to Detective Crider. Is there a reason, Mr. Hudson, other than the benefit of that plea deal that you got, that you're doing this today and yesterday?"

"Yes," said the witness, "because it's the right thing to do."

In fact, on August 8, 2011—a week before the proceedings that ended in a mistrial—H.D. had written a letter to Amico that said unequivocally: "Neveah didn't deserve that. I would go to court for her even if I hadn't got anything out of it."

And that's exactly the final thought Amico wanted to lodge in the minds of the jurors: H.D. might be a low-life, but that didn't mean he was lying. Indeed, he was there testifying once again as a snitch because it was simply the right thing to do.

On re-cross Welton asked a few questions that covered no new ground and scored no new points. That's all she could do. She had, in short, won the battle to keep out that most damning piece of information, but she was losing the war.

For indeed the jury fixed on those final statements made by the jail house snitch: he would have testified even if he had not gotten anything out of it. It was the right thing to do.

* * *

Detective Crider was called to testify for the last time. Yes, he said, it was common for the police to encounter snitches who want something in exchange for information. And no, the police do not accept all such offerings at face value. They first have to corroborate the information that is provided.

That's why he and an investigator from the DA's office had interviewed H.D. extensively on September 23 and October 16 of 2009. And why they had followed-up by checking out the housing logs from the county jail, the bus routes H.D. claimed Angel Ray had used, and other details that convinced them he was telling the truth.

Amico ended her brief exam by asking if H.D. had relayed specific details about how Neveah's body had been covered—details not revealed in the media. Detective Crider replied that Angel Ray had told H.D. that he had "rolled the log on top of Neveah," exactly how the log was positioned on top of her body when it was found.

Welton had only a few questions for the detective. He left the witness stand. The saga of H.D. Hudson ended.

The prosecution had nearly completed its case.

FIFTEEN: ARGUMENTS and INSTRUCTIONS

The pieces of the puzzle don't always fall into place neatly. Scheduling problems and tactical decisions often conspire to preclude a nice chronological delivery of the prosecution's case. So it was with their final witness, a woman named Dawn Bienek, called to the stand to further supplement the story of Jesus Perez. In a perfect world she might have appeared before Dr. Case and H.D. Hudson, closer to the testimony she was there to support.

Either way, Bienek's role as a witness sparked some of the longest and most intense side bar conferences that punctuated the proceedings. The first one consumed 16 pages of transcript and laid the groundwork for the last ditch efforts by Holly Lucas to secure a mistrial—for the second time—for Angel Ray.

The problem was easy to state but hard to solve. Bienek was the probation officer assigned to Angel Ray in connection with his guilty plea to misdemeanor child abuse. She had interviewed him more than once and prepared his presentence report. He had made statements, indeed admissions, to her that were admissible under exceptions to the hearsay rule. The prosecutors wanted to get those admissions before the jury.

At the same time, the defense wanted to keep Bienek off the stand altogether, or minimize her testimony, because obviously she could be damaging to Angel Ray's case. More importantly, Lucas argued, she could not adequately cross-exam Bienek because she could not get into the context of the interviews, or the accuracy of her memory, or even the contents of her report without divulging Angel Ray's misdemeanor conviction and his probation, both of which were clearly inadmissible.

"I cannot," insisted Lucas, "fully execute his right to cross-examination, and at the same time protect him from having his prior conviction" come in. In fact, the whole exercise would be misleading to the jury. It would "open a whole lot of doors" and lead to "improper inference."

Washburn disagreed. She had worked on many cases where parole or probation officers were allowed to testify and the issue was simply sanitized by saying they worked for the state or city. Moreover, she argued, "the information that Ms. Bienek has is highly relevant to this case. Especially given the inferences and implications that have been made by the defense, first of all, that Jesus was somehow coached into making this report. And secondly, that perhaps Ms. Martinez is the one who caused those injuries to Jesus. The defendant makes very specific statements about how injuries would have been caused by him to Jesus. He denies choking or strangling Jesus but he admits to grabbing him around the neck, slapping him on the shoulders, slapping him on the butt, slapping him on the back of his head … There have been plenty of land mines that we've all had to dance around in this case. Plenty of things that both the defense and the People aren't able to question witnesses about that are the truth about what went on that the jury can't hear."

Lucas dug in. Allowing the testimony would "undo what has been fairly effectively done so far in terms of protecting one's right to remain silent."

Amico joined the fray. She argued the issue had already been fully litigated in 2011, when the defense moved to suppress and the court denied the motion, so it was law of the case.

Judge Rappaport sided with the prosecutors. For the record she stated: "I think the relevancy and probative value outweighs the prejudice at this point, given the fact that both Mother and the child were subject to cross-examination and were cross-examined in those areas. In addition, I agree with the prosecution: I've seen many cases where they have a parole or probation officer, and it has to be sanitized."

So Bienek took the stand on Tuesday, May 1, after the noon recess that followed the testimony of H.D. Hudson and Detective Crider. Without eliciting any background, Washburn asked if Bienek had spoken with Angel Ray on October 12, 2005.

"Yes, I did," said Bienek. She identified him as "seated to my left, and he's wearing glasses and a tan shirt."

Washburn asked a series of questions that prompted a series of objections by Lucas. Questions were phrased and rephrased. Still the story came out. Angel Ray had told Bienek that Jesus was grouchy when he woke up. He was uncooperative and wouldn't eat his Lucky Charms. He threw a tantrum. Angel Ray threatened to spank him and did in fact spank him on the butt, shoulders, back, and head—five or six times.

Lucas called for a side bar and reiterated her objections. She argued the questions made it sound like Bienek had interrogated Angel Ray, which would lead to those improper inferences. Judge Rappaport told Washburn to lead the witness so her testimony wouldn't go astray. Washburn tried again and there were more objections, until finally she asked: "Did the defendant ever tell you that he strangled Jesus?"

Bienek answered, "No, he denied it."

Lucas demanded another side bar and moved for a mistrial. The denial part of the answer crossed the line, she said. It again suggested there was some sort of interrogation. "This is highly prejudicial because, again, I can't really confront this woman … without letting the cat out of the bag that this woman is interrogating Mr. Montoya because she's his probation officer."

Judge Rappaport agreed with Washburn that "it doesn't rise to the level of mistrial." She struck the last answer, however.

Back in open court, and a few more questions confirmed Angel Ray had told Bienek that he did not strangle Jesus or tie him up. He did admit, however, that he grabbed Jesus around the neck. Washburn asked the witness, "Did he do anything to demonstrate that? You kind of did something with your hands, so I wanted to be clear. Did he do anything to demonstrate where he grabbed Jesus around the neck?"

"Yes," said Bienek.

"Can you show the jury?"

"Yes. He said he did this." Bienek showed the jury how Angel Ray had shown her. "And shoved him. Grabbed him around the neck and shoved him."

"And was it the front of the neck, the back of the neck or somewhere else?"

"My understanding is the front."

With no further questions, Washburn gave the witness to Lucas for cross-examination. Lucas asked the judge to strike the first part of the last answer, and the judge agreed, though further questions only drove home that it was the front of the neck and not the back. Next Lucas tried to ask questions that would challenge Bienek's memory but she had a hard time being specific since she could not ask openly about the context of the conversations with Angel Ray or about Bienek's report.

Frustrated, Lucas again called for a side bar. She said, "Judge, I'm going to ask you to strike – this is exactly what I was talking about. There is no way I can't fall through some trap door. All I'm trying to do is show to this jury that her memory can't be relied on. And I can't really do that now." She took yet another stab at striking the witness and declaring a mistrial.

Judge Rappaport again refused: "I'm not going to declare a mistrial or strike the witness, but we need to make sure that when the question is asked, it's based on that conversation of what she remembers … We can maybe clarify with her. Okay."

The jury was sent to its room while the judge and lawyers instructed Bienek to avoid certain words, like "report" and "denial," that would suggest questioning or interrogation. If she got confused, she should say, "I don't know how to answer."

The jury returned. Judge Rappaport had neglected to give them the limiting instruction she should have given prior to Bienek's testimony, so she gave it to them at that time. Soon cross-examination was over. On re-direct Washburn asked a few questions to emphasize it was the front of the neck Angel Ray had grabbed, and on re-cross Lucas asked a number of questions to demonstrate Bienek "didn't document anywhere whether it was [the] front or the back."

Then another bench conference. More insistence by Lucas: "It doesn't matter which way I go, there is a trap waiting for me. I cannot successfully execute cross-examination on Mr. Montoya's behalf." There ensued more haggling over the use of words like "report" and "document" and "memorialization."

Finally re-cross ended. Amico stood and said, "On behalf of the People of the State of Colorado, the prosecution rests."

It was the last time she would speak those words. In her next trial she would appear as a judge in Arapahoe County.

Drums didn't roll. There was no drama, no flurry of activity.

The case against Angel Ray had been stated. It had taken nearly three weeks for Amico and Washburn to fully assemble the puzzle, but now all the pieces were in place.

For the jury, it had been grueling to sit through all the witnesses and exhibits, the tears and tragedies, the gruesome details and endless objections. Few were the moments of levity like those supplied by H.D. Hudson.

Still there was that morning when Amico and Washburn showed up in court wearing identical suits and blouses. The jury wondered what was up. In truth nothing was up. The two women had simply been so immersed in the trial that their wardrobes were depleted, so each on her own had rushed out to Target to quickly score something for the next day, and purely by chance they had selected the same outfits. No mystery.

Judge Rappaport didn't wait a beat. She called for a side bar to ask if Lucas wanted "to make any record at this point."

Lucas moved for acquittal, a routine motion, and the judge denied it. She asked if the defense wanted her to give Angel Ray a full advisement, called a *Curtis* advisement," about his right to testify, at that time or at some later time. They decided on a later time, after he had a chance to hear the witnesses called on his behalf, but to ask him if that was okay with him.

In other words, Angel Ray would not have to decide if he would take the stand until later in the proceedings. Asked if that was indeed his preference, he said, "Yes, your honor, it is."

It was one of the few things he actually said on the record.

* * *

The defense of Angel Ray was brief. It lasted roughly three days compared to the three weeks the prosecution had taken. And it was mostly designed to sow the seeds of reasonable doubt in the minds of the jury.

To that end the defense suggested all sorts of ways Neveah could have died other than at the hands of Angel Ray. She could have had a disease or infection. She could have died from some sort of genetic disorder, something they would never know since no one—including Miriam—knew who her father was and since only the most basic DNA testing had been done.

The defense called its own medical expert to speculate over all these ways Neveah might have died. One observer later dismissed this expert's testimony, commenting the "expert" sounded more like a "quack."

Throughout Angel Ray sat motionless, quiet, stone-faced, sometimes wearing his black glasses, sometimes not. After the handful of witnesses who testified on his behalf were finished, he had to decide if he would take the stand in his own defense. At this point the *Curtis* advisement became mandatory.

Since 1984 the Colorado Supreme Court had required the criminal courts of the state to perform a ritual whenever the defendant sought to waive his right to testify. The trial court judge must seek to assure that the waiver is "voluntary, knowing and intentional by advising the defendant outside the presence of the jury that he has a right to testify" and if he wants to do so, then no one—even his counsel—can stop him. Also, he should be told if he does testify, the prosecution will be allowed to cross-examine him, and if he has been convicted of a felony, then the "prosecutor will be entitled to ask him about it and thereby disclose it to the jury." Furthermore, if the felony conviction is disclosed to the jury, then it can be "instructed to consider it only as it bears upon his credibility."

The ritual also required the trial court judge to advise the defendant that "he has a right not to testify," and if he chooses not to testify, then the jury will be instructed that it cannot use his refusal to testify against him.

Judge Rappaport performed the ritual and delivered the *Curtis* advisement. There were no surprises when the time came for Angel Ray's decision. He did not take the stand.

He remained at the defense table, mute.

* * *

Closing arguments consumed four hours on the afternoon of Thursday, May 3. By then everyone was exhausted. Still Amico delivered a passionate repeat of "the hands" and she and Washburn used their arguments to connect the dots for the jury, tying up loose ends, filling in whatever blanks remained.

Lucas did her best to water those seeds of doubt she had tried to plant. She argued Angel Ray was innocent: there were no eye-witnesses to the crimes and witnesses like Miriam and H.D. Hudson lacked credibility. She speculated on all the other possible causes of death. She brought out the life-sized plastic doll and made it throw a tantrum. She even drew gasps from the audience when she suggested Neveah had been laid to rest near peaceful running waters—though everyone knew she had been dumped near a drainage ditch under a log, a tire, and a stone.

These arguments were the last chance for the lawyers to appeal to the jury. And they were the first chance for the family and the witnesses to sit together in open court and hear the whole story. Many were the tears they shed.

The lawyer from the parking lot sat in the second row, fascinated to hear all the things she had not been allowed to hear before. Something about the case had spoken to her and she had followed it as best she could. She felt invested in its outcome.

Andrea Martinez, the mother of Jesus, and her mother sat with Janet, Vera and Cathy. Vera later recalled how much kindness they showed: "The mother just embraced us and told us how sorry she was. And she said she hadn't lived in peace since she got the news about Neveah. And she said, 'Please have some compassion for Miriam 'cause everybody makes mistakes.' And she said, 'I made—the biggest mistake of my life was Ray. Angel Ray Montoya was my biggest mistake.'"

* * *

Judge Rappaport's instructions to the jury came next.

Jury instructions often start with prescribed forms, selected, shuffled, and modified to suit the particulars of the case at hand. Often the prosecutors and defense team offer variations on the forms to the court, slanting the wording this away or that, and often the arguments over these variations cause sparks to fly.

All criminal cases, however, come with typical instructions concerning the presumption of innocence, the burden of proof, the standard of proof, the credibility of witnesses, and the right to remain silent. These go something like this: the law does not require the defendant to prove his innocence. Every defendant is presumed to be innocent unless proven guilty.

The prosecution has the burden of proving each and every element of the crime that is charged beyond a reasonable doubt. It is not enough to show some element is more likely than not; the proof must be more powerful than that. The law does not require absolute certainty, however. Reasonable doubt is based on thoughtful consideration and common sense. Proof beyond a reasonable doubt leaves you firmly convinced.

In deciding if the prosecution has proven all of the elements of the crime, a fair and rational consideration of the evidence or lack of evidence is required. For each witness, credibility is a legitimate issue. Consider his or her knowledge, state of mind, motive, demeanor, and manner while testifying, as well as his or her relationship to the parties and whether his or her testimony is supported or contradicted by other evidence.

And—very important—every defendant has an absolute constitutional right to remain silent. That means he has an absolute right to not testify. You should not consider, for any reason whatsoever, that the defendant did not testify in this case. This should not influence your decision in any way.

After delivering instructions covering these general subjects, Judge Rappaport turned to the substance of the crimes charged. Here the elements of the crimes, as defined by Colorado's General Assembly, reign supreme. They both enable and limit the prosecutors and judges in bringing criminals to justice.

The most important charges against Angel Ray were first degree murder and child abuse resulting in death. Under section 18-3-102 (1) (f) of the state's Criminal Code, a person "commits the crime of murder in the first degree"—a class 1 felony—if the "person knowingly causes the death of a child who has not yet attained twelve years of age and the person committing the offense is one in a position of trust with respect to the victim."

Under section 18-6-401 (1) (a) and (7) (a) (I):

(1) (a) A person commits child abuse if such person causes an injury to a child's life or health, or permits a child to be unreasonably placed in a situation that poses a threat of injury to the child's life or health, or engages in a continued pattern of conduct that results in malnourishment, lack of proper medical care, cruel punishment, mistreatment, or an accumulation of injuries that ultimately results in the death of a child or serious bodily injury to a child.

(7) (a) (I) When a person acts knowingly or recklessly and the child abuse results in death to the child, it is a class 2 felony except as provided in paragraph (c) of this subsection.

So far, so good. Those were the two crimes charged in the Indictment against Angel Ray. However, subsection (7) (c) of section 18-6-401 also says:

(7) (c) When a person knowingly causes the death of a child who has not yet attained twelve years of age and the person committing the offense is one in a position of trust with respect to the child, such person commits the crime of murder in the first degree as described in section 18-3-102 (1) (f).

Ironically, if the General Assembly meant to avoid confusion with its cross-reference to section 18-3-102 (1) (f), it might well have caused exactly the opposite effect. Were these two separate crimes or really just one? Was the second crime, much like manslaughter, a "lesser included offense" of the first? Were the elements of the two crimes so similar that in essence they "merged" into a single offense?

These questions were not mere abstractions. They proved to be more difficult than the General Assembly likely intended. And they triggered important consequences, both legal and practical in nature.

The jury, after receiving their instructions from the judge, retired to deliberate on Friday, May 4.

SIXTEEN: TWELVE TROUBLED WOMEN

Angela Kana, Sam Hudson, Ashley Perez, Kristy Skinner and eight other women sat with their notebooks in the jury room. Until late that afternoon, they would discuss the lawyers and the witnesses and they would take straw votes on the charges against Angel Ray.

They started with Amico. Some jurors thought she and Washburn had overacted at times, but most felt they were simply demonstrating their "emotional investment" in the case. No one doubted their skill or depth of experience.

Sam later said Amico's performance was "phenomenal," adding "it definitely hit a nerve for me." Angela remarked how "thorough" she was, and Ashley recalled Amico was always prepared and organized, every day, day after day, yet showed great compassion throughout the trial. Kristy agreed, saying the veteran prosecutor did "an amazing job."

Washburn also scored highly. For some jurors, she was the one who connected the dots and filled in several of the blanks. Oh, so all that stuff about sunflower seeds and DNA was meant to show Angel Ray had eaten the seeds before he killed Neveah, then he had vomited them after he killed her, and some of the vomit had gotten on the gym shorts he was wearing at the time, which he had carelessly left in the apartment on Logan Street. Indeed, it turned out the "bodily fluid" found on the tissue recovered in the apartment also belonged to Angel Ray.

Lucas and Welton did not score as highly. Many jurors felt frustration over what they thought were too many objections. Some said Welton appeared to be inexperienced and easily confused. But most of their memories centered on Holly Lucas. Some of the jurors "hated her," though most took a more nuanced stance. Sam thought she did a "phenomenal job" with what she had to work with. Sure, she was abrasive sometimes, but that was just her job.

Angela was even more vocal in her defense of the defender. She felt Lucas was "really good" and remarked how important it was to separate emotions from the trial. Here was the engineer looking at it logically. True, some "hated" Lucas and her facial expressions and her body language, but frankly Angela was bothered by that. She believed the jurors should "put that petty stuff aside as women." If a man had acted the same way, they might think he was a "dick" but they wouldn't hold it against him or his client. This trial wasn't about feelings.

Ashley agreed Lucas was "very good at what she does," but she "did not like her in this case." Afterwards she did a bit of research on Lucas and learned she was well regarded, though in the case of Angel Ray—the only time Ashley would see Lucas perform in person—she felt the public defender was unduly rude and not "very professional."

Kristy blended it all together, concluding Lucas "also did a really good job [but] I kind of hated her." Still the jurors agreed their feelings about the lawyers—any of them—should not influence their decisions. Personal quirks were not evidence.

So they turned to the witnesses and exhibits. Of all the women in the case, Miriam drew the most negative reactions. Kristy said she was obviously a "horrible mother." At first there may have been some sympathy for her, but as the case went on she could see "how deceitful she was." In fact, most viewed Miriam's testimony as necessary—the prosecution had to put her on and have her tell her story—but not sufficient.

Detective Crider, by contrast, garnered universal praise. The jurors found him credible, reliable and professional even though he had showed great emotion while testifying. Indeed, he had been called to the stand on several occasions to tie together loose ends and connect the dots by corroborating the testimony of other witnesses. For Angela, he was one of the most important witnesses, the "glue" that held together the testimony of others. And "he was there for that little girl."

Jesus Perez captured the hearts of the jurors. Angela said, "He was just a kid." She recalled how he had walked into the courtroom with his eyes averted from Angel Ray. And how, while on the stand, he would steal glances at the defendant but then he would quickly turn away. Like Detective Crider said, the kid was still plainly afraid of the Angel of Death.

Sam thought Jesus was simply "fantastic … a handsome little fellow, dressed nice for his court appearance." She agreed he appeared to be honest. It did not seem he had been coached. Ashley said she "loved him" and could not imagine how hard it must have been for him to appear. And Kristy went further, remarking it was "really brave of him" to take the stand and "that whole part of the trial was really … one of the things that made me start thinking."

What struck the jury as so persuasive about the testimony of Jesus was precisely what the defense had tried to attack. He was very clear and open about what he did and did not remember. When he did remember something—Angel Ray had choked him —he was adamant about it. The jurors believed him.

Dr. Mary Case stirred controversy. Angela recalled some of the jurors thought she was arrogant but "I liked her." She was simply being confident in her conclusions. Again the engineer saw things in a logical light. She viewed Dr. Case as both an academic from the world of dissertations and as an experienced and "very classy professional." What Angela remembered most about the testimony of Dr. Case was when she raised her voice, insisting she didn't know who killed Neveah—but she knew someone had killed her.

Sam thought Dr. Case "was phenomenal—very on point." In contrast, like other observers, she thought the expert for the defense was "pathetic." Ashley simply declared that Dr. Case "won the case for me." She really knew her stuff and stood her ground even when Lucas "tried to nail her to the wall … and she wasn't having it, either. She was very sure of herself."

Kristy echoed her friends. Dr. Case was an expert with impressive credentials. She was not being arrogant. "I didn't feel that way at all," said Kristy. "I think that women who are very intelligent get called arrogant or bitchy or whatever." Indeed, "I think what made the decision for me was her."

The fashionista was less kind to H.D. Hudson. She called him a "degenerate" and a "horrible person," but also said she believed him. He had nothing to gain by testifying, having already blown his deal with the prosecutors. And he had taken such careful notes about details he could not have made up.

Ashley, by contrast, "liked him a lot. I think he had some good character. He wasn't afraid to stand up to Holly Lucas, either. She really tried to nail him to the wall [as well] and he wasn't having it. He was great."

Sam simply laughed and said, "That kid should do standup, seriously." H.D. had "damning evidence" against Angel Ray and he "handled it like a champ." He was a car thief, not a child abuser, and Sam believed what he said.

Angela perhaps had the most complete view of the snitch. She said she could understand "both sides" of his story. She did not believe he was lying. He had been very open about his past. His notes and details were compelling. He reminded her of her abusive twin, who had gone to prison, and some of his friends. And he knew "the justice system is small." He could end up in the same facility as Angel Ray someday. He was taking a real risk but it was because he truly "felt for this little girl."

Her familiarity with the system also helped Angela solve the mystery of Dawn Bienek. As Lucas had predicted, the jury was not sure what to make of her. All of the other witnesses had been questioned about their background. Not Bienek. How, then, did she know all these damning things about Angel Ray? Eventually Angela put two and two together. Bienek had to be Angel Ray's probation officer—or maybe his parole officer.

And what about the defendant?

Angela called him a "rock" who showed emotion rarely, tearing up only once or twice over the photos of Neveah's body and her recovery, and laughing once near the end of the trial. Ashley agreed he showed "no emotion at all." She would look at him and he wouldn't cry or wince or move even a little. She never saw his tears though she did recall he "giggled" once. Sam said she was "dumbfounded" by Angel Ray's demeanor. He remained stone-faced even when his verdict was read.

Kristy tried to keep an open mind at first, thinking if he didn't kill Neveah, how awful it must be for him. But as the trial progressed, she kept looking at him. Sometimes she would "stare at him in court." He sat stoically, motionless. He never showed regret. He offered no apologies. Near the end Kristy felt it was "sickening" and "frustrating."

Yet every juror insisted it would have made no difference had Angel Ray taken the stand. "I don't think," said Ashley, "his story would have changed my mind." In addition, the judge had instructed them that they could not hold his failure to testify against him, and they took her instructions seriously.

Friday dragged on. The jury took straw votes on each of the charges to get the easy ones out of the way. Abuse of a corpse was the easiest. All agreed Angel Ray was guilty. Child abuse resulting in death was a little harder. Some jurors were confused and wondered if they said yes to that charge, did it mean they had to say yes to the murder charge as well? The other jurors showed them their booklet of instructions was "very clear" on that point and soon they all agreed. Angel Ray was also guilty of child abuse resulting in death.

Murder was all that was left. The jurors could not agree on that charge and wanted to think about it over the weekend. Victim advocate Cindy Torres sent an e-mail blast at 4:04 p.m. to family, friends and witnesses, saying the jury had gone home. "It was very split," said Ashley, "when we left on that Friday."

Some jurors didn't need to think any more about it.

Kristy was one of them. She later said: "It was obvious to all of us at the end of the trial that he was guilty ... and knowingly guilty." Though if that were true, there would have been no deadlock on Friday afternoon.

"It was nice," said Ashley, "because we had the whole weekend to think about it," even though she, too, had made up her mind at the end of the trial. Angel Ray had to be guilty of something. The defense had tried to make it sound as if he had nothing at all to do with Neveah's death. But it was "obvious he had something to do with it." It was not plausible he didn't. There was just too much evidence. It might have been harder if the defense had "acknowledged something."

Still some jurors worried—Sam said she was "very nervous" —that others would back-slide over the weekend. Their worries were well-founded. Monday morning came and "some people," according to Angela, "were starting to renege on their votes for the first two charges."

So the jurors went around the table and one-by-one explained how they got to their votes on each of the charges. Angela said some were "quite emotional" and interrupted often. There was a lot of back-and-forth. The jury's mood was grave. One woman had a photo of her daughter taped to her binder to remind her of the solemnity of her decision.

Ashley later described her own thought process. She had "battled a little" with the murder charge toward the end of Friday because the wording of the statute was a bit confusing to her. Was the crime Angel Ray had committed really murder in the first degree or was it manslaughter, which—unlike child abuse resulting in death—was a true "lesser included offense?" In the end she decided it had to be first degree murder because that was "the only thing that acknowledged she [Neveah] was a child."

At least two of the other jurors were still struggling. The jury foreperson, Dr. Karen Gieseker, took to the dry erase board. She wrote down the elements of the crimes and the definitions of "knowingly" and "recklessly" under Colorado's Criminal Code.

Section 18-1-501(6) said a "person acts 'knowingly' ... with respect to a result of his conduct, when he is aware that his conduct is practically certain to cause the result."

And subsection (8) said a "person acts 'recklessly' when he consciously disregards a substantial and unjustifiable risk that a result will occur or that a circumstance exists."

Dr. Gieseker guided the jurors through a comparison of the elements of the crimes and their mental states. All agreed this comparison was very useful. It clarified the decisions of most.

Ashley later described it this way: "I'd go home and look at my kids and my kids maybe had one or two bruises on them. She [Neveah] had so many. There was no doubt he had done something that caused her to die." For Ashley, the severity of the injuries led her to conclude the intent element of murder was clearly satisfied.

Still that remained the hardest part for some of the jurors.

"People didn't think," Ashley also recalled, "that he was smart enough to know that applying pressure to her neck would kill her. And it was like—he's not stupid by any means. He knew that what he was doing could possibly result in her death. She was a three-year-old."

Kristy again echoed similar sentiments. She said, "I thought some people were just kind of naïve. At the end, when it came down to, you know, whether it was reckless or knowingly, I wanted to beat it into their head. You cannot strangle a three-year-old and not know it could kill her."

Sam agreed the biggest challenge for the jury was the mental element of the murder charge. Several jurors kept saying they didn't think Angel Ray actually meant to kill Neveah. He did not have that specific intent.

One woman confided she had been physically abused, sexually abused and raped. She stated in her experience, when she was being choked, the intent of the man choking her was to put fear into her, not kill her. She had difficulty separating her own experiences from the facts of the case.

The other jurors responded by focusing on the wording of the statutes and their instructions. They insisted a specific intent to kill was not needed. Angel Ray only had to know his actions could kill a child. The hold-out said, "Well, convince me."

And the others said that was exactly what they were doing. They were not asking her to "just go with the flow." Instead, they were, in Sam's words, "just spreading it all out and showing [her] the facts."

Eventually the hold-out agreed. The mental element of acting "knowingly" had been satisfied. Still one more hurdle awaited and the jury was determined to surmount it. They signaled they were going to skip their break and work through the lunch hour if necessary.

The final hurdle involved another hold-out, though in some versions of the tale, she is the same woman who had confided she had been raped and abused. The reality here is less interesting than the vagaries of human memory. And whether it was two jurors or only one hardly matters.

It was the hurdle that mattered. This juror said she could not vote to convict because she could not live with her own feelings of guilt for putting a man away for life.

Angela said all of the others "felt bad" for this juror. They were confident of their votes by then, but that didn't mean they had not struggled in making their own decisions. A man's life was at stake. There were tensions, frustrations, and what-ifs.

Angela finally said to the hold-out: "Well, Neveah is no longer here for the remainder of her life, my life, his life, her mother's life, her grandmother's life ... Where does your reasoning end?"

Others argued—correctly—it was not the province of the jury to worry about the sentence. What they were now discussing was not the evidence they had seen and heard, and what it showed, but the juror's feelings.

The hold-out finally came around and when she did, according to Angela: "She cried her eyes off." By then, in fact, "we all were crying. It was not an easy decision to make."

At 10:08 a.m. Cindy Torres sent another large e-mail blast that said, "Good Morning Folks. We have just been notified we have a verdict. We are on our way up to take it."

Several jurors, including Angela, cried again as the verdicts were read: Guilty of murder in the first degree, guilty of child abuse resulting in death, guilty of abuse of a corpse.

At the time Angela felt "an overwhelming sense of relief and sadness … I just felt sad for all the parties."

Afterwards Judge Rappaport met briefly with the jurors. They asked her many questions. She told them about Angel Ray's history as a sex offender. They learned about the incident in July of 2006 when Neveah was taken to the hospital, bleeding from her vagina. They also learned that Dawn Bienek was indeed Angel Ray's probation officer.

Judge Rappaport would not, however, tell the jurors anything about the discovery of Neveah's body or the deal that Angel Ray had made with the prosecutors. That remained subject to the gag order. So, too, when several jurors saw Detective Crider outside the courthouse, and they talked to him, he refused to answer questions about the *something* that led the police to Lakewood Gulch on that Monday after the murder.

Still the jurors—especially those who had held out the longest—felt a tremendous sense of relief. Sam later said they all felt "a world better" after talking to the judge and "validated" that they had done the right thing.

Kristy agreed they were all "so relieved" to learn what they had learned: "Thank God we made that decision."

* * *

The *Denver Post* reported Janet's statement to the media outside the courtroom: "We got justice. It has been a long time coming, but we got justice for this baby."

Vera added: "We are happy it's over now. My little girl can rest in peace now."

* * *

The lawyer from the parking received an e-mail blast sent by Cindy Torres at 11:06: Angel Ray had been found guilty on all three counts. She also received an invitation to join the prosecution team at the Cap City Tavern.

At 12th and Bannock in the Golden Triangle, only two blocks from the parking lot at 1080 Cherokee and two from police headquarters, Cap City occupies a brick structure built in 1892. It's a hangout for the cops and prosecutors who work nearby.

At roughly 1:30 that afternoon, the lawyer from the parking lot sat at a dark wood table with Amico, Washburn, Torres and Detective Crider. She had not met the detective before, but as a lawyer she had forged a relationship with the prosecutors unlike those of the other witnesses.

There were hugs, tears, and words of congratulations.

The lawyer from the parking asked one simple question: was this case something special to them or did it just feel that way to her because she had never been involved in anything like it before?

Each of the others answered without hesitation: this case—the case of Neveah Gallegos and the Angel of Death—was one of the most profound and intense of their careers.

It was indeed something very special.

SEVENTEEN: SENTENCING and APPEAL

Judge Sheila Rappaport sat in her black robes behind the bench in Courtroom 5A. Her hair was copper-colored and her countenance was stern. She controlled, indeed dominated, everything that happened inside her tidy domain, with its light blue paint over light wood wainscoting.

It was shortly after 1:30 p.m. on Tuesday, May 15, and she had presided over weeks of trial in the case against Angel Ray. She had heard it all and then some.

A no-nonsense judge known for her courteous courtroom demeanor, Judge Rappaport could see the right side of the courtroom—or the left, if facing the bench—was filled with family and friends of Neveah as well as four of the jurors and the lawyer from the parking lot. A reporter or two sat on the opposite side, taking notes.

Angel Ray appeared trim in a gray V-neck prison jumpsuit, not the button-down shirt and khakis he wore during the trial. He was shackled and seemed nervous for the first time.

Mitch Morrissey and Detective Crider were out there in the audience as well. Judge Rappaport realized it was an important case for them. Three sheriffs, two white, one black, two with shaved heads, hovered at the edges of the left side of the courtroom, behind the defendant.

Michelle Amico wore a gray suit and looked very slender, her brown hair streaked, her features sharp. She argued for the maximum possible sentences. The presentence report had been waived so she supplied details the jury never heard. Angel Ray had six prior juvenile offenses, five for indecent exposure. He had spent time in county jail due to the revocation of his probation and failure to register as a sex offender. In the case of Jesus Perez, he had pled guilty to abuse and been sentenced once again to probation, but he had spent 270 days in jail when it was revoked for his failure to comply with its conditions.

There were more failures to register and more convictions.

Amico also—in the words of an e-mail blast sent the next day by victim advocate Cindy Torres—"gave one of the most wonderful impact statements I have ever been a party to. She talked at great length about the impact Nevaeh's [sp] death has had on the Family, The Witnesses, Jurors, and the Community as a whole. It was truly amazing."

Holly Lucas objected to having to hear from more than one of the family members, but Judge Rappaport swept that aside. These people needed to be heard. They had played by the rules throughout the proceedings—indeed, over the years—and they deserved their day in court. What's more, they had to be given a proper vehicle for the display of their emotions.

At least once already, Judge Rappaport had come down from her bench, during the verdict-and-sentencing process, to speak personally to those members of the family who were openly weeping and sobbing. She told them gently but firmly they must stop that kind of display. So now it was their turn.

Janet and Vera spoke with great emotion. They hoped this sort of thing never happened to any other child.

Next Holly Lucas took to the podium and—first thing out of her mouth—announced the defendant intended to appeal. He had always maintained his innocence. He would not be making a statement and she might well, she indicated, have more to say if there were no appeal.

Angel Ray listened, stone-faced, as Lucas told the judge that his pain was as great as that of anyone else. He was an innocent man with many supporters. The system had failed him. In his long history of crime he had never been convicted of sexually touching anyone inappropriately. And his sex offenses all occurred when he was a juvenile.

The law should prevail in this case, not the emotions.

Furthermore, Lucas argued, the charges of murder in the first degree and child abuse resulting in death should be merged.

Some legal wrangling ensued over the merger of those two charges. Arguments were stated for the record.

Then it was Angel Ray's turn. Asked if he wished to make a statement, he said simply, "No, your honor."

Finally Judge Rappaport spoke. This was an emotional case. The evidence was difficult to take. Here was a man who had encouraged two kids to call him daddy, then choked them and killed one of them. She sentenced Angel Ray to life in prison with no possibility of parole for the murder of Neveah.

Then she gave him 48 years for child abuse resulting in death, twice the presumptive sentence, which she doubled due to aggravating circumstances. Angel Ray had a long prior record and a history of dangerous conduct. He showed disrespect for the law and the court's orders.

Then she gave him 12 months for abuse of a corpse.

The sentences would run consecutively, not concurrently.

And there was no legal merger of the two felonies because the elements of the two crimes were sufficiently distinct.

Anyone with well-trained ears could tell Judge Rappaport was making her record for the appeal. She did not add any emotional or elaborate statements about the defendant and his heinous crimes, no lofty rhetoric, no judicial rant. It was all by the book, almost anti-climactic.

Outside the courtroom Janet once again told the media she was glad the trial was over and Neveah had gotten justice.

In the basement of the courthouse, in the prosecutors' Spartan waiting room, a group gathered to share their feelings: Vera, Janet, and other friends and family; the four jurors, including Angela Kana and Dr. Karen Gieseker; the lawyer from the parking lot; Detective Crider; Cindy Torres; Michelle Amico and Christine Washburn.

The waiting room was next to the prosecutor's war room and their Montoya Count-Down was still on the dry erase board, their tally left at 21, the smiley face drawn by Jesus to the right.

District Attorney Mitch Morrissey addressed the group. His mere presence was enough to affirm for them the importance of their case to his office.

Dr. Gieseker read a poem she had written, something none of the prosecutors had ever seen or heard before. It began:

I close my eyes and see your sweet face
I hold out my hand for you
I am so sorry, little one, for all that you endured

And fifteen heart-wrenching lines later, it asked:

Has justice been served, oh little one, has justice been served?

* * *

Angel Ray's lawyers made good on their warning. A formal Notice of Appeal was filed on his behalf on June 25, 2012. From trial defenders Holly Lucas and Sarah Welton the torch had passed to the Colorado State Public Defender's office and to its Chief Appellate Deputy, Karen Taylor. They would be the ones who would scour the massive record in search of errors they could hang their appeal on.

Their Notice of Appeal is short and sweet. The issues to be raised will include "[a]ll issues preserved by objection at trial, sufficiency of the evidence; sentencing; and, any other issues Appellant chooses to raise as plain error." The Designation of Record is equally broad: all pleadings, motions, judgments, and orders; all transcripts from all hearings on all pretrial motions held in 2009, 2010, 2011, and 2012; all transcripts from all three trials—the aborted first trial, the mistrial, and the last trial in 2012; transcripts from voir dire and jury questionnaires; copies of the notebooks provided to the jurors; all exhibits; and the transcript from the sentencing hearing held on May 15.

After many extensions of time granted by the court due to the sheer volume of the nearly five years of records, including the many exhibits, the record was finally "lodged" in the state court of appeals in late May of 2013. The court granted a substantial extension of time for the filing of the opening brief—the brief on behalf of Angel Ray—until late November of 2013. Even if the answer brief from the state and the reply brief from the defense are filed in accordance with the usual rules without further extensions, which is highly unlikely, oral arguments if any would likely not be held for another six months and the court's decision could easily take another six months.

So the quest for justice isn't really over. It will last at least until the middle of 2014. Then theoretically the case could go to the Colorado Supreme Court for further review. And if material issues under the Federal Constitution are raised—like the right to effective cross-examination of certain witnesses or the admission of certain evidence gathered during the police search of the apartment on Logan Street—then again theoretically the case could go to the U.S. Supreme Court.

Throughout these proceedings, the issues to be considered may include issues of fact, the jury's determination of which is seldom reversed on appeal; issues of law, the judge's determination of which is the most fertile grounds for appeal; and so-called mixed questions of law and fact, which really involve the application of the law to the facts.

There is no jury on appeal. Appellate courts sit in panels of three judges or more. Also, the art of appellate advocacy is very different from the art of trial advocacy. So, just as the torch was passed from the trial lawyers to the appellate lawyers on the defense side, so, too, the torch was passed on the prosecutor's side from Michelle Amico and Christine Washburn to the appellate lawyers in the office of the State Attorney General.

In the meantime Angel Ray sits alone in prison. According to a source who is spending some time in the same facility as

Angel Ray, he is not enjoying his incarceration. He is being held in segregation—that destination dreaded so by H.D. Hudson. Allowed into the general population once for lunch, "they nearly got him." Meaning Angel Ray was assaulted and nearly killed.

Child killers, like snitches, do not fare well in prison.

Is it possible, by some stretch of the imagination, that he will be declared wholly innocent and set free by the appellate court? That is hard to imagine given the injuries Neveah suffered prior to her death and the strength of the other evidence against him. Is it possible, nevertheless, the appeals court will overturn his conviction and order yet another trial? Any lawyer will tell you, anything is possible when a case goes on appeal.

But to reverse Angel Ray's conviction, the appellate court must find not only errors made by the trial court, but errors that were both material and prejudicial. Errors that cut in his favor do not count, and neither do errors that are truly minor. As the pleadings, motions, and transcripts from his trial show, however, many were the motions and objections made on his behalf and many were the opportunities given to both Judges Robinson and Rappaport to make an erroneous decision on this particular exhibit or that errant statement.

To repeat: the quest for justice is not really over.

* * *

And what, after all, is justice? Entire college courses are taught on the subject. But ultimately what is justice in any given case—moral and ethical and social justice as well as legal justice—lies in hearts of each of the many individual human beings who are touched by its tragedies and its lessons.

Amico—now Judge Amico—after prevailing in her final case as a prosecutor, said this to the press: "A win would be if we could get the baby back to the family. And we can't."

EIGHTEEN: STOPPING the ABUSE

This book is not a work of journalism. It is not meant to be "fair and balanced," nor does it tell all sides of the story. It tells the story from the limited perspectives of a dozen of the most important participants. If Angel Ray, Miriam, their counsel, or anyone else ever wishes to write his or her side of the story, then he or she should.

This book, instead, is a work of advocacy. In telling the tale of one child's tragedy and the many people whose lives it touched, from the perspectives of those dozen participants who shared their narratives and feelings, it is meant to inspire change: meaningful, lasting change with the goal of stopping the abuse.

Change must occur at the administrative level of all state and local agencies and departments of health and human services, who have "failed to death" so many children while suffering from budget cuts, lack of staffing, lack of statewide coordination, and the other woes of the modern bureaucratic state.

Change must also occur at the legal level, in the courts and the legislatures that must bear the responsibility for many of the inadequacies of the administrative systems. They are the ones, after all, who set the ground rules and make the appropriations for the agencies to begin with.

In short, change must occur in all branches of government—legislative, judicial and executive—and all levels of government, local, state and Federal. Basic definitions of child abuse need to be changed to eliminate outmoded exceptions. The law must make clear the duty of a parent to protect his or her child. And the law must make it easier for state agencies to investigate suspected abuse, and to step in and stop it from continuing.

Nothing short of a fundamental rebalancing of the rights of the parents and the rights of their children is needed to stop the abuse and the killing. Parents and caregivers may have the right to discipline children, but not abuse and kill them.

On Tuesday, May 14, 2013, the State of Colorado took a step in the right direction when Gov. John Hickenlooper signed into law five bills designed to respond to these horrific statistics: over the preceding six years, 202 children had died in the State due to child abuse or neglect; 75 of these children had prior involvement in the child welfare system.

One of the new pieces of legislation established a statewide child abuse reporting hotline. Another expanded the pool of parties who must report suspected abuse to include emergency medical technicians and paramedics. A third enhanced the child fatality review process. Another allowed funds for child welfare services to be allocated more flexibly. And the fifth directly addressed the rights of the child in parental responsibility cases. It required judges in court cases to consider whether the child is emotionally, mentally, and physically safe in the care of a parent, and in custody cases it added the right of the child to reside in a home free from domestic violence and child abuse and neglect.

These improvements—especially the last one, which is the most substantive in nature—are important but not enough. Virtually all improvements to the system, in Colorado and across the nation, are threatened by budget cuts to social services. Often meaningful improvement is sabotaged by lack of adequate funding for implementation.

In July of 2013, Seth Stephens-Davidowitz, an economist with a Ph.D. from Harvard, wrote a deeply provocative piece in *The New York Times*. He challenged the official statistics that suggested child abuse had declined during the Great Recession. Using a "novel technique" for studying child maltreatment, he enlisted Google's "immensely powerful database." He found that searches from victims of child abuse rose when the recession began and rose again whenever unemployment claims rose. He took direct aim at budget cuts: "Budgets were slashed in hard-hit states, particularly on social programs directed at children." Overworked and stretched thin, "it is harder to report cases."

Dr. Stephens-Davidowitz provided four conclusions, starting with the harsh reality that child maltreatment is "yet another cost of the Great Recession, one that will be felt long after the economy fully recovers." Second, we should be skeptical of official statistics. These cases are badly under-reported and when reported often receive less attention than they deserve. Third, "Google search data can fill holes in our understanding of crime generally"—so get ready for Big Data in crime analysis.

Finally "and most important, the contrast between search data and the reported data tells a sad story about social services in this country. Just when more children are searching for help, we decimate the budgets of the very people who might actually do something to protect them."

True, even tragic, and yet: to keep our children safe, we cannot rely on the government in a nation of limited government. We must effect change at the community, the family, and the deepest of individual levels. The Denver police, prosecutors, and community united in bringing Angel Ray to justice for the killing of Neveah, but they did not stop the killing from happening. Criminal laws speak to events that have happened. They address the past. They do little to deter the caregiver who recklessly or maliciously causes the death of a child.

They did little to deter Angel Ray.

What did deter Angel Ray, after the death of Neveah, was the prospect of his own death. In fact, DA Mitch Morrissey, when he was interviewed for this book, commented this was a good case to cite in favor of having a death penalty. For it was the prospect of being tried for his life that motivated Angel Ray to trade the location of Neveah's body for a deal that Morrissey's office would not seek the death penalty. And to insure his fair trial in light of that damaging disclosure, Angel Ray's deal was made subject to a strict gag order that prevented the full story from being told to the jury. So much for Angel Ray.

Still others must undergo deep personal change.

Since 80% of child abuse is perpetrated by parents and a significant percentage after that by care-givers or significant others, the problem of child abuse and, indeed, child killing can only be solved by change in the hearts and the minds and especially the conduct of parents.

Miriam is serving her time for letting it all happen to Neveah and for what she did after it happened. She was the mother who saw the bruises appear on her daughter. She was the mother who witnessed the outward symptoms of the injury to her daughter's mesentery, the result of blunt force trauma. She was the mother who just stepped aside.

Too many are the parents—and too often they are mothers like Miriam—who just step aside and let it happen even though they know it is happening. They know.

They may rationalize it or they may deny it. They may try to talk themselves out of it. They may have low self-esteem and consciously decide to hold onto the "only man" who they think will ever love them.

But they know.

The state, the community, and the family must make it safe for those parents—those mothers—to transform their knowledge into action on behalf of their children. Facilities like the new Rose Andom Center in Denver, which provide services from many public and private agencies under one roof, are a necessary innovation to help in that transformation. They should become widespread and commonplace.

* * *

The coming generations of parents will ultimately bear the responsibility for stopping the abuse and the killing of their children—before it happens. They will be the ones on the front lines of the war against abuse. One of those gladly willing to fight for the cause is Cathy Gallegos.

The daughter of Janet, niece of Vera, sister of Miriam, and aunt of Neveah, Cathy was the third of Neveah's triumvirate. She took care of Neveah more than Miriam ever did, even when Miriam was living at home in the little house on Lipan Street.

Neveah bore a strong resemblance to Cathy, and they were seen together so often in public, that people would ask if Neveah was Cathy's daughter. "No," Cathy would say, "my niece."

Shaped more like Janet than Miriam—rounded but less heavyset—Cathy has deep dark eyes and wears simple glasses. Her long dark hair is usually pulled tight behind her head, and a thick gold chain from which hangs a heavy crucifix often appears outside her oversized T-shirts. She has graduated from high school and aspires to more education, but her mother's health has put those aspirations on hold.

Cathy was 22 at the time of Angel Ray's trial. The next spring found her still living with Janet and working hard at Public Storage to earn enough money to help keep Janet healthy. It's been a struggle. Janet's health has gone up and down ever since she lost Neveah.

Cathy of course regrets being the one who actually gave Neveah back to Miriam days before she was killed, but she later said she could not deny the child to her mother, even though Neveah had begged, "No mama, no mama."

On the morning of Friday, September 21, 2007, after leaving Neveah alone with Angel Ray for the last time, Miriam phoned Cathy from the Sportscastle. She asked Cathy to stop by her apartment on Logan Street later in the day, to check on Neveah because—in Miriam's words—Neveah had a "black eye," and she wanted Cathy to make sure Neveah was okay before returning her to Janet, so Janet wouldn't get mad.

Cathy knew something was wrong, but she never made it to the apartment house. Tragic events intervened. And, it's true, from hindsight Cathy believes Miriam had "prior knowledge" that something was terribly wrong.

Cathy later described the mood of the family during the trial of Angel Ray in 2012: "You could feel the tension, didn't matter what room you were in, you could tell—everyone had their own set of emotions, trying to hold it in. We really couldn't speak with each other regarding what was going on."

Did she actually mean to say they had all truly honored the instructions they had been given?

"Yes," Cathy insisted, "we did. We had literally stuck with [what] they told us—don't talk, you know, don't talk with Miriam, all this stuff. But you could tell, there was [a lot of] wanting to get the case over with, after so long, get justice for Neveah—that's what our main thing was, justice for Neveah."

Looking back at that difficult time, Cathy said, "It was a great year, that year. Angel was able to get what he had coming to him for what he did to my niece."

There finally came a measure of closure for Cathy, "kind of lifted off my shoulders, knowing she got justice. That's what sits in my heart all the time."

Still Cathy thinks about Neveah "all the time … it will always be there." She knows how important it is to stop the abuse and the killing before it happens, and she knows it is her generation—the next generation of parents—who will be on the front lines.

Cathy has this to say to those who wish to join with her: "That there are more resources out there. You just can't stop when you hear the first 'no.' You got to keep going, like my mother did, keep going until you find the right person that will finally listen to you. 'Cause there's always someone that will be willing to help. Don't be scared to impart anything."

Cathy is a quiet person. She likes to keep her head down. On this topic, however, she speaks loudly, with deep conviction: "No child deserves to live a life that they have to live like that."

NOTES and SOURCES

In keeping with the tradition set by the bible of true crime writing—*In Cold Blood* by Truman Capote—footnotes and end notes are not used in the narrative portions of this book. However, great pains were taken when quoting individuals to use only three types of sources: [1] transcripts of witness interviews conducted by investigators, memos about such interviews, official court records, and other official government documents; *or* [2] widely distributed media sources, in which case the specific news outlet and the date of publication or broadcast are almost always identified in the text; *or* [3] personal interviews conducted and recorded by the author. If you see a phrase like "He recalled," the quote likely came from such an interview.

In the expository portions of this book, which occur mostly in the first half, end notes are provided below. However, for the sake of brevity, if the source is adequately identified in the text, it is not repeated in the end notes. For example, if a Colorado statute is identified fully in the text, a more formal citation will not be repeated in the notes. Also, citations to matters of common knowledge or history—like the location of the meadow where Magna Carta was sealed—are omitted.

ONE: THE LAWYER in the PARKING LOT

Pages 14-16:

www.acf.hhs.gov/programs/cb/resource/child-maltreatment-2011

www.childlaw.us/2013/01/child-maltreatment-2011---the-.html

www.kempe.org/index.php?s=10394&item=3982

www.childhelp.org/

TWO: THE FAMILY and ANGEL RAY

Pages 28-31:

Colorado Department of Human Services, Child Fatality Review dated 4/15/08 *accessed at* www.9news.com/assetpool/documents /121111060035_fatality-gallegos.pdf

Pages 32-34:

V. Johnson & C. Hargrove, *The Tort Duty of Parents to Protect Minor Children*, 51 VILLANOVA L. REV. 311-34 (2006)

Colorado Revised Statutes, Title 19 (Children's Code), starting with the definitions set forth in CRS 19-1-103; and Title 26 (Human Services Code)

Colorado Revised Statutes, Title 18 (Criminal Code), especially the definition of "child abuse" set forth in CRS-18-6-401; and Title 16 (Criminal Proceedings Code)

People v. Rolon, 160 Cal. App. 4th 1206, 73 Cal. Rptr. 3rd 358 (Court of Appeals 2008)

Pages 35-36:

W. Wilcox & J. Dew, *Protectors or Perpetrators?* (2008) *accessed at* www.americanvalues.org/pdfs/researchbrief7.pdf

THREE: THE DAY of the MURDER

Pages 46-47:

See H. Abrahams & J. Snowden, *Separation of Powers and Administrative Crimes*, 1 SOUTHERN ILLINOIS L. REV. 1 (1976), for a discussion of the jurisprudence and the history of "common law crimes" in the United States.

Pages 48-49:

References to the U.S. Constitution are self-sufficient, but for a discussion of the "incorporation" of the Bill of Rights through the Fourteenth Amendment, *see, e.g.,* "Judicial Interpretation of the Fourteenth Amendment," *accessed at* www.uscourts.gov/ EducationalResources/ConstitutionResources/LegalLandmarks/ JudicialInterpretationFourteenthAmmendment.aspx.

See also the majority opinion by Justice Benjamin Cardozo in Palko v. Connecticut, 302 U.S. 319 (1937), for the rationale behind the "selective incorporation" of the Bill of Rights through the Fourteenth Amendment.

FOUR: THE POLICE and the SEARCH

Pages 59-60:

For general discussions of the problems arising in connection with the ancient doctrine of the *corpus delecti, see* R. Perkins, *The Corpus Delecti of Murder*, 48 VIRGINIA L. REV. 173 (1962); *and* D. Moran, *In Defense of the Corpus Delecti Rule*, 64 OHIO STATE L.J. 817 (2003).

See also People v. LaRosa, Case No. 11SC664 (Colo. S. Ct. January 14, 2013), for a discussion of the reasons why the Supreme Court of Colorado has abandoned the *corpus delecti* rule in the context of cases involving confessions by the accused.

On the "presumption of innocence," *see* Article 11 of the Universal Declaration of Human Rights (1948), *accessed at* https://www.un.org/en/documents/udhr/index.shtml#a11.

Pages 61-62:

For information on Denver District Attorney Mitch Morrissey, *see* his web site at http://www.denverda.org/ Meet_DA.htm.

Page 63:

For one of the many media reports concerning the search for Neveah's body, *see* http://www.thedenverchannel.com/news/ police-ask-for-public-s-help-to-find-3-year-old.

Page 65:

Morrissey took the position the original gag order prohibiting such disclosure was never intended to be permanent and, furthermore, it had technically been dissolved when Angel Ray filed his Notice of Appeal, which transferred jurisdiction over his case from the trial court to the court of appeals. The interview of Morrissey took place in January of 2013, months after the trial was completed and the notice was filed.

FIVE: THE AUTOPSY and the LOVE BIRDS

Pages 74-75:

The lengthy quote from the *Rocky Mountain News* was *accessed at* http://m.rockymountainnews.com/news/2007/sep/25/montoya-became-sex-offender-as-a-juvenile/.

Pages 77-78:

The lengthy quote from the *Rocky Mountain News* was *accessed at* http://m.rockymountainnews.com/news/2007/Oct/02/neveahs-mom-boyfriend-free/.

SIX: FAILURES and ALTERNATIVES

Pages 80-81:

The lengthy quote from the *Rocky Mountain News* comes from M. Oak Kim, "Critics say signs were there in kids' deaths," Thursday, September 27, 2007, pages 4-5.

Pages 81-83:

The murder of young Chandler Grafner was widely reported. *See* "Chandler may have been in coma for days," by M. McPhee, *The Denver Post, accessed at* http://www.denverpost.com/ recommended/ci_10114960?source=pkg.

Pages 84-86:

Colorado Department of Human Services, "Child Maltreatment Fatality Report 2007," *accessed at* http://www.ncdsv.org/ images/CDHS_ChildMaltreatmentFatalityReport_4-08.pdf

Page 87:

"KMGH gets award for children series," *The Denver Post,* Thursday, April 2, 2009, page 5D; "Report: Denver Human Services Improving," *State Bill News,* November 25, 2009, *accessed at* http://statebillnews.com/2009/11/report-denver-human-services-improving

The Denver Post web site is extremely detailed—and useful—in its compilation of the original stories featured in the series "Failed to Death," its links to various resources and reports concerning such stories, and its many follow-up articles. *See* http://www.denverpost.com/failedtodeath

Pages 88-89:

DeShaney v. Winnebago County Department of Social Services, 489 U.S. 189 (1989)

E. Chemerinsky, *The State-Created Danger Doctrine,* 23 TOURO L. REV. 1 (2007)

Currier v. Doran, 242 F.3d 905 (10th Cir. 2001)

SEVEN: THE PROSECUTORS and the EXPERTS

Pages 97-98:

For the 2011 C.V. of Dr. Case, *see* http://path.slu.edu/upload/uploads/facultycvs/Mary%20Case%20CV%2010-27-11.pdf

"This is what it's like … to perform an autopsy," from a series in *St. Louis Magazine, accessed at* http://www.stlmag.com/St-Louis-Magazine/December-2007/This-Is-What-Its-Like/

EIGHT: THE GRAND JURY and the INDICTMENTS

Pages 107-08:

The lengthy quotes come from M. Kadish, *Behind the Locked Door of an American Grand Jury: Its History, Its Secrecy, and Its Process*, 24 FLORIDA ST. U. L. REV. 1 (1996).

Pages 109-10:

Hurtado v. California, 110 U.S. 516 (1884)

Media Alert, Colorado Judicial Branch, "Grand juries in Colorado state courts," *accessed at* http://www.courts.state.co.us/Media/Alert_ Docs/grand_juries.pdf

Pages 111-12:

See B. Weisz, *State Grand Juries in Colorado: Understanding the Process and Attacking Indictments*, 24 COLORADO LAWYER 63 (2005), for a good discussion of the pros and cons.

Page 114:

http://en.wikipedia.org/wiki/Neveah_Gallegos; www.colorado-supremecourt.com/Regulation/UPL_Injunction_Listing.htm

NINE: ONE PLEA and TWO FALSE STARTS

Pages 122-23:

Sheppard v. Maxwell, 384 U.S. 333 (1966)

TEN: THE JURORS
through
EIGHTEEN: STOPPING the ABUSE

All quotations from individuals are taken from official court transcripts, personal interviews later conducted and recorded by the author, or statements made or reported by the press.

In addition, Pages 213-14:

People v. Curtis, 681 P.2d 504 (Colo. 1984)

Pages 215-16:

See generally http://www.cobar.org/repository/Inside_Bar/Criminal/Attachment%202%20Chapter%203%20%201-04%20071-511.pdf -- for a detailed comparison of existing and proposed jury instructions by the state bar committee charged with making the instructions read in "plain language." This is an interim working document prepared in 2011.

Pages 235-36:

Colorado State Senate, Majority Office, Tuesday, May 14, 2013, "Five essential child protection bills signed into law," *accessed at* http://colorado-senate.org/home/features/five-essential-child-protection-bills-signed-into-law.

Stephens-Davidowitz, "How Googling Unmasks Child Abuse," *The New York Times Sunday Review*, 7/14/2013 at page 5.